Early American Silver and Its Makers

ANTIQUES
Magazine Library

FOLK ART IN AMERICA
Painting and Sculpture
Edited by Jack T. Ericson

EUROPEAN POTTERY & PORCELAIN
Edited by Paul J. Atterbury

Early American Silver and Its Makers

Edited by Jane Bentley Kolter

A Main Street Press Book
Published by Mayflower Books, Inc., USA
New York City

Articles included in this volume are printed as they appeared in the following issues of *The Magazine* Antiques:

Part I: Masterpieces in American Silver—Part I, December, 1948, Part II, February, 1949, Part III, April, 1949; Colonial Silversmiths—Masters and Apprentices, December, 1956; Some Engraved American Silver, Part I, Prior to about 1740, November, 1945; Colonial Cherubium in Silver, April, 1940; Colonial Furniture and Silver, January, 1947; A 1757 Inventory of Silver, January, 1956; Sucket Forks, December, 1942; Two Hoof Spoons, September, 1978; Candlesticks and Snuffers by American Silversmiths, December, 1930; American Silver Spout Cups, August, 1943.

Part II: Early New England Silver, September, 1925; Master and Apprentice: Some Relationships in New England Silversmithing, November, 1955; Jeremiah Dummer, Silversmith, October, 1935; John Edwards, Goldsmith, and His Progeny, April, 1951; A Samuel Casey Coffeepot, April, 1952; Daniel Greenough, Early New Hampshire Silversmith, June, 1942; Verifying a Hull and Sanderson Porringer, September, 1937; A New Form in American Seventeenth-Century Silver, December, 1968; Little-known Masterpieces, VII. A Unique Early Colonial Salt, July, 1922; The Nine Colonial Sugar Boxe, January, 1964.

Part III: The Distinctive Quality of Early New York Silver, May, 1938; Early New York Silver, November, 1924; The Sanders-Garvan Beaker by Cornelis VanderBurch, January, 1935; Cornelius Vanderburgh-Silversmith of New York, Part II, February, 1936; The New York Silver Mark PVB, July, 1933; Two Chafing Dishes by Peter Van Dyck, October, 1936; Peter Van Dyck of New York, Goldsmith, 1684-1750, Part II, June, 1937; Albany Silver, July, 1951; The Demihorse: Mark of a Silversmithing Van Rensselaer?, October, 1960; The Ten Eyck Silversmiths, December, 1942; The Verplanck Cup, December, 1967; New York's Two-handled Paneled Silver Bowls, October, 1961; Further Comments on the Lobate Bowl Form, October, 1966.

Part IV: A Porringer by Cesar Ghiselin, January, 1955; John De Nys, Philadelphia Silversmith, May, 1932; John Nys vs. John Newkirke, December, 1936; An Unrecorded Goldsmith, Jeremiah Elfreth Junior of Philadelphia, January, 1947; Joseph Richardson and Family, Philadelphia Silversmiths, January, 1975; Some Forged Richardson Silver, May, 1961.

First Edition

Library of Congress Catalog Card Number 79-87674
ISBN 8317-2536-2

Produced by The Main Street Press
42 Main Street
Clinton, New Jersey 08809

Published by Mayflower Books, Inc., USA
575 Lexington Avenue
New York City 10022

Contents

Introduction

Early colonial newspapers contain advertisements of goldsmiths, silversmiths, and "juellers" working in America, but these artisans—all members of the same powerful guild, who used their trade designations interchangeably—left us no material evidence of their craft until after the middle of the 17th century. Two silversmiths arrived with the first wave of immigrants to Virginia. What happened to them after they arrived is still a mystery. Perhaps they turned to tobacco farming, which after a slow start became the economic answer to mercantilist dreams. Cash crops from the Southern colonies swelled England's coffers and lined the pockets of those merchants and craftsmen who supplied colonial needs. Most of the Southern colonies, however late they were founded, continued to rely on the mother country for material goods of all sorts. Though silversmiths advertised in Virginia newspapers as early as 1620, and in Charleston, South Carolina, before 1700, none of their products seem to have survived.

New England, on the other hand, never fulfilled the hopes of the mother country. It was not only a poor source of raw materials, but, what is worse, its Calvinist settlers were committed to establishing a self-sufficient society. The arts and crafts were generally safe from the rigorous control imposed on other areas of society. Silversmiths, as eminently respectable citizens, were welcome and were advertising in Boston newspapers by the mid-1630s. Work by such silversmiths as John Hull and Robert Sanderson, for example, survives from the 1650s. Much of the earliest work was preserved by various New England churches, whose central position in their communities made them frequent recipients of gifts and bequests. This fortunate tradition of donation has provided today's collectors and scholars with a great deal of evidence and information about New England silversmithing in the colonial period.

Such pieces, however, must be studied with caution. Most have engraved dates, for example, but such dates were usually added at the time the gift was made—perhaps several years after the piece was fashioned. Many beakers and tankards saw several years of household use before they were delivered to the care of the church (see, for instance, the illustration on p. 11, upper right). Church records sometimes contain references to specific commissions of plate—the usual term for domestic silver. When some recorded piece survives, its precise chronology can be established, and the piece can be analyzed for whatever stylistic innovations it shows. Secular silver can be measured against these bench marks.

Unlike most English silver, American work has no date marks. The colonists had no assay offices to check each piece for purity and to stamp the letter mark which identifies the year a piece was presented for assay and guarantees its quality. In order to date American work, one must generally rely on knowledge of particular craftsmen and their marks, stylistic evidence, and any incidental information which provenance and engraved dates, crests, or initials supply. Even then, nothing is certain. Silversmiths occasionally crafted pieces in an earlier style or engraved long-past dates on modern pieces. To make matters worse, they sometimes engraved contemporary dates on older pieces—anything to satisfy a customer's whim and to confuse the scholars of a later period.

By the 1680s, silversmiths were active in Boston, New York, and, to some extent, in Philadelphia and smaller settlements. They enjoyed a lively trade—so lively, in fact, that English silver continued to be imported, both to meet an overwhelming demand for plate and to serve as a model for colonial craftsmen. English work remained the stylistic standard until well into the 19th century. New fashions introduced in the mother country usually reached America within ten years. Americans made their first venture in a new style by adding *au courant* ornament to a conservatively-shaped piece. Gradually, the newer shapes were absorbed into their somewhat parochial vocabulary of accepted design. By the second quarter of the 18th century, however, Americans were much more in touch with current London tastes.

On the whole, American craftsmen maintained the standards set by the strong goldsmiths' guilds of the Old World. Had they not, undoubtedly, they would not have survived. America was a competitive market, and short-changing customers with underweight pieces, low quality metal, or unattractive plate would have been economic suicide. Although the assay offices were absent in the colonies, Americans held as best they could to the sterling standard of 92.5 percent silver mixed with 7.5 percent copper. They had only a trained eye, scales, and traditional procedures to produce the correct mixture, and the process was further complicated by the lack of pure silver. Every ounce was contaminated with trace elements, including gold, which are removed from silver mined today. (These impurities account for some of the "mellow" color of old silver.)

In 1697, as Louise C. Belden points out in "The Verplanck Cup" (pp. 129-131), the standard of purity for domestic English silver was changed. The new standard required that silversmiths use a purer—and softer—metal than that used in coinage. This discouraged English silversmiths from continuing the wholesale conversion of coins to plate and started a trend toward simpler styles which suited the softer metal. Americans adopted the fashions, but did not necessarily raise the standard of purity.

Colonial methods of working and marketing silver were the same as those of England. Silver was usually made to order, but spoons, simple pieces of jewelry, and a few oddities were available in most shops. Sometimes the customer supplied coins (often Spanish) or old pieces of plate which a silversmith used in filling his commission. Then, of course, the customer only paid for labor.

Teapots, tankards, and other major pieces were almost always commissioned. The silversmith started with an ingot, either imported or cast in his shop from melted coins. He flattened this with innumerable hammer strokes or rolled it out in a "flatting" mill, but such rolling devices were very rare in the colonies. A disc of silver of the required size was cut from the flat sheet, and a mark punched at dead center. The silversmith then began the tedious process of raising the edges of his piece with repeated, overlapping hammer strokes. From time to time he checked his progress with calipers to make sure that the distance from the center punch was uniform throughout the piece. He continued raising and shaping the piece, using a variety of hammers and anvils designed to produce different curves and effects. Whenever the piece became brittle, it was heated and then plunged into a water and sulphuric acid bath to cool it. This annealing process returned the silver to a malleable state and cleaned off any copper that had been pushed to the surface of the silver. Then, using a planishing hammer, the silversmith smoothed the more vigorous marks of the raising hammers from the outside of the piece.

Spouts, finials, porringer handles, and many types of ornament were cast in a fine sand mixture which was compressed into iron-bound boxes, called flasks. Patterns were usually carved in wood or made up in brass, but duplicating another silversmith's product by using parts of his piece as patterns was probably a frequent practice. These cast elements were joined to the body with solder. Wire ornament and reinforcement for rims and bases was made by pulling, or drawing, thin sheets of silver through a die containing holes of the desired diameter. As may be imagined, pulling the silver required considerable strength. A very thin wire might be made in several stages, using apertures of graduated size and working from the largest to the smallest. Finally, this, too, would be soldered into place.

The whole piece received a preliminary polishing before any engraving, chasing, or *repoussé* decoration was added. *Repoussé* is a low relief embossing technique, generally done from the back or inside of the piece, while flat-chasing is accomplished from the front. Punched and granulated textures, used by many early American silversmiths, are specialized forms of chasing. Engraving, on the other hand, actually cut into the silver surface instead of simply pushing the metal around to form a pattern. All of these techniques were part of the repertoire of any colonial silversmith. Most of the earliest artisans had, in fact, been trained under masters in Europe who passed on standards and skills established centuries earlier by medieval guilds.

Like their English and European counterparts, American silversmiths of the colonial period were important members of their communities. At first they were more closely allied with the merchant oligarchy—the customers who supported their livelihood. The silversmith's role, however, changed gradually in the years preceeding the Revolution, and the men who so actively sought a society of greater equality found that their status diminished as that of other artisans increased. It was little consolation that a similar social revolution was occurring in the Old World. The power of the aristocracy was curtailed by the ascent of an influential new class, legitimized solely by wealth. While the middle class patronized the silversmith who provided the necessary evidence of wealth, they chose to lionize the portrait painter who could produce the image of their vanity.

For over fifty years, readers of *The Magazine* ANTIQUES have recognized the contributions of early silversmiths to the development of American culture. Collectors, scholars, and aficionados have contributed greatly to this field, and much of their work has been recorded in the pages of ANTIQUES. *Early American Silver and Its Makers* consolidates some of the best of this work. It is not just a jumping-off place for the study of American silver, but a source of much information not recorded elsewhere.

The volume is divided into four sections. The first is a general view of early American work. Here the masterpieces are highlighted, ornament and form are discussed, and some interesting sidelights are brought into focus. Specific regional characteristics and silversmiths are cited in three sections on New England, New York, and Philadelphia. The last article in the Philadelphia section addresses the problem of forgery. It seems to be an appropriate warning to collectors with which to close the book.

Any small discrepancies which exist between the early articles and more recent research are covered in the introductory text for each section. Corrected biographical dates for craftsmen are listed parenthetically at the first mention of the craftsman's name. Specific information in the introductory texts is consistent with the most recent publications on American silver.

A selective bibliography follows the text. Many of its authors are represented in this anthology. C. Louise Avery, Francis Hill Bigelow, Kathryn C. Buhler, Martha Gandy Fales, Beatrice Garvan, Graham Hood, and John Marshall Phillips have all contributed mightily to the study of American silver and deserve special mention. Their work forms the foundation for this and for all studies on the subject.

I Form and Ornament in Early Silver

Visitors to America in the early 18th century were often surprised at the fashionable scene which greeted them. They viewed the expanding cities and colonial enterprise with some envy and a little scorn. Their jealousy—for surely it was that—was misplaced. By imitating London tastes and manners, the colonists were acting just as British mercantilists had hoped. America was becoming the marketplace of a flourishing empire.

What tourists found, at least among wealthy Americans, was a culture that mimicked the comfortable existence of England's middle class. The colonists expressed their willing adoption of English values and taste by every material means, including silver. Americans preferred good, solid stuff, rather plain, and perhaps a little out of date, a preference which was, nevertheless, an indicator of status and well-being. Plate served another function, too. It was safer to store family wealth in the form of handcrafted silver than to hold it in silver coins. If the unique plate were stolen it might be traced, whereas common coins were untraceable. Silver could be made even more identifiable with engraved arms or crests that proved the noble, or erstwhile noble, lineage of its owner. Similarly, engraved initials and the silversmith's touchmark provided additional proofs of ownership. Newspaper advertisements for missing silver always mentioned marks and requested that a piece be "stopped" by anyone who saw it.

American investment in plainly-shaped silver was founded on good sense. A simple middle-of-the-road piece would stay in fashion longer. Plate could always be melted down and remade when tastes changed, but labor was expensive in the underpopulated colonies, and unnecessary expenses drained private treasuries. So, as in all provincial centers, more conservative silver was commissioned. It could always be enlivened with ornament.

Kathryn C. Buhler, in the first of her two articles in this chapter (pp. 30-33), describes the changing fashions of engraved ornament. These changes usually preceeded whole revolutions in silver style, and silvermakers, in turn, led other craftsmen in adopting innovations. Chinoiserie, for instance, made its American debut on a salver by Boston silversmith Timothy Dwight. Dwight's imaginative animals were engraved about twenty-five years before the craze for japanned furniture hit the colonies, but both derived their inspiration from the Far East trade. Kathryn C. Buhler points out other similarities between furniture and silver in her second selection (pp. 37-40).

Though ornament was appreciated, function was always the key to American preferences. Household furnishings, and, indeed, all one's worldly goods were expected to be useful. Silver combined function and beauty even when completely unadorned. It was a wise choice for drinking vessels since it never affected the taste of potent brews—as pewter and earthenware were likely to do. In fact, physicians recommended that all liquors be taken from silver, and, in an age when alcoholic beverages were about the only safe thing to drink, the exclusiveness of the precious metal and the frequent washing it received probably did make drinking from silver healthier.

Ale was often served in beakers, a form approved in homes and in nonconformist churches alike because it was easy to hold and did not evoke any fearsome associations with dogma or popery. The caudle cup was also accepted in sacred and secular settings. This two-handled cup could be used for caudle—a hot mixture of gruel, sugar, wine, or ale—or any number of other potations passed around the table. Opposing handles simplified the process of passing a community cup from hand to hand.

A number of beakers and two-handled cups are shown in John Marshall Phillips's series of articles, "Masterpieces in American Silver" (pp. 11-25). Phillips also illustrates many of the best early American tankards. This is probably the form most easily recognized by expert and non-expert alike, for it seems to symbolize both the silversmith's art and 18th-century hospitality. The tankard, a lidded mug, shares the alcoholic heritage of beakers and two-handled cups; it was used for the beer, ale, and cider which the colonies produced in abundance.

David Stockwell's inventory (pp. 41-42) records a number of forms made by silversmiths in the Philadelphia area. Most were well-known and fairly common throughout the colonies. Porringers, tankards, salvers, and canns make up the bulk of this list. Less usual are sucket forks, the subject of an article by George Barton Cutten (p. 43), and hoof spoons, a New York form, which Albert Scher describes (pp. 44-46). Very few American examples of either form survive, undoubtedly because both were going out of fashion in England and Europe by the middle of the 17th century—just as American silversmiths were beginning to produce their own interpretations.

Candlesticks are another comparative rarity in early American work. Edward Wenham illustrates several examples in "Candlesticks and Snuffers by American Silversmiths" (pp. 47-49). Since the article's first publication in 1930, a few more rococo candlesticks have come to light. Myer Myers produced several variants, similar to those in figure 11 on p. 49. One pair shows traces of English marks cast into Myers' stamped piece. Obviously, the craftsman used his English patterns literally. Myers also produced a pair of snuffers on feet, illustrated in Graham Hood's *American Silver: A History of Style, 1650-1900*. A few biographical dates in Wenham's article should be revised: John Burt (1693-1746), John Coney (1656-1722), Jacob Hurd (1703-1758), Myer Myers (1723-1795), and Cornelius Kierstede (1675-1757).

V. Isabelle Miller approaches another unusual form in ''American Silver Spout Cups'' (pp. 50-52). She suggests that infants and invalids were likely users, and this is probably the case for the examples shown in figures 10, 11, and 13 on p. 52.

Several of the other cups may have seen more use as posset pots; they resemble Delft pieces of the period. At least one, pictured in figure 1 on p. 50, seems to be a diminutive chocolate pot, perhaps made to serve some late riser who needed a cup of chocolate in bed before getting up to face the day. Like larger capacity models, this pot had a hole in the lid for a stick, called a chocolate mill, which was used to stir up the chocolate shavings just before a cup was poured. A date in the caption of figure 12 on p. 52 requires some adjustment: Joseph Richardson died in 1784. Another change should be made in the caption at the upper right of p. 20: Jacob Hurd worked in Boston, not New York.

BEAKER (*Boston*). The sturdy base molding and broad style of engraved ornament, featuring the Tudor rose, are indicative of the mid-seventeenth century and reflect the English training of Robert Sanderson and his partner, John Hull. *Mabel Brady Garvan collection, Gallery of Fine Arts, Yale University.*

BEAKER (*Boston*). The simplicity of line and refined base molding are indicative of the third quarter of the seventeenth century. An early work by John Coney, this piece served as an ale beaker in the Potter household in Ipswich until 1699, when it was presented to the First Church by Mrs. Potter. *Garvan collection.*

MASTERPIECES IN AMERICAN SILVER

By JOHN MARSHALL PHILLIPS

Part I, Seventeenth-Century Traditions

John Marshall Phillips is director of the Yale Art Gallery and curator of its rich Garvan collections, and teaches a course on the American decorative arts at the University. He is recognized as the outstanding authority on American silver.

ONE HUNDRED PIECES of American silver, ranging in date from the seventeenth to the nineteenth centuries, will be presented in this and three subsequent parts. Those shown here are from the seventeenth century. The selection is based primarily on quality of design and workmanship, but consideration has also been given to physical condition. Some pieces which might otherwise qualify were unfortunately buffed in the nineteenth century, whereas the one hundred chosen have all undergone a minimum of restoration and retain their patina. The selection is further confined to examples now exhibited in public collections. Since many churches have placed their silver on loan in local museums, church pieces have been included. Those shown here were all made originally for domestic use; a later section will be devoted exclusively to ecclesiastical silver.

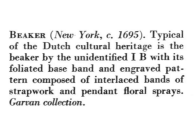

BEAKER (*New York*). The outstanding domestic beaker made in New York was fashioned in 1685 by New York's earliest native-born silversmith, Cornelis van der Burch. The emblems decorating its surface were inspired by the engravings, by Adriaen van der Venne, illustrating the didactic poems of Jacobus Cats, seventeenth-century Dutch best-seller. (See ANTIQUES, February 1935). *Garvan collection.*

BEAKER (*New York, c. 1695*). Typical of the Dutch cultural heritage is the beaker by the unidentified I B with its foliated base band and engraved pattern composed of interlaced bands of strapwork and pendant floral sprays. *Garvan collection.*

PORRINGER (*Boston, c. 1655*). The simple geometric piercing of the handle and the profile of the curved bowl reflect the Commonwealth style as fashioned by Boston's earliest silversmithing partners, John Hull and London-trained Robert Sanderson. *Spalding collection, Museum of Fine Arts, Boston.*

PORRINGER (*New England, c. 1692*). A refinement in the handle design is noticed in that introduced by the Huguenot craftsman René Grignon, who settled in Boston following the revocation of the Edict of Nantes and later worked in Norwich, Connecticut. Its delicately engraved heart motif follows the contemporary handle design of its French counterpart, the *écuelle*. *Mabel Brady Garvan collection, Gallery of Fine Arts, Yale University.*

TANKARD (*Boston*). This generous cider tankard by Robert Sanderson offered a solution for the safekeeping of coins received in trade. At small charge the silversmith could melt and fashion them into pieces both useful and ornamental. *Museum of Fine Arts, Boston.*

TANKARD (*Boston*). Mary Shrimpton's wedding tankard of 1692 by John Coney illustrates a refinement in the base molding, noticeable after 1690, as well as an admirably executed heraldic achievement. *Garvan collection.*

TANKARD (*New York, c. 1698*). This piece by Gerrit Onckelbag interestingly exemplifies a product of the impact of Dutch and English culture: the English providing the form, the Dutch an individualistic treatment of parts and ornament such as the corkscrew thumbpiece, foliated base band, and heraldic mantling. *Metropolitan Museum of Art.*

CAUDLE CUP (*Boston, c. 1652*). Flat chasing and punched ornament, popular in the mid-seventeenth century, were employed by Hull and Sanderson on this caudle cup. The tulip was a favorite design for both metal- and woodworker. *Spalding Collection, Museum of Fine Arts, Boston.*

CAUDLE CUP (*Boston*). By little-known Benjamin Sanderson, Robert's son, this piece shows the use of flat chasing and punched ornament by a first-generation Boston craftsman. *Worcester Art Museum.*

COVERED CAUDLE CUP (*Boston, 1679*). The vigorous design and execution of this generous cup made by John Coney when only twenty-three is evidence of his early skill. The caryatid handles are excellent examples of cast ornament. The Addington arms is one of the earliest heraldic achievements on American silver. *Garvan collection.*

CAUDLE CUP (*Boston*). The repoussé ornament of cherubs and flowers on a somewhat later caudle cup by Coney shows a conservative reflection of the florid Stuart styles in Boston. A cup identical in form and decoration inspired Oliver Wendell Holmes' poem *On Lending a Punch Bowl. Harvard University.*

PUNCHBOWL (*Boston, 1692*). In its lobed rim this bowl by Jeremiah Dummer reflects a Portuguese influence in Boston in the last decade of the century, referred to in contemporary documents as "Spanish." The flat-chased stiff floral pattern suggests Stuart crewel embroidery patterns. *Garvan collection.*

PUNCHBOWL (*New York*). The typical New York punchbowl apparently has no counterpart in Holland. Its distinctive pumpkin shape is decorated with panels usually chased, but plain in this example, fashioned by the Huguenot Bartholomew Le Roux for Quaker clients in New Jersey. *Garvan collection.*

PUNCHBOWL (*New York, c. 1698*). More typical of the style favored by the Knickerbocker families than the Le Roux bowl is that fashioned by Cornelius Kierstede, who enriched the panels of this bowl with repoussé and chased floral patterns of bold design. *Metropolitan Museum of Art.*

PLATE (*Boston*). The broad flat rim with molded edge dates from the last quarter of the seventeenth century. This plate by Coney, engraved with the Eyre arms, is the earliest surviving example of its kind. *Bell collection, Minneapolis Institute of Art.*

PLATE (*Boston*). Almost exotic by contrast with the plate above is this one, with a richly engraved border, from Coney's workshop. The quality of the engraving reflects a more polite way of living than is usually associated with the age of settlement. Detail below. *Pickman collection, Museum of Fine Arts, Boston.*

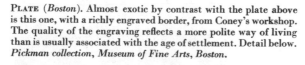

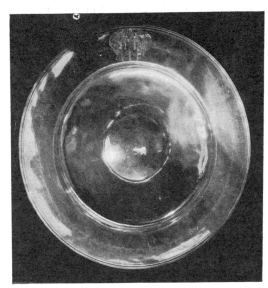

SALVER (*Boston*). The earliest American example of Eastern influence in the *chinoiserie* manner is the engraved design on this salver by Timothy Dwight (*died 1691/2*), which antedates by a quarter-century the japanned furniture designs with Oriental influence. *Pickman collection.*

BASIN (*Boston, 1695*). The rosewater dish or basin was used at feasts before the advent of knives and forks. This one by Dummer was bequeathed in 1717 by the Reverend William Brattle to his Cambridge church, where it has since served as a baptismal basin. *First Parish Church, Cambridge, Massachusetts.*

TUMBLER CUP (*New York, c. 1695*). Form is well adapted to function in this cup by the rare maker, H. H. The form, more usual in Continental than English silver, was popular for wine in New York. *Garvan collection.*

TANKARD COVERS (*New York*). The flat surface of the New York tankard cover invited fine engraved ornament. (*Left*), Jacobus van der Spiegel in 1697 engraved what is thought to be the most handsome cover of his day. *Garvan collection.* (*Right*), a year later Gerrit Onckelbag engraved what purports to be a representation of the *Nassau*, Captain Giles Shelley's ship engaged in Eastern trade. *Metropolitan Museum.*

TOYS (*c. 1690*). Fashioned by an unidentified Boston silversmith for Bethia Shrimpton, these miniatures preserve in their form some designs which have not otherwise survived the whims of fashion, war, or the melting pot. Four other pieces made at the same time are privately owned. *Garvan collection.*

CANDLESTICK (*Boston, 1686*). The close relationship existing between architectural and silver forms is illustrated in the majestic candlestick, one of a pair, executed by Jeremiah Dummer. The clustered shaft is reminiscent of the pilastered central chimney found in contemporary New England houses. This piece is an outstanding example of the mastery of craftsmanship achieved in American silver in the early days of settlement. It compares favorably with contemporary European design and workmanship. *Garvan collection.*

MASTERPIECES IN AMERICAN SILVER

In Public Collections

By JOHN MARSHALL PHILLIPS

Part II, 1700—1750

We here present the second installment of the hundred best pieces of American silver, selected at our request by John Marshall Phillips, director of the Yale University Art Gallery and curator of its Garvan collections. The first part, devoted to silver of the seventeenth century, appeared in December, and our Easter issue in April will feature ecclesiastical silver.

STANDING SALT *(Boston)*. The last vestige of medieval tradition to survive in colonial America was the imposing standing salt, which in accordance with ancient custom was placed in the center of the table before the guest of honor. The sophistication of the American William and Mary style *(1700-1715)* is characterized by the use of the gadrooned band on this example by Jeremiah Dummer *(1645-1718)*. Height, 5½ inches. *Tyler collection, Museum of Fine Arts, Boston.*

TANKARD (*New York*). Conservative Knickerbocker silversmiths followed the seventeenth-century tankard form, retaining the plain flat cover as in this example by Cornelius Kierstede *(1674-1757)*, a master of line and proportion. The crisp quality of its moldings and cast ornament are particularly pleasing. Height, 7⅞ inches. *Garvan collection.*

SUGAR CASTER *(New York, c. 1705)*. The early eighteenth century ushered in a more gracious way of living, as evidenced by the imposing sugar caster, one from a suite of three from the workshop of the Huguenot craftsman, Bartholomew Le Roux *(1663-1713)*. The other two are somewhat smaller. The tall cover of this one is pierced in an elaborate design, and boldly executed gadrooned bands decorate cover and foot. Height, 8¼ inches. *Mabel Brady Garvan collection, Yale University Art Gallery.*

TANKARD *(Boston)*. A slight Swedish influence is to be found in the repoussé handle decoration of this tankard by the American-Swedish silversmith Hendrick Hurst *(1665-1717)*. Typical of many of the Boston tankards dating from the first decade of the eighteenth century are the gadrooned band decorating the cover and the mask and dolphin thumbpiece, symbolic of gaiety and strength. Height, 7 inches. *Pickman collection, Museum of Fine Arts.*   *Left*

TANKARD *(New York)*. The most elaborate of the New York tankards, fashioned about 1705 by Peter van Dyck *(1684-1751)* for the Wendell family of Albany, has in addition to the locally characteristic foliated baseband and corkscrew thumbpiece, a gadrooned band enriching an elaborately engraved cover. The handle is decorated with sculpturesque cast ornament to insure a strong grip when the vessel is full. Height, 7⅛ inches. *Garvan collection.*   *Right*

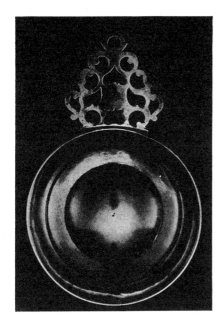

PORRINGER *(Boston)*. The heart, tulip, and crescent moon, ancient symbols of love and chastity, are featured by John Coney *(1655-1722)* in the handle design of this porringer fashioned in 1709 for Henry and Elizabeth Dering of Boston. Length, 8⁹⁄₁₆ inches. *Garvan collection.*

TWO-HANDLED COVERED PORRINGER *(New York)*. The porringer in New York dates from the early eighteenth century. Its earliest handle exhibits an intricate lacy pattern featuring a heart, cross, and diamond. The two handles on this unique example by Jan Niewkerk *(working 1708-1715)*, based on the French écuelle, show the influence of the French settlers and French plate in New York following the revocation of the Edict of Nantes. Length, 11¼ inches. *Clearwater collection, Metropolitan Museum of Art.*

SUGAR BOX *(Boston)*. Almost exotic by comparison with the other utensils of their time are the elaborate sugar or confiture boxes, popular in the early eighteenth century, which recall the custom of serving loaf sugar with black cherry brandy and other stimulating drinks. Stylistically, Coney's box is based upon a form popular in London toward the end of Charles II's reign. The coiled serpent which forms the handle is symbolic of eternity. Length, 8⁷⁄₁₆ inches. *Museum of Fine Arts.*

SUGAR BOX *(Boston)*. Featuring the gadrooned and fluted ornament of its period is the box by Coney's contemporary, Edward Winslow *(1669-1753)*, fashioned for his family use. No counterpart in design, with its embossed medallions depicting St. George and the dragon, has as yet been found among English or Continental plate. Three other boxes of similar design but with slight variations, two dated *1702*, by Winslow are known. Length, 7¼ inches. *Garvan collection.*

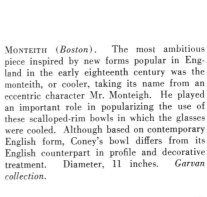

MONTEITH *(Boston)*. The most ambitious piece inspired by new forms popular in England in the early eighteenth century was the monteith, or cooler, taking its name from an eccentric character Mr. Monteigh. He played an important role in popularizing the use of these scalloped-rim bowls in which the glasses were cooled. Although based on contemporary English form, Coney's bowl differs from its English counterpart in profile and decorative treatment. Diameter, 11 inches. *Garvan collection.*

TWO-HANDLED COVERED CUP (*Boston*). The spirit of the baroque with its gadrooned and fluted ornament is ably interpreted by Coney in this "grace cup" of 1701, presented to Harvard by its benefactor, Lieutenant Governor William Stoughton, in that year and engraved with his arms. It remains today the finest piece in Harvard's collection of American silver. Height, 10 inches. *Harvard University*.

TWO-HANDLED COVERED CUP (*Boston*). Slightly later in period than the Coney cup and somewhat bolder in design is Edward Winslow's use of gadrooned ornament to achieve a variety of surface pattern with its resultant play of light and shade. Height, 11 inches. *Garvan collection*.

TWO-HANDLED COVERED CUP (*Boston*). Symbolic of the Queen Anne period is Jacob Hurd's masterpiece, a covered cup, architectonic in scale with finely cast handles and domed cover with bell-shaped finial. The plain surface of the cup is enriched with a finely molded band below a decorative inscription. A presentation piece for a naval victory of 1744 at the outbreak of King George's War, it is the noblest of the pieces in its period. Height, 15⅛ inches. *Garvan collection*.

CHOCOLATE POT (*Boston*). The counterpoise of plain and richly ornamented surfaces of the William and Mary style is ably demonstrated by Winslow in the chocolate pot made for the Hutchinson family. A silver chain is attached to the acorn finial, originally removable for the insertion of a stick to crush and stir the chocolate. Height, 9½ inches. *Clearwater collection*.

CHOCOLATE POT (*Boston*). The early influence of Oriental ceramic shapes on silver is shown in the chocolate pot fashioned in 1701 by John Coney for Mrs. Tailer of Boston from a legacy of twelve pounds. The lower jointure of the handle is masked by cut-card ornament, the curve of the spout is complemented by the use of graduated beaded ornament. Height, 7⅞ inches. *Museum of Fine Arts*.

TEAPOT (*New York*). The popularity of tea early in the eighteenth century introduced new forms for the silversmith's skill. The early shape favored in New York was based upon Dutch forms. In this example van Dyck has employed ornamental strapwork, a decorative treatment popular in London with his contemporary Anglo-French silversmiths, to enrich the cover. Height, 8 inches. *Garvan collection.*

COFFEEPOT (*New York*). The simplicity of the American expression of the Queen Anne style emphasizes the richness of the metal, enhanced by fine moldings or engraving as shown in this coffeepot by Charles Le Roux (*1689-1745*). Height, 11 inches. *Garvan collection.*

TEAPOT (*Boston*). During the 1725-1750 period the Bostonians favored the simple globular shape for teapots, as in this example by Jacob Hurd (*1702-1758*). The simplicity of its surface is enriched by armorial bearings—in this instance, the Pepperell arms as borne by the father of Sir William, the hero of Louisburg. The spout is sometimes varied by the use of a polygonal shape. Height, 5 inches. *Garvan collection.*

TEAKETTLE (*New York*). Reminiscent of the hospitality of eighteenth-century New York is the kettle made for the de Peyster family by Cornelius Kierstede. It is fashioned on generous lines, and has a turned handle of cherry wood and a notably individualistic treatment of the spout. Height, 10¼ inches. *Metropolitan Museum of Art.*

CHAFING DISH (*Boston*). The quality of pierced ornament is best seen in the chafing dish, an accessory of the early kettle and also used in the preparation of hot drinks such as caudle, posset, and chocolate. The finest of these designs was that popularized by Coney as shown in the example made for his family use. Diameter, 5⁵⁄₁₆ inches. *Garvan collection.*

PUNCHBOWL (*New Haven*). The outstanding piece of silver fashioned in colonial Connecticut was the work of the migratory silversmith Cornelius Kierstede who settled in New Haven in the late 1720's, becoming the earliest resident silversmith. Based stylistically on the bowls of New York with its stiff floral panels, it was a gift from the Yale College Class of 1746 to their sole tutor, Thomas Darling, upon his retirement in 1745. Diameter, 7½ inches. *Yale University.*

SUGAR DISH (*New York*). A further instance of the influence of Oriental ceramics is the translation of the Chinese tea bowl into a sugar container by Simeon Soumain (*1685-1750*). The beauty of the bowl's form is further enhanced by the neatly engraved cipher *E C*, of its original owner, Elizabeth Cruger. Height, 4¼ inches. *Garvan collection.*

TEA TRAY (*Boston*). An accessory to the popular tea table and its service was the rectangular footed tray with its beautifully molded incurved rim. Hurd featured in his engraved border the characteristic Queen Anne shell, a popular motif in both wood and metal. Diameter, 12½ inches. *Garvan collection.*

INKSTAND (*Boston*). The graceful design and beautifully cast lion supports of Coney's inkstand or standish with its containers for ink, wafer, and sand, made for Governor Belcher, illustrate the mastery of workmanship attained by the colonial craftsmen and recall the age when the fine art of letter-writing played an important part in daily life. Height, 4¼ inches. *Metropolitan Museum of Art.*

MASTERPIECES IN AMERICAN SILVER

In Public Collections

By JOHN MARSHALL PHILLIPS

Part III, Ecclesiastical Silver

The ecclesiastical silver illustrated in this issue has been selected from pieces made for presentation to churches and does not include the secular pieces which found their way through bequests into church collections. Many of these have been discussed in the preceding parts of this series, which appeared in December 1948 and February 1949.

BEAKER *(New York)*. The Dutch colonists of New York also favored the beaker for a communion vessel but copied the traditional Holland beaker with its elaborately engraved ornament, featuring an interlaced strapwork band and three oval panels portraying Faith, Hope, and Charity. The example here illustrated was made in 1684 by Jurian Blanck, an early New York craftsman. Height, 7 inches. *First Reformed Church, Brooklyn, New York.*

BEAKER *(Boston)*. In Nonconformist New England the secular form of the beaker was adopted as a popular vessel for communion. Approximately five hundred examples have survived. The earliest type had a straight body slightly curved at the lip with a flat bottom, as in this one by John Hull and Robert Sanderson, fashioned in 1659 for their church. The body is decorated with a broad granulated band, a form of decoration introduced into England from Scandinavia and Germany. Height, 3⅞ inches. *The First Church of Boston.*

BEAKER *(Boston)*. By the late seventeenth century the church beaker in New England was taller, with a finely molded base, as in the example fashioned by Jeremiah Dummer and presented to the First Church, Ipswich, Massachusetts. Height, 6¼ inches. *Garvan collection.*

STANDING CUP *(Boston)*. Vying in popularity with the beaker in New England was the secular wine cup based upon a style popular in England in the reign of Charles I. Several English examples are still preserved in the Boston churches, and undoubtedly one of these was the model for John Hull and Robert Sanderson, who in 1674 fashioned this for the Newman Congregational Church at Rehoboth, Rhode Island. Height, 7¼ inches. *Garvan collection.*

BEAKER *(New York)*. The conservatism of Knickerbocker families alluded to by Washington Irving is evidenced in the continuation of the seventeenth-century form with its richly engraved surface, as late as 1731 when this example, one of a pair, was fashioned by Henricus Boelen to replace the pewter beakers in use until that time. Height, 6½ inches. *Reformed Church, Bergen, New Jersey.*

STANDING CUP *(Boston)*. The impact of the William and Mary style in silver is first evidenced in these standing cups. One example dated 1700, in the collection of the Museum of Fine Arts, was made by Dummer, who in 1701 also made the one illustrated. It demonstrates his masterful use of gadrooned and fluted ornament to accent the curved lines of the cup and create a contrast in surface values. Height, 8 1/16 inches. *First Parish Church, Dorchester, Massachusetts.*

BEAKER *(Boston)*. A variant in gadrooned pattern is found in this beaker by Dummer, in which he combines the bold repousse ornament of the gadroon with a flat granulated band. One of six made in 1705. Height, 5¾ inches. *North Congregational Church, Portsmouth, New Hampshire.*

TANKARD *(Boston)*. The Congregational churches were slow in accepting the form of the flagon, using the secular tankard for this purpose before 1711. Two such tankards by John Coney with gadrooned covers were purchased in 1705 by the church committee as "vessels for ye Communion Table." Height, 6¼ inches. *First Parish, Unitarian, Cambridge, Massachusetts.*

TWO-HANDLED CUP *(Boston)*. The frequent bequest of gourd-shaped caudle cups to the New England churches in time established a style, as evidenced in this example made in 1707 by Edward Winslow. Height, 4⅝ inches. *Church of Christ, Congregational, Milford, Connecticut.*

TWO-HANDLED CUP *(Boston)*. The seventeenth-century gourd shape was discarded early in the eighteenth century for the inverted bell shape of the William and Mary style with its typical gadrooned and fluted ornament. Although most of the surviving examples in church plate were secular in origin, this one by William Cowell, Sr. *(1682-1736)* is inscribed *F. C.* for the Farmington Church. Height, 4¼ inches. *Church of Christ, Congregational, Farmington, Connecticut.*

TWO-HANDLED CUP *(Boston)*. The simplicity associated with the Queen Anne style is evidenced in the example made in 1726 by George Hanners Sr. The quality of the casting of the handles is noteworthy. Height, 5 inches. *First Congregational Church, Woburn, Massachusetts.*

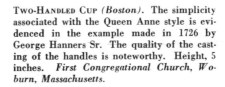

BAPTISMAL BASIN *(Newport)*. Unique in form is the baptismal basin of oval body with two loop handles, fashioned in 1734 by Daniel Russell. Length, 14¾ inches. *Trinity Church, Newport, Rhode Island.*

FLAGON *(Boston)*. The introduction of flagons into the Puritan churches of New England did not occur until the first quarter of the eighteenth century. An early example with flat cover and molded finial by Edward Winslow was presented to Brattle Street Church in 1713. Height, 11⅞ inches. *Museum of Fine Arts, Boston.*

FLAGON *(Boston)*. Typical of the Queen Anne style in flagons is the example by John Potwine, its elongated body decorated with molded bands, its domed cover surmounted by a bell-shaped finial. The small engraved panel below the donor's arms is suggestive of New England tombstone ornament. Height, 13½ inches. *Garvan collection.*

BAPTISMAL BASIN *(Philadelphia)*. The deep baptismal basin with flat shallow rim was made in 1712 by Irish-born Philip Syng. Diameter, 14¾ inches. *Christ Church, Philadelphia.*

BAPTISMAL BASIN *(New York)*. Based on a Dutch model is this basin made in 1694 by Jacobus van der Spiegel. Its broad flat rim with molded edge is beautifully engraved with a poetical verse in Low Dutch explaining the meaning of baptism. At one time in the loan collection of the South Reformed Dutch Church of New York, which no longer exists, and now at the Metropolitan Museum of Art. Diameter, 10⅜ inches.

BAPTISMAL BASIN *(Boston)*. Based upon English styles is the shallow basin with domed center and broad rim, uot unlike the rosewater dishes of the seventeenth century. It was a gift in 1716 to the Brattle Street Church, and is a fine example of the craftsmanship of its maker, William Cowell Sr. Diameter, 13 inches. *Museum of Fine Arts.*

MUG *(Boston)*. Few mugs were made for churches. Among the earliest are two made by Benjamin Hiller in 1714 and 1715 and presented by his parents-in-law to their church. Height, 3⅞ inches. *First Baptist Church, Boston.*

BEAKER *(Newport)*. The simplicity of the Queen Anne style lasted well past the middle of the eighteenth century. Typical of its pleasing form and functional design is the beaker, one of three fashioned in 1760 by Thomas Arnold for the Newman Congregational Church. Height, 4½ inches. *Garvan collection.*

BEAKER *(New London)*. The use of curved lines during the rococo period is shown in the flaring lip of the tulip-shaped body and the wide splayed foot of this beaker made in 1773 by John Gardiner of New London, Connecticut. It was used in the celebration of the sacrament by Bishop Samuel Seabury, a graduate of Yale in 1748, the first American bishop of the Protestant Episcopal Church. Height, 5⅛ inches. *Berkeley Divinity School, New Haven.*   *Left*

BEAKER *(Boston)*. In sharp contrast to the curved lines in Gardiner's beaker of 1773 is Revere's beaker of 1795, with its ovoid body and reeded rim, illustrating the classical influences of the Federal period. Height, 5½ inches. *Garvan collection.*   *Right*

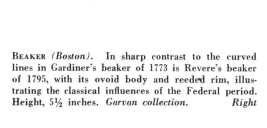

ALMS DISH *(Boston)*. The boldly engraved inscription and rocaille engraving of the Hancock arms on this alms dish, made by John Coburn in 1764 for the Brattle Street Church, typify the rococo ornament of the period. Diameter, 13⅛ inches. *Museum of Fine Arts.*

STANDING CUP *(Boston)*. Church cup made in 1758 and copied at the express desire of the donor from an elaborate seventeenth-century French chalice presented to the Old South Church in that year. The donor, Rev. Thomas Prince, pastor of the church, directed in his will "a Piece of Plate of the Form and Height of the last presented to ye sd church. I would have it plain and to hold a full pint." Perhaps its felicity of execution is due to the fact that it was fashioned by Paul Revere, son of the French-born Apollos Rivoire. Height, 9½ inches. *Old South Church, Boston.*

TWO-HANDLED COVERED CUP *(Boston)*. Typical of the Federal period and its classically inspired style is the use of the ovoid body, urn finial, reeded molding, engraved ornament, and Roman lettering. One of a pair made about 1795 by Joseph Loring for the Brattle Street Church. Height, 11¾ inches. *Garvan collection.*

CROWNS OF THE LAW *(New York)*. Exotic by contrast with the simple forms used in the New England churches are the elaborately ornamented Crowns of the Law, with repoussé and pierced designs, made by Myer Myers about 1765. They are still in use as crowns or ornaments for the wooden rollers around which the Pentateuch is rolled. Height, 14 inches. *Touro Synagogue, Newport, Rhode Island.*

Caudle cup by Hull and Sanderson, earliest Boston silversmiths, both from London. Inscribed *The gift of Eliezer Moody to the Church in Dedham. 1720.* Height 3-13/16 inches. *Lent by the Dedham churches.*

Colonial silversmiths

—masters and apprentices

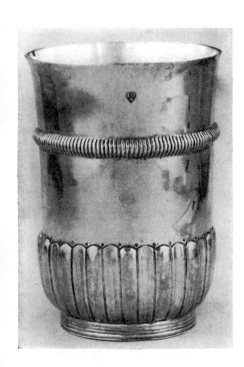

Beaker, one of a pair by Jeremiah Dummer, Boston, who was apprenticed to Hull and Sanderson. Engraved in small semi-script on the bottom *Church of Dedham.* Height, 5⅝ inches. *Lent by the Dedham churches.*

Beaker by John Edwards, Boston, who was trained by Dummer. Mark, IE crowned. Engraved, *The gift of Hannah Ware to the church in Dedham, 1722.* Height, 4¼ inches. *Lent by the Dedham churches.*

Photographs by courtesy of the Museum of Fine Arts, Boston; except as noted, pieces are from the museum's collection.

Church cup or beaker by Joseph Kneeland, Boston. Inscribed *The Gift of Mr. Thomas Metcalf to ye first Church in Dedham.* Metcalf also presented a caudle cup by Dummer to this Dedham church. Five maker's marks, imperfectly stamped, are crisscrossed on the bottom. Not enough of Kneeland's work is known to indicate who his master was. Height, 6 inches. *Lent by the Dedham churches.*

Teapot, c. 1765, by Benjamin Burt, Boston, who learned his trade from his father John Burt, an apprentice of John Coney. Teapot has repoussé decoration on shoulder. Engraved on reverse *OB to SB* under a double-headed eagle (Obadiah Brown of Providence to his daughter). A similar teapot exhibited has the Brown arms in a foliate cartouche on one side, *OB to AB* under the crest on the other; a porringer and cream pot in the Clearwater collection are similarly engraved. Height, 5⅝ inches. *Lent by Mr. and Mrs. Mark Bortman.*

Teapot by Jacob Hurd, Boston, whose apprenticeship remains a puzzle. Marked HURD in small rectangle. Engraved with Fayerweather arms in foliate cartouche, and in similar device on other side *The Gift of Edwᵈ Tyng Esqʳ to H. Fayerweather . . . 9, 1745.* Height, 5¼ inches. *Lent anonymously.*

In 1906 THERE WAS HELD at the Museum of Fine Arts in Boston a loan exhibition of American silver of the seventeenth and eighteenth centuries which has become a landmark in the antiquarian history of this country. Some ninety craftsmen were represented, from John Hull to Paul Revere; those of Boston were most numerous, and works by smiths of Newburyport, Newport, New York, and Philadelphia were also included. In the introduction to the catalogue, R. T. H. Halsey wrote, "The Museum of Fine Arts, Boston, has demonstrated by this exhibition that the art of the silversmith was highly developed during our early colonial days, and that the craftsmanship of our early native born artisans deserves wider recognition by our Museums than hitherto accorded."

Recognition has indeed become wider in the fifty years since then. Some of the pieces shown for the first time in 1906 have since been many times exhibited and published. Some that then belonged to descendants of the original owners are now proudly installed in museum collections. Knowledge and appreciation of the work of our early silversmiths have so greatly increased that one might suppose all the significant pieces surviving had been displayed and recorded—but that is far from true.

In observance of the fiftieth anniversary of that first silver show, the Museum of Fine Arts is currently holding another loan exhibition of American silver, and it contains a remarkable number of examples that have never before been on public view. Entitled *Colonial Silversmiths—Masters and Apprentices*, the show gives a fresh approach to the study of our early silver by emphasizing the craft relationships among the smiths, particularly those of New England. It will continue through December 30.

From the pieces on view, a few have been selected for illustration here and on the frontispiece of this issue. All these are previously unpublished, except in the catalogue of the current exhibition. Notes and comment about them are supplied by Kathryn C. Buhler, assistant curator of decorative arts at the museum, who organized and catalogued the exhibition. Craft relationships among the Boston silversmiths, masters and apprentices, were first discussed by Mrs. Buhler at the Antiques Forum in Williamsburg in 1955, and in ANTIQUES for November of that year.   A. W.

Tankard (1700-1710) by John Noyes, Boston, who learned his craft from Dummer, and married the sister of another Dummer apprentice, John Edwards. This tankard with reeded cover resembles examples by Coney, Burt (Coney's pupil), and Winslow (apprenticed probably to Dummer). Engraved *S/WA* for William and Abigail (Fowle) Smith. Their son, Reverend William Smith, married Elizabeth Quincy and bequeathed a silver tankard to his daughter Abigail, "wife of Honorable John Adams Esq. of Braintree." Height, 5½ inches. *Lent by the Adams National Historic Site.*

Teakettle, c. 1720, with cut-card decoration. Unmarked, but credited to New York because of its style and generous size. The spout is distinctive; perhaps a marked kettle with spout cast from the same mold may turn up to identify the maker of this handsome piece. Height, 9½ inches. *Lent anonymously.*

Porringer by Jeremiah Dummer (c. 1670-1680), with unique handle of early design. Engraved *NG* on handle, and underside of handle *B/EM* for Ebenezer and Mary (Turner) Bowdich. Length, 6⅝ inches.

Pair of porringers by Samuel Casey of Newport, an apprentice of Jacob Hurd. Engraved on handles *S/RE*, perhaps for Robert Staunton of Richmond, Rhode Island, and Elizabeth Whitehorne of Kingston who were married January 16, 1757. Length, 7½ inches. *Lent by Philip H. Hammerslough.*

Sauceboat, one of a pair by Joseph Richardson, Sr. (1711-1784). A simple American version of an English form, engraved with cipher *C W* on side. Length, 7¾ inches. *Lent by Mr. and Mrs. Mark Bortman.*

Sugar bowl and coffeepot by London-trained Simeon Soumain (c. 1685-1750) who worked in New York after 1706. Made for John Odell of Stratfield and Connecticut Farms, New Jersey, these pieces were taken to the Maritime Provinces by his Loyalist son, Jonathan, and remained there in the family until recently. Height of pot, 10⅝ inches. Another Soumain sugar bowl in this Chinese rice-bowl form is at Yale. The tall tapered coffeepot is seamed on the side, and has an unusual lid.

Pair of candlesticks by Joseph and Nathaniel Richardson (1771-1791). Of columnar form, reeded, with gadrooning on bobêches and bases; engraved with script *MB* on bases. Height 5½ inches. *Gift in memory of Dr. George Clymer, by his wife, Mrs. Clymer.*

Pair of trifid spoons by one of Philadelphia's earliest silversmiths, the Huguenot Cesar Ghiselin (c. 1670-1734). Engraved *L/RP*. Length, 8 inches. *Gift in memory of Dr. George Clymer by his wife, Mrs. Clymer.*

SOME ENGRAVED AMERICAN SILVER

Part I. Prior to about 1740

By KATHRYN C. BUHLER

ENGRAVING ON SILVER FOLLOWS, in the main, definite styles at given times and it is these generalities which seem pertinent to an article on the subject however much one is more intrigued by the exceptions which occur to all rules. The technical side of engraving was explained in a pictorial demonstration in the January, 1942 issue of ANTIQUES and to those who have access to a file of The Magazine both the usual and unusual results are available in generous array. These may be divided into three categories: inscriptive, decorative, and heraldic; the first and last were doubtless primarily for purposes of identification, yet sometimes the first and always the last filled the second requirement too.

The earliest colonial silversmiths whose work is known to us were the partners, John Hull and Robert Sanderson, of Boston; and, if one may draw conclusions from the few existing examples of their work, heraldry was not their "hobby horse," in the somewhat derisive words of that Salem diarist, the Reverend William Bentley. They engraved block initials; or inscriptions on the rims of cups in a simple and forthright style; a typical example (*Fig. 1*) bears distinct relation to the lettering of John Hull's signature. Others of their pieces, discounting of course the engraving added by later generations, are in quite another script which, despite the absence of comparable handwriting, we may assume to be Sanderson's since it seems improbable that an apprentice would be entrusted with this important task.

Even in the abbreviations of these inscriptions one imagines the austerity of New England life; but oddly enough this early period was the one wherein our colonial silversmiths were most inclined to elaboration and ornamentation but in embossing and repoussé work perhaps more than in engraving. Hull and Sanderson also engraved the decorative designs of strapwork and foliage on beakers derived from those Dutch examples long adopted in England and some even then in New England possession (ANTIQUES, September, 1925, pp. 158, 159). One (*Fig. 2*) made in Amsterdam in 1637, owned by the First Church of Boston, has been recorded as "probably the 'silver tunn' bequeathed by the Rev. John Cotton in 1652" (E. Alfred Jones, *The Old Silver of American Churches,* 1913), but I herewith record my belief that the Boston silversmith, Robert Sanderson, had this Dutch beaker among his household goods for it is engraved with initials suitable for himself and his wife and the latter is found to have bequeathed, in 1694, a silver beaker to the First Church. Many of these beakers were made by New York silversmiths working in their native traditions; two of them have been minutely described, and their designs identified as motifs from published books, by Mrs. Russel Hastings in ANTIQUES (February, 1935, p. 52), and by Miss Edna Donnell in the Bulletin of the Metropolitan Museum of Art (February, 1938).

Despite the greater wealth of ornament on much New York silver, there too simple inscriptions, sometimes duly abbreviated, were engraved, as on the bowl of a spoon (*Fig. 3*) by Cornelius Vanderburgh commemorating the death of Olof Stevense Van Cortlandt in 1684. Funeral spoons are met not infrequently in early New York, and occasional ones are extant from a later period, but in New England the preference seems to have been, as gifts to bearers, relatives, or friends at a funeral of importance, for rings, either engraved or enameled.

Sanderson, on a tankard with initials pricked in a method common at this time, engraved on its lid (*Fig. 4*) flowers reminiscent of embroidery designs or of those executed in flat-carving on seventeenth-century chests, wainscot chairs, and even the stalwart cupboards whereon such silver would gleam indeed in an ill-lit room. Al-

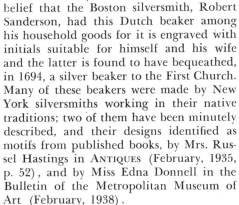

FIG. 1 (*top, above*)— INSCRIPTION on church cup by Hull and Sanderson (*Boston, fl. 1652-1683*). *This and Figures 3, 7, 9, 12, 17, 18, 19, from the Mabel Brady Garvan Collection, Yale University Art Gallery.*

FIG. 2 (*center*) — BEAKER made in Amsterdam in 1637. *From the collection of the First Church in Boston.*

FIG. 3 (*bottom*) INSCRIPTION on funeral spoon by Cornelius Vanderburgh (*New York, 1653-1699*).

FIG. 4 (*below*) — TANKARD COVER by Robert Sanderson (*Boston, 1608-1693*). *This and Figures 5, 6, 8, 10, 13, 14, 15, from the Museum of Fine Arts, Boston.*

though similarly decorated lids are comparatively rare among the large number of New England tankards surviving, others by Dummer, Dwight, Hurst, and Rouse come instantly to mind and seem to justify the inclusion of this type here. Similar flowers, recognizable even by the layman as tulips and carnations, were engraved a generation later on the rim of a plate by the excellent Boston silversmith, John Coney (*Fig. 5*). Although all silversmiths were capable of engraving, for better or worse, their own production, certain of them were pre-eminent in that art and Coney was one of these. Yet in the detailed inventory of his tools, which amounted to over £150, his "gravers" were valued at but 5/ 10d—even adding his sand cushion at 2/, it is a small proportion for the skill they demonstrated. The initials on the plate, in the triangular arrangement of the surname over husband's and wife's given names, are enclosed in a "plumed" or "feathered" cartouche modified to give, perhaps, better balance with the cherubs' delicate wings. Another version of this cartouche, described by C. C. Oman in his *English Domestic Silver* as "elaboration and conventionalization of the crossed palm-leaves," encloses, appropriately, the arms of Edward Palmes of New London, on a plate by Edward Winslow (*Fig. 6*). An interesting comparison is the freer execution of this cartouche on the New York tankard by Jesse Kip illustrated by John M. Phillips in ANTIQUES (July, 1943, p. 19).

Early New England heraldic engraving is well exemplified on the tankard (*Fig. 8*) made by John Coney for Mary Browne, sometime before her marriage in 1699 to Benjamin Lynde since the arms are those of Browne and her maiden initials are on the bottom. The acanthus is here shown with the helmet of proper heraldic *mantling*, that is, suggesting a mantle or cloak depending from the helmet. Mr. Oman

FIG. 6 (*right, above*)—PALMES ARMS on a plate by Edward Winslow (*Boston, 1669-1753*).

FIG. 7 (*right, center*) — WENDELL ARMS on a tankard by Peter Van Dyck (*New York, c. 1705*).

FIG. 8 (*right, below*) — BROWNE ARMS on a tankard by John Coney (*Boston, before 1699*).

FIG. 9 (*below*) — TANKARD COVER by Jacobus Vander Spiegel (*New York, 1697*). Made for Hendrick and Wyntje (Rhee) Myer.

FIG. 5 (*above*) — PLATE by John Coney (*Boston, 1655/6-1722*).

illustrates an English example of the acanthus cartouche engraved about 1650, a quarter of a century earlier than the feathered designs he cites, yet they were simultaneously popular in the colonies. An acanthus cartouche with its regional addition of pomegranates or small fruits (*Fig. 7*) was engraved by Peter Van Dyck of New York on the Wendell family tankard which has a characteristically rich cover executed in repoussé work. A tankard by Jacobus Vander Spiegel has a similar heraldic cartouche and an engraved cover in the New York taste for exuberant decoration (*Fig. 9*). Its tousle-headed cherub with sturdy wings is as much in contrast to Coney's prim-mouthed lad as are the heraldic cartouches, or the cypher monogram on the cover of the New York tankard to the plain block letters on the bottom of the New England one. An even more restrained New England cartouche is on the salver by Thomas Savage (ANTIQUES, August, 1942, Frontispiece); a second era of engraving is seen in the added script initials.

Although there are rare instances in New England of the use of cyphers, the above-mentioned triangular arrangement of block letters was preponderantly popular there until the mid-eighteenth century, and has never been completely abandoned. Sometimes these universally popular block initials were placed to add a decorative note; as often, probably, they appear on the bottom of a piece only to denote ownership. Certainly the most striking lettered engraving by a colonial silversmith is on the rim of the unique baptismal basin wrought by Jacobus Vander Spiegel for the South Reformed Church in New Yor¹ illus-

trated by Miss C. Louise Avery in ANTIQUES (November, 1924, p. 247).

Coney engraved in 1701 an inscription on a chocolate pot in a freer script than is found from the previous century. On the bottom, it was definitely not for decoration but was commemorative as well as identifying since it recorded *The gift of Wm. Stoughton Esquire to Mrs. Sarah Tailer: 701* in response to his bequest in 1701 giving "as a particular remembrance of me twelve pounds to buy a piece of Plate." Similar lettering was engraved in a quaintly arranged inscription on the bowl of a church cup made by Jeremiah Dummer of Boston who made many such cups with gadrooned surbases, some inscribed, some heraldically engraved, and some left plain. That both Dummer and Coney were commissioned to engrave plates for paper currency indicates in their own day an acknowledged proficiency in this art. Coney's, dated 1690, has upright lettering and the now familiar Indian seal of Massachusetts. Dummer's in 1709 combines block and script lettering in the manner that became popular on silver; variety in the shapes of the state seal depicted proved the existence of more than one plate used in "Printing 6,550 Sheets of bills of Credit" as recorded by the Council Board of Connecticut.

Many inscriptions on eighteenth-century silver were enclosed, sometimes in the cartouches used for heraldry, often in simple lined circles or the more decorative framing designs such as are seen on the four flagons made by as many local silversmiths for the Church in Brattle Street, Boston, 1711, 1712, and 1713. One (*Fig. 10*) was made by Nathaniel Morse, described at his death as "an ingenious Engraver" but today better known for his silver of which more has been found than of his prints. The others are by John Noyes, John Edwards, and Edward Winslow, in the order of their dating, and are to the casual observer

FIG. 10 (*left*) — INSCRIPTION on Nathaniel Morse flagon (*Boston, c. 1685-1748*).
FIG. 11 (*below*) — CARTOUCHE on tankard by Johannis Nys (*Philadelphia, fl. 1700-1723*). *From the Historical Society of Pennsylvania. Photograph courtesy of Mr. Harrold E. Gillingham.*

FIG. 12 (*above*) — CARTOUCHE on cup by Charles Le Roux (*New York, 1689-1745*).

as nearly alike as four flagons even by the same man might be; but the engraving, though of the same design and lettering, on each is by a noticeably different hand.

The plumed and acanthus cartouches of the seventeenth and early eighteenth centuries were superseded by one of quite another form, with symmetrical scrolls and an elliptical or circular center which, if unconventional heraldically, was none the less effectively used for armorial bearings. Johannis Nys, one of Philadelphia's first silversmiths, engraved this design to enclose a reversed cypher monogram on a tankard (*Fig. 11*) made for George and Mary Emlen who were married in 1717. Coney engraved it to enclose Henry Flynt's arms on the two-handled cup presented by his pupils in 1718, and emphasizing the English influence on all colonial plate of this era is the similar device engraved by Charles Le Roux of New York on a cup bearing Frederick dePeyster's cypher (*Fig. 12*) made about 1731. The Bostonian John Edwards used another variant of it for an inscription on a church cup (*Fig. 13*), in form similar to the pair he made in 1732 for the Church in Brattle Street on which the inscription is in the old-style feather cartouche surmounted by the ever-popular cherub's head. In 1739 his son Samuel was commissioned to make a pair of cups, at a cost of £49, 7d, for the same Church in Lynde Street, and he copied his father's cartouche for their similar inscription. At the same time he engraved, at a charge of £1, 1s, the donor's arms on his father's cup (*Fig. 14*) in a cartouche of surprisingly different effect for its somewhat similar elements.

A related cartouche with a shield-shaped enclosure of arms was engraved by Jacob Hurd on a globular teapot (*Fig. 15*) in 1737 which he further embellished with a decorative band around the rim. The mask is still a favorite device, but bellflowers or shells are often found in its place here. A Philadelphia cartouche on a cann by Philip Syng (*Fig. 16*) adds birds, as are found on New York pieces, and beasts; with a pendent mask, sterner visaged than the youthful cherubs of earlier designs but by its outline of wings related to them. The beasts are hardly akin to the supporters of the British royal arms, yet even this coat was executed by American silversmiths. It is

FIG. 13 (*above*) — CARTOUCHE on cup by John Edwards (*Boston, 1671-1746*).

FIG. 14 (*right*) — HALL ARMS engraved by Samuel Edwards (*Boston, 1705-1762*).

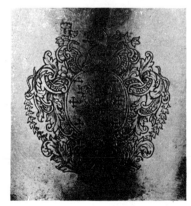

known today on the New York and Boston Admiralty Oars and on a gorget by Barent Ten Eyck illustrated by Doctor George B. Cutten in Antiques (December 1942, p. 302).

The complex cypher seen within cartouches (*Figs. 9, 11, and 12*) was even by itself a very decorative device which had, at least since the mid-seventeenth century, been deemed of sufficient interest to be the subject of a number of publications both Continental and English. Peter Van Dyck, about 1710, fitted a cypher (*Fig. 18*) to the curved sides of his charming teapot which in its simplicity contrasts interestingly with his tankard. The puzzling effect of its reversed letters makes one wonder if he strove for the first or second definition which was to be given in Bailey's dictionary of 1782: "The letters of a person's name interwoven together as in a seal" or "Ciphers are certain odd marks and characters in which letters are written that they may not be understood in case they should be intercepted." An even more baffling effect was occasionally obtained by early New York silversmiths with a number of interlaced letters in cursive formation. The initials on the teapot are those of Johannis Van Brugh and are repeated, perhaps for surer identity, in block letters and triangular formation with his wife's initial, on the bottom — as are also the Emlens' initials on the bottom of their tankard.

Samuel Sympson of London, in 1726, published "A New Book of Cyphers More Compleat and Regular than any yet Extant. Wherein the Whole Alphabet (Twice over,) Consisting of Six Hundred Cyphers, is variously Changed, Interwoven and Reversed. Being a

FIG. 18 (*below*) — TEAPOT (*c. 1710*) by Peter Van Dyck (*New York, 1684-1750/1*).

FIG. 19 (*bottom of page*) — GOLD LOCKETS by Daniel Russell, John Noyes, and Joseph Richardson.

FIG. 16 (*top, above*) — MADDOX ARMS on cann by Philip Syng (*Philadelphia, 1703-1789*). *From the collection of Mrs. A. K. Peck, Jr.*

FIG. 17 (*above*) — SUGAR BOWL by Simeon Soumain (*New York, c. 1685-c. 1750*).

FIG. 15 (*above*) — TEAPOT by Jacob Hurd (*1737*). Henchman arms.

Work very Entertaining to such as are Curious, and Useful to all sorts of Artificers in general." He used only two-letter combinations and all reversed; a Rhode Island silversmith, Samuel Casey, followed his design so exactly, although in repoussé, that it is evident he had access to the London volume. Simeon Soumain of New York engraved a similar two-letter cypher (*Fig. 17*) for Elizabeth Cruger on a sugar bowl shaped "in the Chinese taste." Although chinoiserie engraving had had its marked vogue in England (see Antiques, November 1943, p. 221), little is known among colonial plate, which, however, was frequently wrought in Oriental form.

Other engravings of a charm not to be overlooked are those found on the contemporarily-termed "small work" or "pocket-cases." In the words of Lewis Janvier, "goldsmith newly come from London" to Charleston, South Carolina, in 1734, they were: "Snuff boxes . . Patch-boxes, Tooth-picker cases, Sissar-cases, Thimble and Needle cases," to which we may add, from examples existing today, nutmeg-grater cases, tobacco boxes, and freedom boxes. These were engraved in designs varying from elaborately framed armorial bearings to the simple conventionalized flower designs found also engraved or chased on gold lockets (*Fig 19*) and buttons.

(The engraving on early American silver bears a direct relation to the form, and like the form follows a definite stylistic development. Part II of this article, to appear next month, will trace that development up to 1810.)

COLONIAL CHERUBIM IN SILVER

By MARSHALL DAVIDSON

Except as noted, illustrations from the Metropolitan Museum of Art

A DECORATIVE detail that adds to the distinctive character of colonial silver tankards is the cast cherub head or mask that was frequently applied to the tip of the handle. While European precedent for this treatment can be found, the practice in America during the late seventeenth and early eighteenth centuries was so general that it became a typical feature of our native silver. The smiths of New England, New York, and occasionally Pennsylvania all employed this method of adding a fillip to their handiwork, despite marked regional differences in other respects. While the New England craftsmen used a greater variety of forms to ornament the handle tip, those of the New York region often went a step further in decorating the curve of the handle as well, with a lion rampant or an elaborate arrangement of a mask with swags and pendent clusters of fruit and flowers. This practice is reminiscent of German and Scandinavian styles. In one instance, that of a tankard recently given to the Museum of the City of New York by Mrs. J. Amory Haskell, a double profile, possibly cut from a contemporary William and Mary coin, is applied to the curve of the handle in place of the more usual type of ornament.

While the idea of applying decoration in this manner finds European precedent, the actual forms under discussion have appeared to be in the nature of creative contributions by the colonial silversmiths. In any event, the same cherub heads, masks, and other figures seem not to have found favor among

FIG. 1 — "APPLIQUE DE CABINET" (*late 17th century*). Mask and pendent ornament, cast and chiseled bronze. From *Le Bronze*, catalogue of metalwork in the Musée des Arts Decoratifs, Paris

FIG. 2 — MASK AND PENDENT. Cast silver ornament applied to handle of a tankard by Cornelius Kierstede (*New York, 1675–1757*)

FIG. 3 — "APPLIQUE DE PENDULE" (*late 17th century*). Winged cherub-head ornament, cast and chiseled bronze. From *Le Bronze*

FIG. 4 (*below*) — WINGED CHERUB HEADS. Cast silver ornaments, applied to handle tip of silver tankards. A and B, New England types, by John Coney (*Boston, 1655/6–1722*) and by Edward Webb (*Boston, d. 1718*). 4, B

from the Mabel Brady Garvan collection, Yale Gallery of Fine Arts. C and D, New York type, by Gerrit Onckelbag (*New York, 1670–1732*) and by Cornelius Kierstede

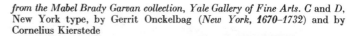

the silversmiths of other countries. The cherub heads that bedeck the scalloped rim of the Coney monteith at Yale and a number of comparable English bowls, it is true, are of the same general type, though used differently.

In ANTIQUES for February 1935, Mrs. Russel Hastings has shown that the engraved decorations on the Vandenburgh-Sanders-Garvan beaker were copied directly from illustrations of the writings of Jacobus Cats (*1577–1660*), the Dutch John Bunyan. Similarly, Miss Edna Donnell has proved that engraved plates by Adriaen Muntinck, Dutch silversmith and engraver of the early seventeenth century, were followed by Gerrit Onckelbag in the decoration of two beakers made in 1697 for the Reformed Protestant Dutch Church at Flatbush (*Bulletin* of the Metropolitan Museum of Art, Vol. XXXIII, no. 2, *pp. 47–50*). Undoubtedly other motives that appear on colonial silver, such as heraldic designs, ciphers, or the elaborate patterns engraved on the lids of a group of tankards by Benjamin Wynkoop, Jacobus Van der Spiegel, "I. B.," and others, will ultimately be traced to some such imported models. That the cast appliqués under consideration were also derived from English or Continental forms is only logical.

In *Le Bronze*, the second part of a catalogue of metalwork in the Musée des Arts Decoratifs in Paris, appears a very pertinent illustration (Plate XXVI, *Fig. 256*) of a chiseled bronze *applique de cabinet* dating from the late seventeenth century (*Fig. 1*). From a comparison of this with one of the typical mask-and-pendent ornaments from a New York tankard (*Fig. 2*), it is obvious that the central elements of the French design below the mask, consisting of a cluster

FIG. 7 (*below, left*) — MASK AND PENDENT. Cast silver ornament applied to handle of a tankard by Peter Van Dyck (*New York, 1684–1750*). *From the Minneapolis Institute of Fine Arts*

FIG. 8 (*below, right*) — CHERUB HEAD AND PENDENT. Cast silver ornament, applied to handle of a tankard by Peter Van Inburgh (*New York, 1689–1740*). *From the Yale Gallery of Fine Arts*

FIG. 9 (*above*) — MASK WITHOUT PENDENT. Cast silver ornament applied to handle tip of a tankard by Jacobus Van der Spiegel (*New York, 1668–1708*). *From the Yale Gallery of Fine Arts*

of fruit and flowers and three floral termini, correspond exactly with elements of the tankard decoration. Although the mask and some of the appendant features of the French bronze are different, the particular details noted are line for line alike.

Interestingly enough, in the same plate with this illustration in *Le Bronze* is another (*Fig. 258*) showing a winged cherub head of a type frequently found on the spandrels of English and Dutch clocks and on occasional brass box locks of the late seventeenth and early eighteenth centuries (*Fig. 3*). Here again the central portion of the French design corresponds curl for curl and feature for feature with another of the ornamental forms found on tankards by at least a score of New York makers — in this case with one of the cherub heads customarily found on the handle tip, as previously mentioned (*Fig. 4, C and D*). Though shorn of the wings and accompanying scroll designs, the tankard appliqués usually show vestiges of these abbreviated members. A direct comparison of clocks and tankards makes this relation even more obvious than it appears in the illustrations.

The fact that these winged cherub heads are such a very common feature of tall-case and bracket clocks of the period suggests a further possibility. *English Domestic Clocks* by Cescinsky and Webster illustrates numerous examples not only of this same cast form but of several variants. One of these shows a more neatly combed

FIG. 5 (*above*) — DIAL OF CLOCK BY "EDWARDUS EAST, LONDINI" (*c. 1676*). From *English Domestic Clocks*, by Cescinsky and Webster, London, 1913. Compare with Figures 3, 4, C, and 4, D

FIG. 6 (*left*) — APPLIQUÉ ON CASE OF CLOCK BY A. FROMANTEEL (*late 17th century*). Sketched from an illustration in Britten's *Old Clocks and Watches*, 6th edition, 1932. This, like Figures 1, 3, and 5, suggest probable sources of the similar decorations used by colonial silversmiths

coiffure, obviously analogous to the cherub heads frequently found on New England silver tankards (*Fig. 4, A and B*). In both the clocks and tankards these small ornaments vary considerably in quality. Some, such as Figures 2 and 4, A, show a refinement of detail indicative of good casting and a thoughtful use of chasing or chiseling, while others seem much cruder, as a result of wear or faulty casting or of frequent recasting (*Fig. 4, B*). The basic types, however, as they were repeated in colonial silverwork, can be discerned with adequate certainty wherever they recur.

Still more interesting are two items illustrated in F. J. Britten's *Old Clocks and Watches*, both made by London clockmakers of the late seventeenth and early eighteenth centuries. One is of a clock by A. Fromanteel (*Fig. 502*, sixth edition); the other is a portable barometer by Daniel Quare (*Fig. 499*, sixth edition; also illustrated in the *Dictionary of English Furniture*). Applied to the jambs of the clock hood and to the feet of the barometer appears nothing but the elaborate mask-and-pendent decoration that is considered a distinguishing feature of certain New York tankards. In these two pieces the same elements noted in the case of the bronze *applique de cabinet* are repeated, but here the complete design coincides with that on the New York tankards. Unfortunately it has not been possible to procure photographs from abroad suitable for illustration of either clock or barometer. But while the figures in Britten's book are not adequate for clear photographic reproduction, they do serve to remove any doubt in the matter, and, without taking undue liberties, it has been possible to reproduce the essential details in a sketch here illustrated (*Fig. 6*).

As the accompanying illustrations show, the topmost portion of the clock-barometer design, above the mask, has been omitted in the case of most New York tankards, although the other elements remain intact. The Peter Van Dyck tankard at the Minneapolis Institute of Fine Arts, however, provides a rare instance in which this top portion is swung down below the mask in place of the customary pendent and swags (*Fig. 7*). In at least one case, that of the Peter Van Inburgh tankard at Yale (*Fig. 8*), the mask has been replaced by the cherub head usually associated with the handle tip. In several other pieces the mask has, in turn, been detached from its swags and pendents and used alone on the handle tip (*Figs. 9 and 10*). Occasionally the two lateral floral termini are omitted, and the combination of the different ele-

ments may otherwise vary according to the maker's whim.

In all these cases the correspondence in size, outlines, and details is so remarkable, making any necessary allowances for wear or chasing, that one naturally concludes the colonial work to be castings from imported originals. That is far more likely than that some unheralded American sculptor-in-miniature might have carved forms identical with these examples from abroad for use by colonial silversmiths. But the question of why the latter chose to employ such engaging ornaments in this rather novel manner carries interesting implications too numerous to discuss here.

From what source the brassfounders, who undoubtedly supplied the clockmakers with their spandrel mounts, derived the design for their molds is not definitely known. Suffice it to say that the example illustrated in *Le Bronze* is apparently from France, home of much fine design and workmanship in ormolu. However, use of this particular form and closely related forms is far more typical of English and Dutch clock decoration than French, and the somewhat similar cherub and scroll escutcheons on much fine English (and probably Dutch) furniture of the William and Mary Period also comes to mind. The mask-and-pendent composition is rather more French in character. Although many other instances of its use on clocks and other pieces could undoubtedly be found, in the only illustrations that have come to light (aside from the related example shown in *Le Bronze*), it appears on the work of London clockmakers.

No claim to completeness can be made for this brief discussion. One continues to wonder what

FIG. 10 — SILVER TANKARD. By Simeon Soumaine (*New York, 1685–c. 1750*). Showing cast mask-and-pendent ornament applied to the curve of the handle, and mask applied to handle tip

the immediate source may be for the familiar dolphin-and-mask thumbpiece used by New England silversmiths on their tankards, and for the lion passant or rampant frequently found on the handle curves of New York tankards. These and other contemporary motives were, of course, only part of the art vocabulary of the time, used and reused in many different media. It is hardly surprising that the silversmiths and their patrons found them agreeable and fashionable. Doubtless they were less concerned than we with the question of immediate prototypes and analogues. But however simply these cast forms were adapted from European models, the imagination with which they are used and combined with other decorative features on colonial tankards is the equivalent of creative design. Something more than whimsy must have prompted the choice and manner of application of these details.

COLONIAL FURNITURE AND SILVER

A Study of Parallels and Divergences

By KATHRYN C. BUHLER

COLONIAL CABINETMAKERS AND SILVERSMITHS employed, in their widely disparate products, certain identical elements of design or decoration. This observation raises the question whether our forebears were consciously striving in the direction of the "matching sets" with which we are surfeited today, or whether the manifest similarities were merely the unconscious result of a common taste.

An answer to the question calls for close comparison between examples of early furniture and contemporary items of silverwork. To begin near the beginning, let us look at the furniture of Thomas Dennis of Ipswich, Massachusetts (*c. 1638-1706*), one of the earliest identified American cabinetmakers. His work, recorded with satisfying thoroughness in ANTIQUES by the late Doctor Irving P. Lyon (November, December 1937; February, April, June, August 1938) exhibits moldings on chests similar to those on the silver beakers wrought in 1693 for the First Church in his town by the unidentified silversmith IA (*Fig. 1*).

But the contrast between the usually severely simple silver of early New England and the richly ornamented furniture of Dennis' recorded work is greater in effect than is their similarity, although one may cite many details of like treatment. Consider, for example, a wainscot chair ascribed to Dennis (*Fig. 2*). The bulbous turnings of the supports find their contemporary parallels in the stems of silver standing cups. The framing panels of conventionalized pattern on the Ipswich chair back are definitely reminiscent of the designs on basebands of bowls and tankards wrought by the then distant New York silversmiths. This chair's shaped crest might well find its outline in the serrated rim of a typical silver tankard cover. These simple turned finials are very like those with which early eighteenth-century silversmiths topped the lids of their products. Dennis also used a vase-form finial found on silver only in the later years of the century when cabinetmakers and silversmiths wrought flame-like finials of similar form.

Dennis ornamented some of his furniture with panels in definitely geometric design; although writers for years have referred to "geometric" handles on silver porringers, it is difficult to see any real relation between them. One is more apt to see a connection between the frequent heart-shaped holes in porringer handles and a detail of ornament applied to the stiles of a Connecticut cupboard of the late seventeenth century (*Fig. 3*). The conventionalized tulips carved on the panels of this same type of cupboard have been compared with those in panels on a caudle cup by Hull and Sanderson (*Fig. 4*), Boston's earliest identified silversmiths (John Hull, *1624-1683*; Robert Sanderson, *1608-1693*). The matted or pitted background of this and other early silver pieces can hardly be considered as a model for the punchwork much used a century later in wood by the carver Samuel McIntire — but we must for the present leave aside the Federal period to which McIntire belongs, for the colonial era alone offers more than ample material for our consideration.

THE RELATIONSHIP between pewter and silver, or silver and ceramics, or ceramics and glass, in a given era is fairly apparent, because of their similarity of size, shape, and function. One may also see, if one looks for it, a distinct relationship between contemporary objects of two quite different kinds — as, for instance, between furniture and silver. A Queen Anne highboy is as expressive of its era as is a Queen Anne teapot, and there is consequently a recognizable affinity between them, though their similarity is less one of form than of decorative detail. Because comparison of colonial furniture and silver is not often made and may be instructive, we asked Mrs. Buhler to consider the extent of their relationship, how it came about, and why. Here are her conclusions.
—THE EDITOR

Applied spindles on early furniture were sometimes sufficiently plain to be compared with the "rat-tail" drops on spoon bowls or below handle joinings on silver, though on furniture spindles were purely ornamental, while on silver the drops had a functional purpose, to strengthen a joint. Furniture spindles in baluster form are not dissimilar to the turned drops below hinges on tankard handles, though they are usually more elongated. The silversmith's applied "cut-card" ornament, also favored in early styles near handles or at the base of a finial, is obviously not a practical device for a cabinetmaker; yet the looking-glass maker for a longer period of years cut outlines in his crested frames similar to those of cut-card work on silver. Bosses were favored by both crafts, but in diverse ways. In furniture we find them applied, like the spindles. In silver they may be an integral part of the surface, almost an element of the form, as in John Coney's sugar box (*Fig. 5*). This box also illustrates a type of hinge which at this time the silversmith was using more commonly than the cabinetmaker; the latter's doors or lids were wont to swing on wooden or roughly finished iron pegs. Neat hinges in brass at the sides of mahogany doors were used later, when the silversmith was carefully concealing the hinges on teapot lids, though on tankards he continued to flaunt their use.

Spiral turnings are found on colonial furniture; the New York chest on stand (*Fig. 6*) shows a freer spiral than Coney curled for these sugar-box feet or than silversmiths used for tankard thumbpieces; but the chest's globular feet bring to mind those on nineteenth-century silver teapots. On other pieces of silver Coney was well ahead of his cabinetmaking contemporaries in the use of claw-and-ball feet (no new thing on European furniture) but his were a practical combination, on chafing dishes, of silver claws grasping insulating balls of wood. Oddly, when claw-and-ball feet were favored by the cabinetmaker, silversmiths rarely used them; a notable exception, the only known New England piece of its period to have them, is the little creampot by Samuel Casey (*Fig. 8*). Its scallop-cut rim, a treatment also found commonly and with a wider swing on sauceboats, is repeated in the skirt of a contemporary claw-and-ball foot desk (*Fig. 7*). The masks which provide a rather unusual embellishment for the carved knees of this desk repeat a motif which had long been cast or engraved on silversmiths' production (see ANTIQUES, April 1940, p. 184).

In silver, at least as early as 1700 here, the spiral embossing known as gadrooning was effectively employed. Dummer is noted for his use of it on bowls and bases of cups; and Revere and his contemporaries, in New York and Philadelphia as well as in Boston, edged coffeepot lids and other rims with this rope-like design. On chair and table rails of the 1760's it probably had its most successful furniture use, but this universally popular ornament had appeared in rudimentary form on furniture in the late 1600's, in the applied slanting segments under the top and shelf of the cupboard (*Fig. 3*).

FIG. 1—"IA" BEAKER, made for the First Church in Ipswich (1693). *From the Mabel Brady Garvan Collection, Yale University Art Gallery.*

FIG. 2 — WAINSCOT CHAIR, ascribed to Thomas Dennis of Ipswich. *From the Essex Institute.*

FIG. 3 — PRESS CUPBOARD (*Connecticut, late 1600's*). *This and Figures 4, 5, 7, 8, 9, 10, 11, 12, and 13, from the Museum of Fine Arts, Boston.*

FIG. 5 — SILVER SUGAR BOX, by John Coney (*1655/56-1722*).

FIG. 6 — CHEST ON FRAME. Gumwood (*New York, late seventeenth century*). *From the Metropolitan Museum of Art.*

FIG. 4 — SIVER CAUDLE CUP (*c. 1675*). By Hull and Sanderson (*in partnership 1652-1683*).

Fig. 7 — Mahogany
Desk (*c. 1760*).

Fig. 8—Silver Cream-
pot, by Samuel Casey
(*c.1724-c.1770*).

Fig. 11 — Walnut Tip-Top Table, by Jonathan
Gavet (*Salem, c. 1784*).

Fig. 9 — Cherry Tea Table (*c. 1740*).

Fig. 10 — Silver Tray, by Myer Myers (*1723-
1795*). *M. and M. Karolik collection.*

Fig. 12 — Silver Cast-
er, by Rufus Greene
(*1707-1777*).

As tea drinking ushered in new forms for the silversmith, so did it introduce a range of charming little tables for the cabinetmaker. Many simple molded salvers of the early eighteenth century are reflected in the tray top of the little folding cherry table (*Fig. 9*). One finds, I think, the silversmith first essaying a scalloped rim on a tray when he replaced the salver's funnel-shaped foot or base by three or four small scrolled feet. A tray by Simeon Soumaine (*1685-c.1750*), illustrated by Miss C. Louise Avery in the catalogue of *Early New York Silver* (1931), has four c-scrolled legs on shell-like feet and a shaped rim with a simple molding. Shortly the silversmith was adding shells to his rim (*Fig. 10*) but the cabinetmaker expended his elaboration in carving the bulbous turned pedestal and the knees of his comparatively simple scallop top table (the scallop a reference to the general outline, not, as one might think from certain silver examples, to the type of shell). Shells on furniture were by no means overlooked, however; one finds them carved on knees and rails, on blockings and in cabinets, in growing profusion throughout the so-called Queen Anne and Chippendale periods. The blocked bracket foot of many Chippendale-style chests and secretary-bookcases is seen on London silver trays of the early Georgian era but I do not know them on an American piece. On the whole, feet in silver and in wood are surprisingly dissimilar at given periods.

Another Chippendale characteristic — a pierced gallery on a table top — seems definitely to have influenced the Philadelphia silversmiths who added pierced galleries to their teapots and sugar bowls in a manner as effective as it is individual.

Silver, in the early eighteenth century, began to curve; outstanding in this trend were the straight-sided mugs which gave way almost entirely to bulbous canns. Yet in furniture the bombé piece, of similar contour, is exceptional. The reason for the cabinetmaker's straight lines is obvious — but the colonial silversmith usually hammered up his straight-sided pieces in the same painstaking fashion as his curved, so that neither form was for him a short-cut to accomplishment.

While the piercings of a porringer handle were primarily a practical measure, to serve as insulation against hot contents of the bowl, the piercings of a chair splat, which weakened the structural member, were solely for ornamental effect. Touches of carving which elaborate chair backs dim the similarity between the splat piercing and that on the so-called "keyhole" porringer handle — but the comparison is not so far-fetched as at first thought it seems. And the high-shouldered vase-shaped caster, more commonly of London make than American, and in outline akin to New England's gallipot shapes in silver, is

not unlike the vase-shaped splats of contemporary Queen Anne chairs.

Turnings on tea tables and lightstands show a feeling for another vase form found in silver. Rufus Greene's chunky little caster made in the second quarter of the eighteenth century (*Fig. 12*) agrees nicely with the heretofore unpublished tip-top table by Jonathan Gavet (*Fig. 11*). Beneath the top of this table is an aging paper neatly inscribed *This stand was bought of Jonathan Gavet Dec' 15th 1784 by my Grandfather Thomas Holmes. Cost £1.8.0. Joseph Ropes, Salem, Ap. 7, 1890.* And again we are indebted to Mrs. Mabel M. Swan for identifying Gavet as in the cabinetmaking rather than the retailing or second-hand business. For let it be noted that by this evidence of date, the silver and furniture forms are a generation, perhaps even half a century, apart.

In the early days the universal vogue for *chinoiserie* is reflected in a few known pieces of japanned furniture, although many fewer pieces survive today than records indicate were fashioned in the Colonies. In ornamentation on silver it seems to have been an even rarer expression of colonial taste, though in form it is frequently encountered. A salver made by Timothy Dwight (*Fig. 13*) has a fascinating border of engraved flowers separating mythical and Eastern animals, but although the last are generically like those depicted on furniture they were apparently derived neither from life nor from the japanners' sources. Silver was more often engraved than embossed, whereas the japanners' designs were in low relief, as were usually the furniture carvers'. An exception is the incised skirt-rail, with the ever-popular scroll considerably enriched, on a dressing table made in Philadelphia (*Fig. 14*). As near a match as could be is the scroll design executed in silver on a sugar bowl (*Fig. 15*) by Charles Oliver Bruff who from 1760 to 1765 was sojourning not far distant in Elizabethtown, New Jersey. There is no indication that the two pieces are not now together for the first time but, though Chippendale used this scroll innumerable times in his published *Director*, his was a borrowing from the French, and one source for such a universal detail would seem highly improbable.

Shall we, then, conclude that the overlappings and repetitions in colonial furniture and silver design occurred by chance or by intent? They were frequently not simultaneous, and there is apparently little evidence of the use of common sources of design. It seems to me that we must acknowledge, and certainly appreciate, the congeniality of general taste; but that so far as common motifs in both are concerned, in the words of the novelist, "any similarity . . . is purely coincidental."

FIG. 13 — SILVER SALVER with border of engraved flowers and animals, by Timothy Dwight (1654-1691/2).

FIG. 14 — MAHOGANY DRESSING TABLE (*Philadelphia, c. 1760-1770*). *Collection of Mr. and Mrs. Andrew Varick Stout.*

FIG. 15 — SILVER SUGAR BOWL, by Charles Oliver Bruff (*c. 1765*). *Collection of Mr. and Mrs. Nicholas Rutgers Jr.*

BY DAVID STOCKWELL

A 1757 inventory of silver

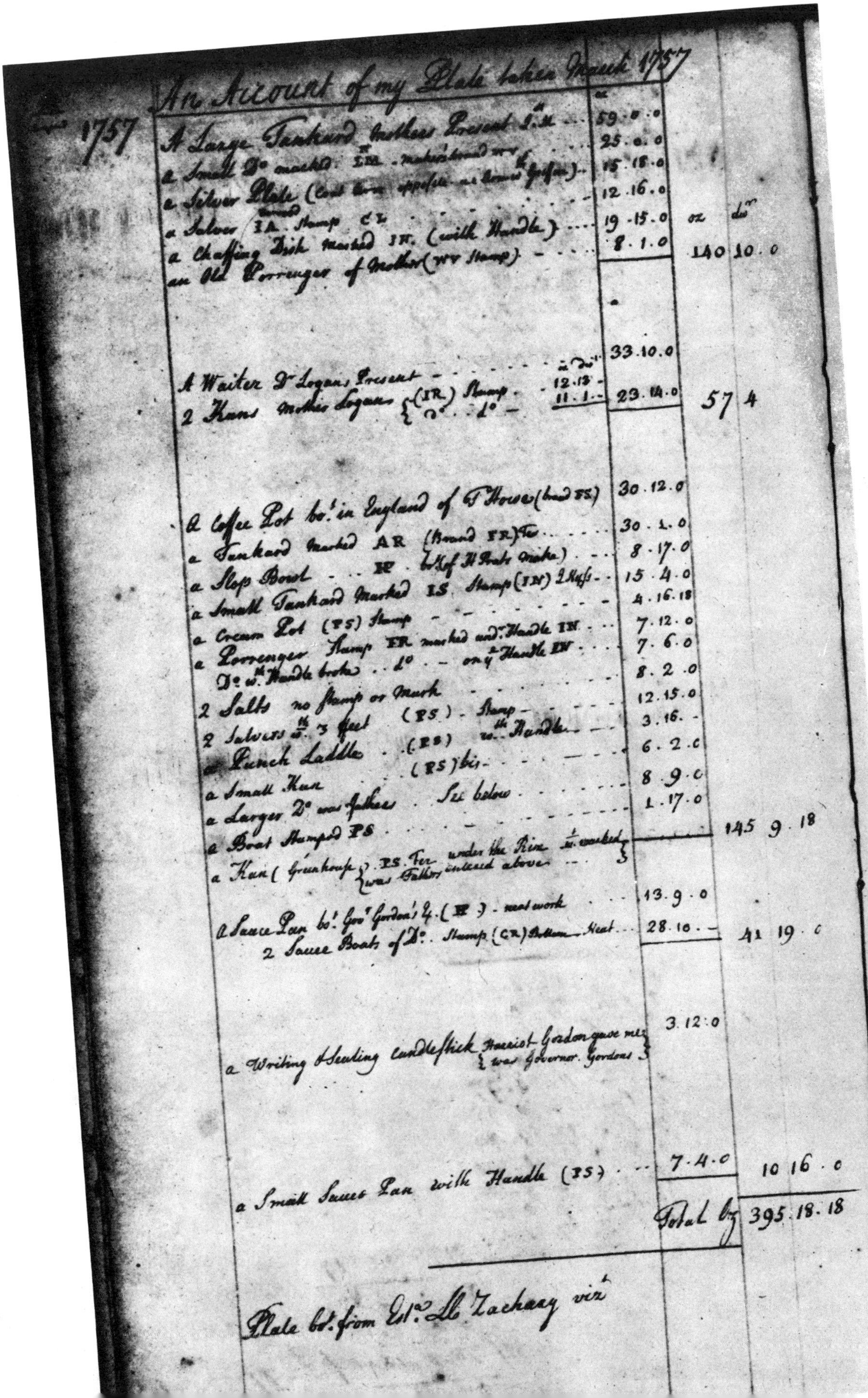
An Account of my Plate taken March 1757

1757 A Large Tankard Mothers Present ... oz 59.0.0
a Small Do marked ... 25.0.0
a Silver Plate ... 15.18.0
a Salver ... Stamp ... 12.16.0
a Chaffing Dish marked ... (with Handle) ... 19.15.0
an Old Porringer of Mother (... Stamp) ... 8.1.0 ... 140 10.0

A Waiter Dr Logans Present ... 33.10.0
2 Cans mother Logans {(IR) Stamp 12.13 / Do 11.1} ... 23.14.0 ... 57 4

a Coffee Pot bot in England of ... 30.12.0
a Tankard marked AR ... 30.1.0
a Slop Bowl ... 8.17.0
a Small Tankard marked IS Stamp ... 15.4.0
a Cream Pot (PS) Stamp ... 4.16.18
a Porringer Stamp ... 7.12.0
Do wth Handle broke ... 7.6.0
2 Salts no Stamp or Mark ... 8.2.0
2 Salvers ... 3 feet (PS) Stamp ... 12.15.0
a Punch Ladle (PS) wth Handle ... 3.16.-
a Small Can (PS) ... 6.2.0
a Larger Do was father ... See below ... 8.9.0
a Boat Stamped PS ... 1.17.0 ... 145 9.18
a Can ... PS ... was Fathers entered above

a Sauce Pan bot Govr Gordon's ... 13.9.0
2 Sauce Boats of Do Stamp (GR) ... 28.10.- ... 41 19.0

a Writing & Sealing candlestick Harriot Gordon gave me {was Governor Gordons} ... 3.12.0

a Small Sauce Pan with Handle (PS) ... 7.4.0 ... 10 16.0

Total oz 395.18.18

Plate bot from Estate ... Zachary viz

IT HAS LONG BEEN THE LAMENT of collectors of antique silver that early inventories give exceedingly meager descriptions, usually only a bare list of items and their weights. When a detailed inventory does turn up it is an important find—one that may fit an entirely new piece into the old jigsaw puzzle of the past.

Such a find is the hitherto unpublished and uncatalogued inventory of the silver of Isaac Norris, Jr. (1701-1766) of Philadelphia. A son-in-law of Penn's representative James Logan, who was mayor of Philadelphia, chief justice of the Supreme Court of Pennsylvania, and acting governor of Pennsylvania, Norris too was one of the great men of his day—statesman, scholar, and wealthy merchant. His silver inventory, headed *An Account of my Plate taken March 1757*, is an entry in one of his account books now in the manuscript collection of the Library Company of Philadelphia. I am indebted to the curator of the Ridgway Branch of the Library Company, Edwin Wolf II, for calling the document to my attention, and for his interest and aid in identifying many of the family initials recorded in it.

Twenty-nine items of silver are listed, with their weights in ounces, and in most cases with identifying notes. Norris and his contemporaries used the word "mark" not as we do today, to indicate the maker's identification, but only for the owner's initials. Of these it is reasonable to interpret I N as Isaac Norris. The initials N/I M on "A Large Tankard Mothers Present" would stand for Isaac Sr. and his wife, Mary Lloyd Norris. Isaac Jr.'s wife had been Sarah Logan; I S has not been identified as an individual but the letters might stand for Isaac and Sarah, with the N for Norris omitted. "Mother Logan" would be Sarah's mother, and "Dr. Logan" was undoubtedly Dr. William Logan of Bristol, her uncle. A R may have been a member of the Read family; "Mother Logan" had been Sarah Read.

Besides recording such "marks," Norris noted the maker's "stamp" or "brand" on most of the pieces, using these terms as we use "mark" or "touch." W V must be William Vilant, who was working in Philadelphia in 1725. C L and C R may both stand for Charles Le Roux

(1689-1745) of New York, or C R may have been Christopher Robert (1708-1763) of New York. No Philadelphia smith using these initials is recorded by Ensko. F R and I R are certainly members of the great Richardson family of silversmiths—Francis (1681-1729), who came to Philadelphia from New York in 1710; or his son Francis Jr. (b. 1708); and his better-known son, Joseph Richardson, Sr. (1711-1784). (Joseph Jr. was not born until 1752.) The "Coffee Pot" branded F S was "bot in England"; its maker was probably the London smith Francis Spilsbury (w. 1729-c.1743). A "Slop Bowl" stamped with conjoined HP is identified as "of H Prats make," and a "sauce pan" similarly stamped rates the only personal comment in the inventory: "neat work." I do not know of one example surviving today of the work of Henry Pratt (1708-1749) of Philadelphia, who was the father of the painter Matthew Pratt.

The initials I N occur in the inventory not only as the *mark* of the owner, but also as the *brand* of a maker, as Norris used the terms. He identifies the maker I N as "I. Nyss"; Johannis Nys (1671-1734) was one of the earliest of the Philadelphia smiths, coming from New York about 1695. Eight items in the inventory bear the P S stamp, which must be that of Philip Syng, Sr. or Jr. The elder Syng (1676-1739) came to Philadelphia in 1714 with his sons; Philip Jr. (1703-1789) was working there by 1726. Either of them could have made the "Kan" which "was father's," as the senior Norris lived till 1735.

Already an heirloom when Isaac Norris, Jr., recorded it in 1757, this can and the "Old Porringer of Mother" and all the other pieces enumerated doubtless passed to the next generation and the next. Probably some were lost or destroyed in time, and some traveled far out along the spreading branches of the family tree. But two, at least, came straight down in the Norris-Logan family for over a century and a half, until they were acquired by the late Maurice Brix. Recently sold at the auction of his collection, they can be readily identified with items in the Norris inventory. They are illustrated here, along with another family piece similar to one listed. It would be exciting if in time other items could be traced.

Silver flat-top tankard of William Vilant (w. 1725) of Philadelphia; engraved with initials *N/I M* and stamped twice on rim with maker's mark, wv in a heart; height 6¾ inches. Listed as the second item in the inventory: "a Small D° [tankard] marked IᴺM—maker's brand wv . . . 25.0.0 oz."

Silver piecrust-edge salver by Philip Syng, Jr. (1703-1789) of Philadelphia; on three scroll-and-hoof feet; engraved with crest of Isaac Norris, Jr; maker's mark PS stamped three times underneath; diameter, 7 7/8 inches. The inventory lists "2 Salvers w.ᵗʰ 3 feet. (P S.) Stamp . . . 12.15.0 oz."

Silver pear-shape can by Philip Syng, Sr. (1 1739) of Philadelphia; inscribed on base I I L; marked PS three times under rim; he 4¼ inches. Presented by Isaac Norris to James gan (1674-1751), this piece was not, of co among the former's plate in 1757, but is prob similar to two Syng items listed in his inven "a Small Kan . . . (PS) bis [twice] . . . 6.2.0 and "a Larger D° was fathers . . . PS. Ter [t times] under the Rim . . . 8.9.0. oz."

SUCKET FORKS

By GEORGE BARTON CUTTEN

Dr. Cutten's research has added greatly to our knowledge of early silversmiths in various parts of the country. Following his published records of New York State craftsmen, he has been investigating those of North Carolina and Virginia. He has lived in Chapel Hill since retiring from the presidency of Colgate University which he held for many years.

A SUCKET FORK is in a way a cross between a fork and a spoon. In fact, there are grounds for believing that its use formed the opening wedge for the introduction of table forks in England. Queen Elizabeth is reported to have been the first English sovereign to use a fork. For this she was sharply reprimanded by a clergyman, who declared that forks were "a tool of the devil" and an insult to God, who had already given us fingers with which to eat. The record of a visit Elizabeth made to a certain John Puckering, knight of the realm, mentions a "spoone and forcke of agatte" which she took away with her.

The name "sucket" comes from preserved plums or grapes served in thick syrup, very popular in the sixteenth and seventeenth centuries with aristocratic ladies. Eating them with the fingers must have been quite messy. The sucket fork provided a handy utensil, with a fork for the fruit and a spoon for the syrup. At first the name "spoon" was used, with the word "fork" as an auxiliary, but later the "fork" triumphed in popular usage.

These "fork-spoons" were never very common, even in England. In the inventories of the king's plate are a few "sucket spones with fork joyned together," and the next to the last item in the Jewel Book of Henry VIII is "One Spone wt suckett forke at thend of silver and gilt." By the time the first American ones were made, sucket forks were almost obsolete in England, and the fashion evidently did not last long here. The few extant American examples which can be definitely dated were all made at least two hundred and twenty-five years ago.

There are only ten American sucket forks whose makers can be identified. Four of them are by Bartholomew Le Roux, who was born in Amsterdam, Holland, about 1663, the son of a French Huguenot goldsmith. Le Roux came to New York some time before June 6, 1687, on which date he was made a freeman. In 1693 he purchased the property at the corner of Broadway and Beaver Lane, where he lived and worked. He held several city offices, and served as assistant alderman from 1702 until his death in 1713.

In the collection of Mrs. Julian L. Coolidge is a pair of sucket forks by William Rouse of Boston. We do not know very much about Rouse. The following terse announcement appeared in the *Boston News-Letter*, January 20, 1704: "William Rouse, goldsmith, died in Boston." His estate was appraised by John Coney, and the total inventory amounted to £575,11,6.

Johannis Nys also made a pair of sucket forks. This silversmith has been an elusive and at times mythical figure, no doubt due to the different spellings of his name, which has appeared as Neuss, Nice, deNice, Nis, Niss, Neys, deNoys, and Dennis. He was probably a French Huguenot, who came to this country via Holland. He is supposed to have served his apprenticeship in New York, and about 1698 went to Philadelphia, where he remained until 1723. It was at this time that these sucket forks would most likely have been made. William Penn was among Nys' patrons; his name appears in Penn's account book in 1700. From Philadelphia Nys went to Delaware, and died in Kent County in 1734.

The final extant pair of sucket forks was made by Jesse Kip *(1660-1722)*. He was born in New York and baptized in the Dutch Reformed Church on December 19, 1660, and continued to live and work in New York, in the North Ward. Kip was first identified in an article by John Marshall Phillips in ANTIQUES (July 1943).

The lengths of these sucket forks vary from 4¾ to 6¼ inches, with shafts from 2 to 4 inches. All have two-tined forks, and bowls with rat tails; with the exception of those on the Le Roux examples the rat tails are short.

Three other sucket forks have been located, but the makers are not known. These are all in museum collections.

SUCKET FORKS, two of four extant, by Bartholomew Le Roux *(1663-1713)* of New York. Length, 4¾ inches. All but one stamped with maker's mark, *BR*. Probably originally from a set of six, made for Gertrude Schuyler, daughter of Colonel Peter P. Schuyler, Albany's first mayor, before her marriage in 1714 to Peter Lansing. Initials *GS* engraved on all four. In addition the initials *P/EL*, for Peter and Elizabeth Lansing, appear on two of them. This arrangement was peculiar to Albany silversmiths, who seem to have preferred it to the more usual arrangement with surname initial above. *Author's collection.*

Two hoof spoons

BY ALBERT SCHER

WHEN HELEN BURR SMITH wrote about silver spoons with hoof-shape terminals in ANTIQUES in 1944 there were only four of these interesting survivals from seventeenth-century Dutch New York households known in America.[1] Now two more hoof spoons have come to light.

One bears the initials of the unidentified first owner, *F·A*, in seventeenth-century lettering on the flat of the hoof, but is otherwise unmarked (Figs. 1, 1a). It appears to be identical to a spoon made by Ahasuerus Hendricks (Figs. 2, 2a) that was discussed and illustrated in Miss Smith's article, except that the bowl of the spoon in Figure 1 is slightly larger than that of the Hendricks example. In both cases, the hand-wrought fig-shape bowl is neatly soldered to a rattail extension of the handle—a construction feature typical of seventeenth-century New York spoons.

The fig shape of the bowl attests to the early date of the spoon. John Marshall Phillips wrote, ". . . the earliest form [of spoon made in America] has a deep fig-shaped bowl. . . . This style, popular in England during the Commonwealth, dates back to the fifteenth century." [2] And Miss Smith pointed out, "Because of its fig-shaped bowl, the Hendricks spoon is thought by experts to be probably earlier than the other hoof-handled spoons" known in 1944, and possibly even earlier than the oldest known American spoon, which was made about 1664 by John Hull (1624–1683) and Robert Sanderson (1608–1693) of Boston.[3] Close examination of the spoon shown in Figure 1 reveals that the angle formed where the cast handle joins the bowl is greater than that on the Hendricks spoon. This has suggested to some experts that this spoon is even older than the Hendricks example.

The second newly discovered hoof spoon (Figs. 3, 3a) is one of the few pieces of silver—and the oldest spoon—known to have been made by Bartholomew Le Roux, the first of a distinguished family of early

Fig. 1. Silver hoof spoon, probably New York, seventeenth century. Length 6 9/16 inches. Inscribed *F·A* on the flat of the hoof. It is nearly identical to the spoon shown in Figs. 2, 2a. *Private collection; photograph by Meyers Studio.*

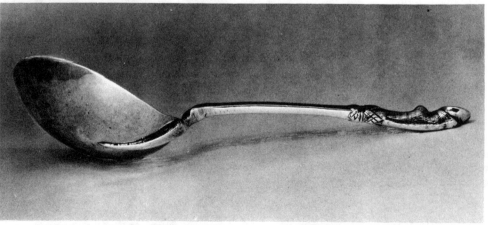

Fig. 1a. Side view of the spoon shown in Fig. 1. *Meyers Studio photograph.*

American silversmiths.[4] His family was of French descent and had lived for some time in Holland [5] before moving to England, where Le Roux was trained.[6] A skilled craftsman by the time he arrived in New York,[7] where he was married in 1688, his known silver shows that he could work in both the Dutch and English traditions. For instance, a two-handled bowl with paneled sides (in the Mabel Brady Garvan Collection at Yale University) is designed in true Dutch style,[8] while a richly decorated caster marked by Le Roux, also in the Garvan Collection, is very similar in design to an English example in the Victoria and Albert Museum.[9] Le Roux's hoof spoon is an interesting blend of the two styles. Typical of hoof spoons made in England, but not of those made in Holland, the flat of the hoof faces the back of the spoon. On the other hand, the series of graceful molded lobes at the base of the cast handle is a feature of seventeenth-century Dutch spoons.

The recently discovered hoof spoons are both in excellent condition, which suggests that they were presentation pieces rarely—if ever—used for eating. It is known that silver spoons were given as gifts to mark special occasions in the Old World, and many of these traditions were brought to America in the seventeenth century. For example, Dutch godparents gave a *gebortelepel*, or birth spoon, to a newborn child;[10] newlyweds were often given a silver spoon; and an engraved silver spoon was commonly presented to each pallbearer at a funeral.[11]

However, the penchant of seventeenth-century Dutch painters for realistic still lifes gives us proof that hoof spoons, at least, were pressed into everyday use on occasion. *Still Life with Glass and Metalware,* by Jan Jansz. Den Uyl (c. 1595–c. 1640) [12] and a still life of about 1637 by Willem Claesz Heda (1594–c. 1682) [13] both include hoof spoons in scenes of a meal in progress. It is difficult to determine whether the spoons in the paintings are silver or pewter, but their presence in works by these seventeenth-century artists helps to date this type of spoon. Joyce Fleur of the Haags Gemeentemuseum in The Hague feels that silver spoons, possibly hoof spoons, may have been used to eat the brandy-soaked raisins that rich Dutchmen served on feast days in silver bowls similar to the one by Bartholomew Le Roux mentioned above.

According to John Emery, hoof spoons are probably ultimately derived from spoons made in Greco-Roman times, particularly in Pompeii, although the Pompeian form does not include a realistic animal's leg. The immediate prototype for the Dutch spoons, he says, came out of Italy early in the seventeenth century. Hoof spoons quickly became very popular

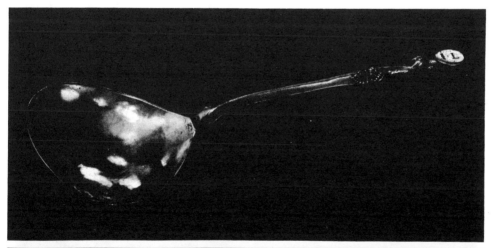

Fig. 2. Silver hoof spoon made by Ahasuerus Hendricks (w. c. 1675–1727), New York, c. 1680–1700. Length 6½ inches. Marked AH conjoined on the back of the bowl (Fig. 2a); inscribed on the flat of the hoof *I•L* for the first owner, possibly Johannes Lansing. *Yale University Art Gallery, Mabel Brady Garvan Collection.*

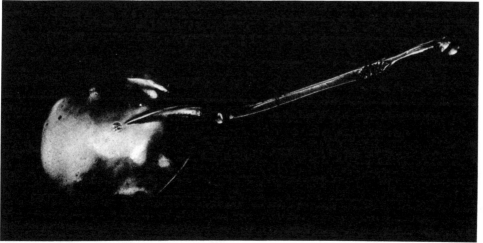

Fig. 2a. Reverse of the spoon shown in Fig. 2.

in Holland and remained in vogue until about 1660, when they were replaced by spoons with grotesque figures for terminals.[14]

During the seventeenth century the Netherlands enjoyed a period of unequaled wealth. It is not surprising, therefore, that Dutchmen who came to America brought not only such symbols of their prosperity as silver spoons, but also their Old World traditions and attitudes. Silver hoof spoons are rare, fascinating reminders of this early Dutch influence in America.

---

[1] ANTIQUES, June 1944, pp. 292-294. Of the four, three are now in the Mabel Brady Garvan Collection at Yale University: one made by Jacobus van der Spiegel, one by Ahasuerus Hendricks, and one attributed to Jurian Blanck Jr., all of New York City. The fourth spoon, made by B. Brasser of Amsterdam, is at the Albany Institute of History and Art.

[2] *American Silver* (New York, 1949), p. 28.

[3] ANTIQUES, June 1944, p. 292. The Hull and Sanderson spoon of c. 1664 is in the Essex Institute, Salem, Massachusetts. A similar spoon by Hull and Sanderson is in the Henry Francis du Pont Winterthur Museum.

[4] His sons Charles (1689–1745) and John (b. 1695) and his grandson and namesake Bartholomew Le Roux II (1717–1763) all became recognized silversmiths in America, as did his apprentice, and later son-in-law, Peter Van Dyck (1684–1751).

[5] Helen Burr Smith found in *Reitstap Armorial Genealogy* (vol. 2, p. 622) that the Dutch government granted the Le Roux family the right to bear a coat of arms.

[6] Most sources state that Bartholomew Le Roux was born in London in or about 1663. However, according to Helen Burr Smith's research files, Bartholomew's father, Pierre, moved from Amsterdam to London in 1680, was made a naturalized British subject in 1682, and was joined in England by his wife, Jane, and their children about 1685. If this is true, Bartholomew could not have been born in London.

[7] He came to New York with his younger brother Pieter and soon set up shop on Broadway near Beaver Lane, now 27 Broadway. (This information was generously provided by Helen Burr Smith.)

[8] An article about this type of bowl appeared in ANTIQUES for October 1961, pp. 341-345.

[9] The Victoria and Albert's caster is illustrated in Charles Oman, *English Silversmiths' Work Civil and Domestic: An Introduction* (London, 1965, No. 93). I have been able to locate references to only two other pieces of silver by Le Roux: a salt mentioned in C. Louise Avery, *Early American Silver* (New York, 1968 ed., p. 162 and Pl. LX); and a wavy-end spoon discovered by Robert Alan Green ("An Early New York Spoon," *The Magazine Silver*, November-December 1973, pp. 6-7). However, I have not been able to examine either piece.

[10] See J. W. Frederiks, *Dutch Silver* (The Hague, 1960), vol. 3, No. 242.

[11] John Marshall Phillips, "Dutch-New York Spoons," *Bulletin of the Associates in Fine Arts at Yale University* (June 1937), pp. 11-13.

[12] The painting is in the Museum of Fine Arts, Boston.

[13] The painting is in the Louvre, Paris.

[14] *European Spoons Before 1700* (Edinburgh, 1976), pp. 33, 36, 65, 151.

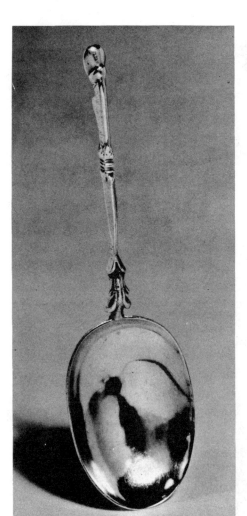

Fig. 3. Silver hoof spoon made by Bartholomew Le Roux (1663–1713), New York, 1688–1690. Length 6½ inches. Marked BR in oval and inscribed *IVB* conjoined on the back of the bowl (Fig. 3a). *Private collection.*

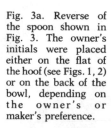

Fig. 3a. Reverse of the spoon shown in Fig. 3. The owner's initials were placed either on the flat of the hoof (see Figs. 1, 2) or on the back of the bowl, depending on the owner's or maker's preference.

Candlesticks and Snuffers by American Silversmiths

By Edward Wenham

IN VIEW of the fact that no very populous centres existed in this country in pre-Revolutionary times, the surviving quantity of early native silver articles indicates that our Colonial ancestors were strongly inclined to favor silver tableware. But, at the same time, we may safely conclude that the precious metal was largely restricted to objects of everyday use. Despite careful searching, few early specimens of purely ornamental American silver have been discovered and equally few more personal articles, such as were made in France and England.

Even silver candlesticks seem to have been regarded as a more or less unnecessary luxury, since they rank among the rarest types of early American silverwork — a point that needs no further evidence, at least to me, than the persistence called for to obtain photographs for illustrating these notes. Hence I would here express my special obligation to those collectors and others who have permitted publication of pieces in their possession. Additional examples are known, but no great number; and it is a matter for regret to those engaged in historical research that some owners object to the publication of their rare belongings.

Apparently no silver candlesticks were made in America prior to the second half of the seventeenth century. The earliest is the work of Jeremiah Dummer (*1645–1718*) and follows the columnar form found in England from about 1660 (*Fig. 1*). Here Dummer employed a clustered shaft rising from a knurled flange supported on a low convex spreading plinth. Concerning the source from which this Boston craftsman derived his inspiration, there can be little doubt, since two pricket candlesticks (*Fig. 2*), basically the same in style and dated *1663*, are still preserved in Salisbury Cathedral, England. But whereas the latter are more than two feet high, and the

stem of each is divided into two sections by a large cushion, Dummer reproduced only the lower half, to the top of which he fitted a wide, square, knurled pan, closely resembling the projecting flange below. He also omitted the ball feet of the English prototypes, and, in place of the circular depression appearing in the originals, substituted a plain, flat platform. Even so, the American work displays a remarkable likeness to the candlesticks in the English cathedral, particularly in the graceful molding of the slightly domical plinth, the knurling of the flange and grease pan, and the narrow molded band around the shaft.

Fondness for an architectural form is manifest in American candlesticks for some time. We find it, for instance, in a pair made by Isaac Hutton (*1767–1855*) of Albany, New York (*Fig. 3*). But though now historically important, these two plainly show that candlesticks were not looked upon as of commanding consequence; their function was to serve as supports for candles. In design and construction they are simple in the extreme. In place of the finely molded bases, often octagonal, and the well proportioned flutings that mark the work of contemporary English silversmiths, Hutton was content to produce a tapering fluted tube supported on an equally unadorned concave foot with a shallow square plinth. Then, too, though he supplied the customary square removable nozzles, or *bobèches*, he omitted the abacus, which English columnar candlesticks invariably have.

In suggesting that early American silver candlesticks were intended to be chiefly useful rather than significant as decorative articles of domestic plate, I would emphasize the fact that, aside from the Dummer stick, which is some eleven inches tall, they seldom attain to more than seven inches. A reason is found in the former custom of enclosing the

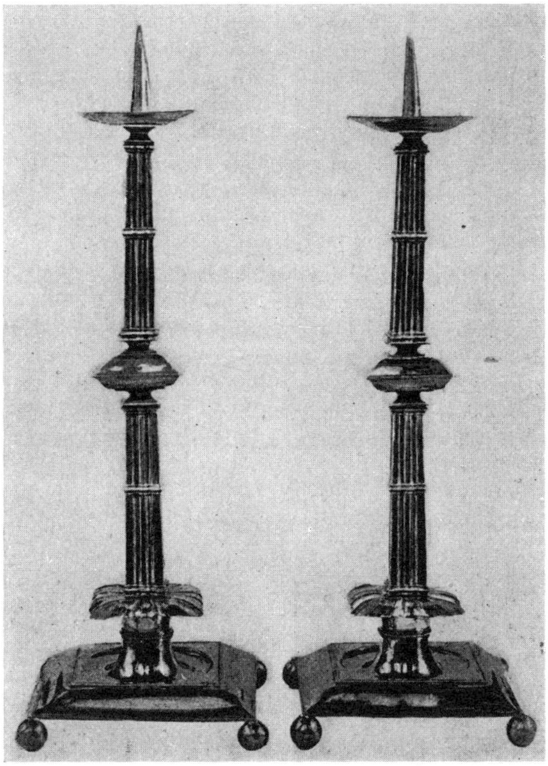

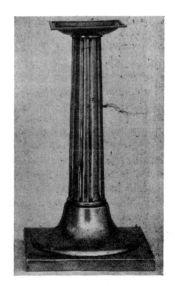

Fig. 1 (left) — First of Its Group (*c. 1680*)
   The earliest known American silver candlestick. By Jeremiah Dummer. *From the Museum of Fine Arts, Boston*

Fig. 2 (centre) — Pricket Candlesticks (*1663*)
   More than twenty-four inches high. The lower half of the stem was apparently the inspiration for the candlestick by Dummer (*Fig. 1*). *From Salisbury Cathedral, England*

Fig. 3 (right) — Simple Columnar Candlestick (*c. 1820*)
   One of a pair by Isaac Hutton. Probably intended to represent a Doric column, but with a hint of the early clustered form.
   From the Clearwater Collection in the Metropolitan Museum of Art

Fig. 4 — Baluster Candlestick (c. 1720)
By Bartholomew Schaats.
From the collection of Clapp & Graham

Fig. 5 — Octagonal Baluster Candlesticks
(*early eighteenth century*)
By John Burt. A simple but faultlessly proportioned pair, similar in general to Figure 4, but with the faceted sides unbroken from candleholder to base.
From the Fogg Art Museum

Fig. 6 — Baluster Candlesticks
(*early eighteenth century*)
By John Coney. An exceptional pair. Elaboration is achieved by the skilled disposition of simple forms. Study of these sticks will reveal an advanced technical ability.
From the Museum of Fine Arts, Boston

lighted candle within a large glass "chimney," or "hurricane shade," to protect the flame from drafts.

Candlesticks that might well cause any of us to disregard the tenth commandment are those made by American eighteenth-century craftsmen in the baluster form popular in England during the Queen Anne and early Georgian periods. If somewhat more ornamental than their predecessors, the American sticks were sufficiently restrained to comply with the austere tendencies of our native silver. Only recently, an unusual pair (*Fig. 4*) by Bartholomew Schaats of New York City (*1670–1758*) was fortunately discovered. Here is displayed a marked departure from the usual baluster form — the more common moldings are lacking, and the stems are somewhat individual in shape. The balusters are an octagonal pyriform on a high, plain foot with a molded, octagonal base, the same outline being repeated in the exceptionally deep candleholder. All the moldings are well executed, and the conical foot adds an element of grace.

Two others (*Fig. 5*), by John Burt (*1691–1745*), have similar octagonal pyriform baluster stems, but their faceted sides are continued unbroken from the candleholder to the base.

Some cast candlesticks that have come to my notice in American collections follow the English forms current during the first half of the eighteenth century. They are invariably fairly heavy, since they were made by pouring molten silver into a mold, the ornamental parts being afterwards carefully cleaned and finished by hand. But, if some of our native baluster shapes reveal a concession to contemporary decorative styles, they at no time assumed the rococo elaborations developed by the English silversmiths. Instead, American craftsmen seem to have relied for their effects upon the introduction of variously shaped members in the stems and the addition of clearly defined moldings to the bases of their creations.

Careful proportions and an interesting and satisfactorily balanced outline are achieved in a pair (*Fig. 6*) by John Coney of Boston (*1655–1722*). Here we find an unusually elaborate baluster, on a short conical foot that rises from a flat platform supported by a wide molded base. This pair indicates an advanced technique in modeling. Another piece (*Fig. 7*), also attributed to Coney, has a much less imposing baluster, and retains the wide projecting flange, which, like the base, displays gadrooning arranged spirally. This latter stick combines the flange of the English columnar shafts with the gadroon and baluster of the late seventeenth century.

A fine pair (*Fig. 9*) by Jacob Hurd of Boston (*1702–1758*) illustrates the use of concave flutings in the stem and stepped moldings on the base. The fluted motive is repeated in the high domical foot, which continues the line of the molded domical base instead of rising abruptly from a flat platform. On the other hand, the form of the single candlestick (*Fig. 10*), also by Hurd, while undoubtedly derived from a similar source, shows a reeded stem supported on a plain conical foot, which rises from a finely modeled base outlined by a series of cyma curves. Nor is it difficult to see in the reeding a reminiscence of the fluted columnar type of the previous century.

I include among the illustrations a pair of candlesticks (*Fig. 11*) that belong to the more ornate type derived from the English rococo. These are marked M M, impressed four times on the

Fig. 7 — Baluster Stick
Attributed to John Coney.
From the Museum of Fine Arts, Boston

Fig. 8 — English Columnar Candlesticks
(*late seventeenth century*)
Showing heavy column, gadrooning, and domical base.
From the Brooklyn Museum

Fig. 9 — Fluted Baluster Stems (*c. 1735*)

By Jacob Hurd of Boston. Concave flutings on the stems and stepped moldings on the bases. Here is a faint suggestion of the rococo, which never really appears in American silver. *From the Clearwater Collection in the Metropolitan Museum of Art*

Fig. 10 — Fluted Baluster Stem

By Jacob Hurd. Admirable from all aspects.
From the Clearwater Collection, Metropolitan Museum

Fig. 11 — Cast Baluster Candlesticks (*c. 1750*)

Attributed to Myer Myers of New York. The mark M M is impressed four times on the underside of the base. Basically related to the forms of Figure 9; but more obviously ornamental.
From the Ginsburg and Levy collection

underside of the base, and were probably the work of Myer Myers of New York City (*active 1746–1790*). If they are compared with Jacob Hurd's work shown in Figure 9, a like use of the incurved flutes in the baluster will be apparent, as well as a similarity in the shapes of the candleholders and the bases. But here the resemblance ceases. Hurd's sticks are dependent entirely upon flutings and moldings for ornamentation, whereas on the others foliated forms are applied to the shoulders, and the bases take the contour of the scallop shells with which the four corners are decorated. It is also interesting to note that Myers' pieces have a cushionlike knop recalling the Salisbury Cathedral candlesticks (*Fig. 2*).

Of silver snuffers by early American makers there are even fewer specimens than of candlesticks. Nevertheless, silver snuffers and their small accompanying stands, or trays, have been found, and, to judge from the snuffer stand of Figure 12, they were occasionally objects of embellishment.

This snuffer follows the form used in England at the end of the seventeenth century. It was made by Cornelius Kierstede (*1674–1753*), who, from such records as exist, appears to have been in business in New York City and, after 1722, in New Haven, Connecticut. That he was a craftsman of no little skill and versatility is evident from the style of this stand. The stem is a large bulbous knop corresponding in shape to the legs of late Tudor and early Stuart tables. Surmounting

the knop is a rectangular box to hold the wide blade of the snuffers, which fitted vertically with handles uppermost.

Below the stem is a molded and embossed projecting flange concealing the joint to the concave spreading foot, which, in turn, is supported on a molded base, the latter closely resembling English saltcellars of the late seventeenth century. The decoration of this piece is also noteworthy. The side of the snuffer box is enriched with an applied double-headed eagle flanked by acanthus leaves. Renaissance feeling is shown in the style of the moldings and the ornamentation of the flange and base.

Figure 13 pictures a portable candlestick by Joseph Lownes of Philadelphia (*active c. 1780–1816*). The disproportion between the graceful tray and the unduly heavy candle socket almost suggests that this is a composite piece, made by fitting candleholder, conical extinguisher, and snuffer support to an already existing tray. Furthermore, such canoe-shaped trays were generally intended for the occupancy of snuffers only.

Note. Several of the candlesticks here shown have already been illustrated and described in Bigelow's *Historic Silver of the Colonies*, which, though it was published in 1917, still retains its place as the only comprehensive work in its field. It is Mr. Bigelow who first pointed out the resemblance between the Dummer candlestick (*Fig. 1*) and the more monumental English specimens in Salisbury Cathedral. The manner in which a New England silversmith became acquainted with such a model, however, remains something of a mystery. Either he must have relied upon some now unknown drawing or engraving, or have had the good fortune to encounter on his native heath some imported modifications of the Salisbury prototypes.

In a note to ANTIQUES, Mr. Wenham remarks on the scarcity of silver snuffers of early American make. Apparently, he observes, the Colonists preferred to spend their money on more ostentatious silver utensils and to depend upon steel as the material for such purely practical articles as snuffers. This is a reasonable surmise. *Historic Silver of the Colonies*, furthermore, mentions only one pair of American silver snuffers, part of an outfit made by John Burt of Boston in 1720. They are of the scissor type without feet — the latter conveniences, which raised the snuffers far enough above the tray to be easily grasped, having come into use no earlier than the reign of George III. — *The Editor.*

Fig. 12 — Snuffer Stand (*early eighteenth century*)
By Cornelius Kierstede.
From the Metropolitan Museum of Art

Fig. 13 — Portable Candle Tray and Equipment (*late eighteenth century*)
Bearing the mark of Joseph Lownes of Philadelphia. A not entirely successful work.
From the Metropolitan Museum of Art

AMERICAN SILVER SPOUT CUPS

By V. ISABELLE MILLER

THE SILVER SPOUT CUPS of our forefathers are exceedingly rare and seldom found outside of museum collections. Like certain other early vessels, they have no counterpart in today's silver forms. They were apparently made to feed invalids and small children, as their shape made it possible to serve their contents easily to someone in a recumbent position. These practical articles were made almost entirely in the first quarter of the eighteenth century, and while their forms varied slightly, the slight differences point only to the individual taste and craftsmanship of the smiths who made them.

Spout cups might be compared both to mugs with a spout and to the more shapely pear-shaped teapots. The spout, however, differs from those of teapots in that it is generally S-curved, coming from low on the bowl. This enables the contents to be poured by tilting the cup slightly. The spouts are set at

FIG. 1 — SPOUT CUP BY JOHN EDWARDS (*Boston, 1671-1746*). Exemplifying the early type; made about 1700. Beautiful cut-card decoration on the slightly domed cover, surmounted by turned finial. A small circular hole in the lid, with a tiny cover turning on a pin, permits insertion of a stick to stir the contents. *From the Worcester Art Museum.*

right angles to the handle; the only known exception is here exemplified in the interesting item shown in Figure 12.

Spout cups are small, varying from about 3½ to 6 inches in height. Most of them have covers, though a few were made without, notably the one by Edward Winslow (*1669-1753*) of Boston (*Fig. 10*). This one does not seem to need a fitted cover, as the lip flares gracefully. A similar cup exists, made by Moody Russell (*1694-1761*), of Barnstable, Massachusetts (*Fig. 11*). Russell was apprenticed to Winslow, which may account for the similarity of the two cups.

The silversmiths who fashioned these cups were artists, and most of the examples which we illustrate, notably Figures 6 and 7, show well-balanced proportions. The majority were made by New England silversmiths; the two exceptions discovered to date are the one made in Philadelphia (*Fig. 12*) and an interesting example made by Jacob Boelen in New York City (*Fig. 2*).

The Boelen spout cup illustrates Dutch characteristics in its more or less squat shape. The New Yorker who made it, probably to special order, may well have seen New England examples, though he fashioned it in his own style. It is unusual, too, in that the spout has a cap attached by a chain to the upper edge of the cup cover.

Since most of the American spout cups are of New England origin, it is

FIG. 2 (*above*) — SPOUT CUP BY JACOB BOELEN (*New York, 1654-1729*). Contemporary initials, *L* over *WDE*, and date *1714* are engraved on one side of the neck. The history of this piece is difficult to trace; though it has come down in the present owner's family, the initials do not seem to fit in her family genealogy. *Lent by the owner, Mrs. Leonard Twynham, to the Museum of the City of New York.*

FIG. 3 (left) — SPOUT CUP BY JERE-
MIAH DUMMER (Boston, 1645-1718).
Lent anonymously to the 1939 ex-
hibition of New England silver at the
Yale University Art Gallery.

FIG. 4 (below, left) — SPOUT CUP
BY JEREMIAH DUMMER. From the
Museum of Fine Arts, Boston.

FIG. 5 (right) — SPOUT CUP BY JOHN
DIXWELL (Boston, 1680-1725). From
the Minneapolis Institute of Arts.

FIG. 6 (below, center) — SPOUT CUP
BY JOHN CONEY (Boston, 1655/56-
1722). Note transition in form from
the squat shape of earliest examples,
through the more attenuated shape,
with highly domed cover, of this and
Figure 7, to the pear shape of Figures
8 and 9. From the Minneapolis Institute of Art.

FIG. 7 (below, right) — SPOUT CUP
BY NATHANIEL MORSE (Boston, c.
1685-1748). Figures 7 to 10 from the
Mabel Brady Garvan collection, Yale
University Art Gallery.

likely that their inspiration is purely English. But though English spout cups exist, they are exceedingly rare. Thomas Lumley of London writes that during his twenty years of association with English silver, he has "seen and handled only about half a dozen examples . . . One made by William Andrews in London in 1701 had a plain straight-sided body, rather like a mug, and had no cover. There also exists one rare example with a cover, made at Plymouth [England], now in a private collection, dating about 1680. It is of the Charles II tankard type and the only one of its kind in English silver that I know." We find an illustration of a spout cup in Jackson's *History of English Plate* (*Vol. I, p. 264*), in a group of pieces made at Norwich, England. It is a rare and unusual piece.

Spout cups were also produced in England in Lambeth and Bristol delft pottery toward the end of the seventeenth century and the beginning of the eighteenth. An interesting though later ceramic feeding cup is an item in blue transfer-printed Staffordshire ware made by Josiah Spode (*Fig. 13*).

Ladies of the household of those early days in America were well versed in the art of brewing hot drinks and possets. They could fill the spout cup with the hot liquid and easily carry it, without chilling, to the invalid, who was always cared for in the home. Spout cups filled a definite need and the craftsmen who made them ably demonstrated their skill in fashioning them as handsome pieces of Colonial silver.

FIG. 8 (*above, left*) — SPOUT CUP BY BENJAMIN HILLER (*Boston, 1687-1745*).

FIG. 9 (*left, center*) — SPOUT CUP BY WILLIAM COWELL JR. (*Boston, 1713-1761*).

FIG. 10 (*right*) — SPOUT CUP BY EDWARD WINSLOW (*Boston, 1669-1753*). This and Figures 11 and 12 are unusual in having no cover.

FIG. 11 (*below*) — SPOUT CUP BY MOODY RUSSELL (*Barnstable, Massachusetts, 1694-1761*). Very similar to Figure 10. Russell was apprenticed to Winslow. *From the Cleveland Museum of Art.*

FIG. 12 (*left*) — SPOUT CUP BY JOSEPH RICHARDSON (*Philadelphia, 1711-1770*). This and Figure 2 are the only known American silver spout cups made elsewhere than in New England. Engraved with the Pemberton crest. Unusual in shape, and in placement of the handle. So far as known, this cup never had a cover. *From the collection of Walter M. Jeffords; photograph courtesy of James Graham & Sons, Inc.*

FIG. 13 (*right*) — SPODE EARTHENWARE FEEDING CUP (*Staffordshire, early nineteenth century*). Transfer-printed decoration in blue. *Lent by Mrs. E. Hollingsworth Siter to the Philadelphia Museum of Art.*

II New England Silver and Its Makers

The Puritans who settled New England brought their dissenting ideas to the New World, but the customs and habits they introduced were, nevertheless, thoroughly English. Once survival was certain, the dour, Spartan existence which the word "Puritan" conjures up practically disappeared. In fact, the Calvinistic association of material wealth with general spiritual worthiness insured well-furnished households, good libraries, and plenty of silver. Possessions were the tangible evidence of God's favor, and use of silver proved the point.

The plain style favored in Commonwealth England was reflected in Puritan silver, but only in the few forms and motifs, such as the tulip, adopted by New England craftsmen. These preferences found their way into all the decorative arts, and some forms and motifs remained vestigially in the design vocabulary long after Europe had abandoned them.

As Francis Hill Bigelow points out (pp. 55-58), 17th-century silver objects share a number of decorative motifs with furniture made in the northern colonies. The stylized flowers which silversmiths chased or engraved on small two-handled cups are similar to those on Hadley chests and other relief-carved furniture of the period. Such continuity in design elements illustrates the regional characteristics which gradually developed and were expressed in the several colonial centers.

One factor which strongly influenced regional stylistic characteristics was the apprenticeship system. In the Old World, roles were well defined; no one had access to a craft or trade without serving seven years' training under an acknowledged master. This early stage of apprenticeship was followed by a less-regulated journeyman phase during which the aspiring artisan was usually paid a wage but still worked under a master's supervision. Finally, the craftsman could be accepted as a freeman of the guild and might, in turn, eventually train his own apprentices. Any apprentice who progressed beyond the rudiments of the craft was a valuable assistant; he added significantly to the productivity of a shop.

In America, the apprenticeship system suffered from neglect; without guild organizations, requirements were more difficult to enforce. The journeyman phase was practically discarded since labor-hungry frontier towns granted freedoms readily. Moreover, there were few masters available to train youths. As a result, the influence of those few spread geometrically with each apprentice who left the shop. On the other hand, there *was* a measure of stability. The

quality of American silver remained high, and most masters seemed to take their responsibilities seriously. In Boston, especially, training was a solemn duty, regulated not only by the town meeting, but also by the church.

Jeremiah Dummer, the first successful apprentice of Sanderson and Hull—Boston's earliest silversmiths—is the subject of an article by Hermann F. Clarke (pp. 64-67). Dummer's life is typical of those led by many contemporary silversmiths. He came from a prosperous family and entered a trade which reflected his already high social status. Once established, Dummer expanded his business, became a full-scale merchant, and finally became extremely active in local affairs. He held public offices, printed money, and was, indeed, a key member of his community.

Silversmiths acted as bankers and often dealt with the most powerful men in their communities. They developed mutual bonds of trust and respect. Occasionally, however, opportunity and their skills betrayed them. In "A Samuel Casey Coffeepot" (pp. 73-75), Gregor Norman-Wilcox mentions that Casey was one craftsman who succumbed to the ever-present temptation of silversmiths and engravers. Casey turned to counterfeiting and ended his career under a cloud.

While urban silversmiths, like the Edwards family of Boston, are well documented and left considerable surviving silver, those from smaller communities, like Daniel Greenough, of Portsmouth, New Hampshire, are harder to trace. Frank O. Spinney (pp. 76-78) discovered that Greenough combined silversmithing with gentlemanly pursuits. He also acquired a blacksmith shop—a rare occurrence of diversification among silversmiths. Usually, when an American silversmith wished to expand his business ventures, he imported quantities of plate, scales, or small fancy items from England to bolster his sales. Ironworking did not suit the "elite" among artisans.

The latter part of this section focuses on specific forms and pieces produced in New England. The particular types are, in America, unique products of northern craftsmen who perhaps owe their distinction to the early settlement of Boston and quick adoption of all the ostentation a cultured lifestyle demanded. By the time other colonial centers had acquired the wealth and air of permanence achieved in Boston by 1710, skillets, standing salts, and sugar boxes were largely out of fashion. Mrs. Russel Hastings' detective work in "Verifying a Hull and Sanderson Porringer" (pp. 79-81), is quite adept. Graham Hood (pp. 82-84) describes a more recently discovered silver skillet, one of only two known complete examples, both of which were made in Boston. Samuel Woodhouse, Jr., and Horace H. F. Jayne (pp. 85-87) explore the development of the standing salt with emphasis on an American example by John Edwards and John Allen, both of Boston. Two other similar pieces have since come to light, crafted by Jeremiah Dummer and Edward Winslow between 1695 and 1710. Both Allen and Winslow may have been trained by Dummer.

Another form which seems to have been attempted only by New England smiths is the sugar box. Kathryn C. Buhler (pp. 88-91) discusses the nine known boxes in the last article in this section. Here, especially, the consummate skill of New England artisans is evident. The sugar box is among the most ambitious forms in early American silver; it closely appoaches the high style of contemporary silvermaking in England.

Early New England Silver

By Francis Hill Bigelow*

THE characteristics of such objects as were made by the early New England silversmiths are directly traceable to the mother country, old England. It is known that many of the well-to-do immigrants brought with them those early standing cups belonging to the First and Old South Churches at Boston.†

John Hull (1624–83) was among the earliest of these New England silversmiths, and also a wealthy trader. In all probability he had sent to him from England examples of the prevailing fashions there in silverware to serve as copies. During the Commonwealth (1649–60) objects were, generally speaking, devoid of decoration, but after the restoration of Charles II (1660–85) a noticeable change took place and ornamentation was the rule.

Illustrated upon the cover is an English tankard with the London date-letter for 1658–59. The embossed (or repoussé) decoration of vertical acanthus leaves at the base became popular in England between the years 1670 and 1695 and was probably at that time added to the tankard.‡ An American tankard of this description was wrought by Timothy Dwight (1654–91) of Boston, an apprentice of John Hull, for John Stedman, who was born in 1601 and died in 1693. It was, perhaps, made about 1680–85. A similar decoration is shown upon the beaker illustrated in Figure 65 of *American Silver of the XVII and XVIII Centuries*, published by the Metropolitan Museum

of Art, New York. The beaker is doubtless of New England origin, as it was found there; though the attribution to Shem Drowne of Boston is probably erroneous. There seems to be no evidence that Drowne was a silversmith; and doubtless a craftsman with the same initials will in time come to light, that will more satisfactorily identify the maker.

Many objects wrought by the Boston silversmiths were decorated with vertical or spiral fluting on the lower part of the body, as in the two-handled cup (*Fig. 2*), made by John Coney (1655–1722) of Boston. This form of decoration was fashionable in England toward the end of the reign of Charles II (1660–85). The cup was the gift of William Stoughton, who died in 1701, to Harvard College.

Frequently a fluted or corded band surrounds the body below the lip, as may be seen in a similar cup made by Edward Winslow (1669–1753).* Such bands were often used to surround the edges of patens and the shoulders of tankards; they are shown on the foot of the two-handled cup (*Fig. 2*) and upon the cover. These narrower decorations while similar to the wider flutings of the body are commonly referred to as *gadrooning*.

Cast and chased handles with human heads upon the shoulders were commonly used in the reign of Charles II.

A caudle cup (*Fig. 3*) made by Jeremiah Dummer (1645–1718) of Boston shows spiral fluting (called in the trade *bat's wing*) on the lower portion of the body—the alternating flutes being convex and concave. The handles are cast, and are another type of those common at the time of Charles II. This cup has an engraved inscription on the bottom, *Benjamin Coffin to R. G.* The latter initials

Fig. 1 — AMERICAN SILVER TANKARD
Made by Timothy Dwight of Boston (*1654–91*). This should be compared with the English tankard shown on the cover.

---

*The photographs used were taken under Mr. Bigelow's supervision; some of them for *Old Silver of American Churches*, and some for a contemplated volume on *Domestic Silver* by E. Alfred Jones.

†These are illustrated in *Old Silver of American Churches* by E. Alfred Jones and therein described. These English cups were copied in shape, if not in decoration, by the New England craftsmen.

‡In the collection of Lord Swaythling is a tankard with the London date-letter for 1645–46 with similar decoration.

*Illustrated in *Historic Silver of the Colonies* (Fig. 114).

are for Ruth Gardner of Nantucket, who married James Coffin in 1692. It is of the straight sided type of caudle cup which originated in England in the reign of Charles I (1625–49).

The more usual style of caudle cup is gourd-shaped, and may be traced to the reign of Henry VIII; but its great popularity in England was during the reign of Charles II, when, next to the tankard, it was as a drinking vessel thought indispensable in every household. The bodies were sometimes boldly embossed with sprays of tulips and carnations as

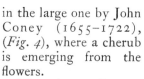

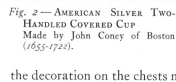

Fig. 2 — AMERICAN SILVER TWO-HANDLED COVERED CUP
Made by John Coney of Boston (*1655-1722*).

in the large one by John Coney (1655–1722), (*Fig. 4*), where a cherub is emerging from the flowers.

Often the caudle cups were decorated with "punched" ornament by being embossed with somewhat crude designs composed of lobes and dots struck with a hammer and round-ended punches on the outside of the object, forming a series of depressions, as in the band of Figure 5, which appeared as raised dots on the inside; they were often arranged in patterns.

Other caudle cups are slightly embossed with sprays of flowers often on a matted surface, and are only remotely like the ornament on English plate. The floral designs resemble, to some extent, the decoration on the chests made in New England during the last quarter of the seventeenth century. The caudle cup in Figure 5, wrought by Sanderson and Hull, was made for Augustin and Elizabeth Clement, residents of Dorchester in 1635. The husband died in 1674 and his widow gave the cup to the First Church there, in 1678.

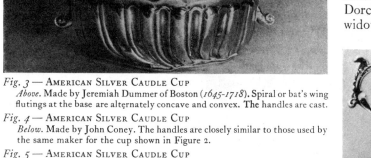

Fig. 3 — AMERICAN SILVER CAUDLE CUP
Above. Made by Jeremiah Dummer of Boston (*1645-1718*). Spiral or bat's wing flutings at the base are alternately concave and convex. The handles are cast.

Fig. 4 — AMERICAN SILVER CAUDLE CUP
Below. Made by John Coney. The handles are closely similar to those used by the same maker for the cup shown in Figure 2.

Fig. 5 — AMERICAN SILVER CAUDLE CUP
At the right. Made by Sanderson and Hull previous to 1674. Decorated with punched dots and with flowers in compartments.

The caudle cup in Figure 6 was made by Robert Sanderson (1608–95) or by his son (1652–1714); the date engraved upon it *19th Sept. 81* is that of John Foster, whose initials and those of his niece Silence Baker are also engraved upon the bottom. The cup was given to the Hollis Street Church in 1744 at the death of Silence Baker.

An ornamentation that first appeared in England during the reign of Charles I (1625–49) and lasted into the reign of William and Mary (1689–94) was called *granulated.*

A broad, matted or granulated band surrounds the body, leaving the lip and base plain, as on the English standing cup illustrated in *Old Silver of American Churches* with the London date-letter for 1639–40 and belonging to the First Church of Boston. Robert Sanderson (1608–93) and John Hull (1624–83) of Boston made a pair of beakers with similar decoration for Thomas Lake of Dorchester. At his decease in 1679 these beakers were given to the First Church

Fig. 6 — AMERICAN SILVER CAUDLE CUP
Made by Robert Sanderson or by his son (*1652-1714*). Decorated with punched dots and with flowers upon a matted ground.

of that town. Jeremiah Dummer (1645–1718) an apprentice of Sanderson and Hull wrought a similar beaker that was the gift to the church at Salem of Francis Skerry, who died in 1684. Another beaker (*Fig. 7*) made by Sanderson and Hull is dated 1659 and belongs to the First Church, Boston.

English beakers with the granulated band were made in small numbers in the Stuart period between 1660 and 1680. In Scandinavia and Germany in the seventeenth century such decoration was used on tankards and other vessels.

Another ornamentation found on English plate between the years 1660 and 1690, and in isolated examples as late as 1720, consists of appliqué foliage or "cut card" work, resembling in effect that of a pattern cut out of cardboard and applied, as in the tankard illustrated in Figure 9, made by Jeremiah Dummer.

The initials of the original owners are those of Rowland and Elizabeth (Saltonstall) Cotton, who were married in 1693. It is not impossible, since the arms of Saltonstall are contemporarily engraved upon the front, that the tankard may have belonged to the second Richard Saltonstall, who left America in 1682 and died in England in 1694. The other two shields of arms are of later date.

Cut card foliage of this kind may be seen on New England furniture of the last quarter of the seven-

teenth century, especially in Connecticut; and some of the flat brass plates (with bale handles) used on furniture during the eighteenth century were probably derived from that earlier decoration.

The New England silversmiths somewhat rarely used engraving as a form of decoration, getting their inspiration from such Dutch examples as had been brought hither by the early immigrants. The beaker (*Fig. 10*), made by John Hull (1624–83), did not come into possession of the Rehoboth Church until 1754.

A smaller beaker (*Fig. 8*), with the initials for Philip and Thankful Withington who were married in 1682, was made by David Jesse of Boston who died in 1705. It is engraved below the lip with a band of scrolled foliage from which depend acanthus leaves alternating with vandyke ornaments. After the early period, New England silver more closely resembles that of other sections.

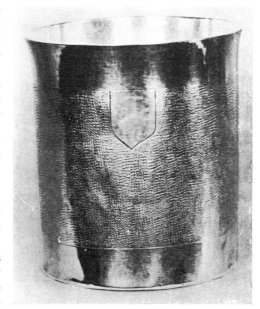

Fig. 7 — AMERICAN SILVER BEAKER
At the left. Made by Sanderson and Hull. An extremely simple form, the decoration of which consists of a broad granular or matted band and a plain shield enclosing the date 1659.

Fig. 8 — AMERICAN SILVER BEAKER
Above. Made by David Jesse of Boston prior to 1705. Engraved with foliated scrolls and depending acanthus forms.

57

Fig. 9 — AMERICAN SILVER TANKARD
Made by Jeremiah Dummer. On the lid and at the base of the handle occurs
an applied flat ornament known as cut card work.

Fig. 10 — AMERICAN SILVER BEAKER
Made by John Hull, *(1624-83)*. Elaborately engraved with band ornament and foliated scrolls.

Master and apprentice:

some relationships

in New England

silversmithing

BY KATHRYN C. BUHLER

Caudle cup with cast handles by Hull and Sanderson.

Caudle cup with cast handles
by Hull and Sanderson's apprentice Jeremiah Dummer.

THE OFTEN-QUOTED EDICT of the Boston Town Meeting of 1660, anent the need to serve a seven years' apprenticeship and be twenty-one years of age to begin a craft or trade, concluded with these words: "that all Indentures made between any master and servant shall bee brought in and enrolled in the Towne's Records." Yet these rolls are today unknown and, except in rare instances, the relationships between masters and their pupils in the goldsmith's art have received scant notice.

The dean of Boston masters, Robert Sanderson, was disclosed as an apprentice in London by E. Alfred Jones (ANTIQUES, May 1943). His partner, John Hull, in a sometimes retrospective diary, recorded that he "fell to learning (by the help of my brother), and to practising the trade of a goldsmith, and, through God's help, obtained that ability in it, as I was able to get my living by it." Hull's [half-]brother, London-trained Richard Storer, apparently soon returned to England, leaving only the skill of his pupil to cause him to be remembered here. Although Hull seems not to have had the required formal training, he undertook to provide it for his pupils, two of whom were noted in the same diary in 1659: "I received into my house Jeremie Dummer and Samuel Paddy, to serve me as apprentices eight years. The Lord make me faithful in discharge of this new trust committed to me, and let his blessing be to me and them." Yet a letter from Hull to Paddy in 1681 suggests that not all apprentices became masters: "Had you abode here and followed your calling, you might have been worth many hundred pounds of clear estate and you might have enjoyed many more helpes for your sole. Mr. Dummer lives in good fashion, hath a wife and three children and a good estate, is a member of the church and like to be very useful in his generation."

The few known contracts between masters and apprentices bear definite relation to those of the Old World on which they were doubtless patterned. This rather free quotation is from Boston in the 1660's: "By his own free will and the consent of his father . . . put himself

Except as noted, illustrations are from the Boston Museum of Fine Arts.

Engraved tankard lid by Robert Sanderson.

to learn his Art . . . After the manner of an Apprentice to serve . . . . term of seven years . . . his [master's] lawful commands gladly do; he shall do not damage to his master nor see it to be done by others [without] . . . he shall make known the same to his Master; He shall not waste the goods of his Master nor lend them unlawfully to any: He shall not commit fornication nor contract Matrimony within the said term; He shall not play at any unlawful game whereby his master may have losse: he shall not haunt Taverns, Alehouses nor places of gaming nor absent himselfe from the service of his Master Day nor night unlawfully. But in all things . . . he shall behave himself towards his said Master . . . and the said Master [shall teach] his said Apprentize in the Art & Occupation . . . which he now useth . . . Finding to his Apprentize Meat & Drink, Washing Lodging & apparrell both linning & wooling & all other necessaries . . . And at the end of the term, the said Master . . . shall give unto the said Apprentize Two Sutes of apparell to all parts of his body, the one for working Dayes the other for Lords Dayes fitt & Convenient . . . there shall be Foure new shirts & Two new paier of Shooes" and the minimum tools of the trade.

While I feel considerable temerity in assigning undocumented apprentices to a master, I hope the suggestions given here may awaken a new interest and instigate further discussion or even refutation. If one tends to attribute many men as apprentices to the few master craftsmen in each generation whose surviving work is outstanding in quality and quantity, is it not reasonable to assume that this great output may be due in part to a large number of learning, and helping, hands?

It has been suggested that Sanderson was the partner who chiefly taught the first colonial apprentices, and Dummer engraved a tankard lid very like the one by Sanderson illustrated here. Many other pieces of Jeremy's fashioning give evidence of his training. His simplest porringer handle copies the only cut one by his masters known; plain caudle cups by master and pupil have even

Engraved salver (detail) by
Hull and Sanderson's apprentice Timothy Dwight.

Engraved plate (detail) by John Coney, trained probably by Hull and Sanders

been confused by the first writers on the craft. For the handles of certain cups, Dummer used the exact casting on the Hull and Sanderson cup shown; but since his appear at the close of the century, the mold was probably acquired from his masters' estate rather than used in their workshop.

Perhaps the use of the graver in drawing and shading offers the safest clue to master-pupil relationships, and by this means Timothy Dwight (1654-1691/2), known to have been apprenticed to Hull and Sanderson, is further associated with his masters. The floral renderings on Dwight's salver, one of only two known pieces of his work, are comparable to those on the Sanderson tankard lid. Let us look, too, at the flowers on the plate by John Coney (1656-1722), another of this first generation of native goldsmiths. Coney occupied a place unique in his age, if one may judge from the variety of his surviving pieces as well as the known names of his important patrons. His master is apparently not contemporarily recorded; the recent argument, that he probably learned from Dummer because eventually they married sisters,

seems neither specious nor confirmed by their work. Coney was born in January 1656; in 1670 he could well have been apprenticed to the first partnership. Hull died in 1683, the elder partner lived another decade; their famous "pine tree shillings" had ceased to be minted, but surely it is significant that Coney's estate included "an engine for coining." Coney's and Dwight's apprenticeship years would have overlapped considerably; another similarity in their work is in the cast lions used for feet on a standish by Coney and a thumbpiece on a tankard by Dwight, but unknown on other colonial plate.

Hull had only one child who lived to maturity, Hannah (1657/8-1717); she married Samuel Sewall (1652-1729/30) and continued to live at home. Sanderson had three sons whom he trained in his craft; only Benjamin's (1649-1678) work is known today, and only Robert (1654-1714) survived his father. A cup by Benjamin (in the Worcester Art Museum) and one made by Coney for the Stratford, Connecticut, church are perhaps the earliest evidence of a kinship between Coney's work and that of a known Sanderson apprentice.

Communion silver made for the Church in Brattle Street, Boston. Baptismal basin by William Cowell, 1716. Flagons by John Noyes, 1711; Nathaniel Morse, 1711; Edward Winslow, 1712; John Edwards, 1713. Morse was probably apprenticed to Coney, all the others to Dummer.

Tankard by John Coney.

Tankard by Benjamin Hiller, probably trained by Coney.

It seems logical to assume that Sewall would have patronized his father-in-law's trainees. The warm ties that existed between a master's family and his apprentices are often evidenced by the latter's marriage to a daughter. Failing that, a daughter would surely give her patronage (or encourage her husband to give his) to the men she had known almost as brothers. Thus there seems to be significance in Samuel Sewall's orders from "Cousin Dummer" and Mr. Coney; and, when these ceased working, from men who had probably been their apprentices. Captain Edward Winslow (1669-1753) is next in Sewall's orders, and Winslow's training has been attributed by John Marshall Phillips to Dummer. Each wrought noteworthy pieces unique to himself, yet neither is particularly noted for his engraving skill, and certain conspicuous differences between their products seem coincidental. The belief once held, that Winslow had been apprenticed in London, is unsubstantiated. There is, moreover, a distinct relation between Dummer's work and that of Peter Oliver (1682-1712), and a chocolate pot by Oliver in the form and decoration of the two known ones by Winslow seems to link these three.

John Edwards (1671-1746), a chirurgeon's son, and John Noyes (1674-1749), son of a cooper, are other probable pupils of Dummer, and with Winslow represent the start of a second generation of native craftsmen. Edwards made a gadrooned standing cup now in a South Carolina church, and his earliest porringer handles follow Dummer's styles. Furthermore, Dummer's son, William, turned to John Edwards for his first church gift in 1726; surely he would have patronized an apprentice of his father. Sewall also recorded purchases from Edwards, who made the Sewall tankard owned by the Old South Church.

Noyes' family stemmed from Newbury where the Dummers, too, maintained their associations, and Noyes married Edwards' sister, whom he might easily have met when the two were apprentices together for half their span. Dummer made a tankard and a standing salt for Rebecca Russell, Noyes later made a clasp of gold for her. Winslow, Edwards, and Noyes made three of the flagons for the Brattle Street Church illustrated; the fourth is the work of Nathaniel Morse (c. 1685-1748), believed trained by Coney. All four flagons are so alike, but for their marks and minute differences in their engraving, as to appear to be the work of one man. Peter Oliver, who was Edwards' first cousin, had made a similar flagon for the Second Church in Boston, also in 1711; no earlier flagons of colonial fashioning are known. Another of Dummer's presumed apprentices was William Cowell (1682-1736) who, besides making pieces very like Dummer's, used marks similar in character to his. Two of Dummer's pupils whose work is unknown are recorded: Daniel Cookin, mentioned in Sewall's diary in 1696, and Kiliaen van Rensselaer (1663-1719) of Albany. In 1682, Stephanus van Cortlandt wrote to his sister: "The man to whom I recommended your son Kiliaen at Boston hanged himself, so that Mr. Patichall and Mr. Usher have apprenticed him to one Mr. Jeremy Dummer. It seems that Kiliaen is not used to living as plainly as they do here." Another relative wrote: "We received a letter from Kiliaen. He is not sorry that he went away. He is with a good master but earns no money . . . he himself writes that he sees a fine opportunity for the trade in silversmiths' work. Mr. Utscher and Mr. Paterschall are sureties for him in case he should undertake some big piece of work and spoil it, so that he would have to stand the loss." This is an aspect not suggested in any consideration of goldsmiths or apprentices, nor hinted in Hull's and Sewall's diaries. Kiliaen's mother later wrote that she "let him set up the silversmith's shop in the country," but no mark is known that can be attributed to him.

Above, spoon by Samuel Casey,
probably Hurd's apprentice.

Left, spoons by Jacob Hurd.
Owned by Mr. & Mrs. Francis S. Dane.

Coney's last and best-known apprentice, mentioned in the inventory of his estate as Paul Rivoire, was the Huguenot lad christened Apollos at Riancaud, France, in 1702. Earlier, Samuel Vernon (1683-1737) of Rhode Island was probably a Coney apprentice, as Benjamin Hiller (born 1687/8) has long been considered; Andrew Tyler (1692-1741) can also be assigned to this master on the basis of their work. John Burt (1692/3-1745) for his Sever chafing dishes, cast candlesticks, and, less conspicuously, his two-handled cup at Harvard, can surely be considered Coney's pupil; one who, in certain instances, almost outdid his master in the fineness of his engraving. Three of his sons were trained in the craft. Samuel (1724-1754) and William (1726-1751), though dying early, each produced pieces distinctly akin to the father's. Benjamin Burt (1729-1805) was a lifelong rival of Rivoire's son, the patriot Revere.

Through the rest of the age of craftsmanship other master-apprentice relationships among silversmiths may be established, some definitely on the basis of documentary record, others tentatively on the basis of similarity of work, family connections, or other associations. Jacob Hurd (1703-1758), who took Coney's place in importance of both his work and his patrons, seems to have had his tutelage with Dummer's pupil John Edwards. Among Hurd's known apprentices were Houghton Perkins (1735-1778) and Daniel Henchman (1730-1775). A small spoon made by Perkins for his master's daughter Ann has been treasured by her descendants, with the elaborate spoon by Samuel Casey shown here, inscribed *Ann Hurd 1751*. The likeness of this Casey spoon to the

Hurd pair illustrated, as well as a similarity in repoussé creampots by the two makers, has led to attribution of Casey's training to Hurd.

Thomas Edwards (1701/2-1755) and his brother Samuel (1705-1762) were no doubt pupils of their father John, and John's grandson, Joseph Jr. (1737-1783), was trained by one of his uncles. Also trained by his own father was Paul Revere, the patriot. Among his apprentices were his younger brother, Thomas, and Thomas Eayres, who became his son-in-law.

Perhaps in post-Revolutionary days contracts became less rigorous. The Reverend William Bentley of Salem records the apprenticeships of his brother Thomas (1764-1804) and his brother-in-law Robert Dawes (born 1767) to Stephen Emery "then in high reputation," and he continues: "My Brother made all the proficiency in his art known in his time and added such other parts as his fruitful invention assisted & was a good Engraver. . . In all this time he was taught nothing which led to correct his manners & a taste for songs & social glee soon gave a wrong bent to his genius." Bentley's brother-in-law was to encounter that other foe of craftsmanship, the machine age: "I visited Richard's factory . . . where my B-in-law D. works. I found several of the new machines in this building."

Yet Joseph Foster in his letter to the Lancaster Church in 1809 reflects the integrity of the craftsmen's tradition: "I have made [the cups] a little heavier than proposed. I was unwilling after having made the bodies a little to heavy for 7 oz. to make the feet thin to keep them down to that weight . . . I hope they will be approved."

Jeremiah Dummer, Silversmith (1645-1718)

By HERMANN F. CLARKE

Note. The accompanying summary of the life and work of Jeremiah Dummer is but the forerunner of a book that Mr. Clarke has been preparing ever since the publication of his definitive volume on John Coney in 1932. The steadily mounting interest among American collectors in the fine silver of colonial days has encouraged measures of research that have achieved almost sensational discoveries. (Witness, for example, not only Mr. Clarke's exhaustive studies in book form, but such all-important revelations as are afforded by Mrs. Russel Hastings' article on the *PVB* mark, in ANTIQUES for July 1933, and that on the Sanders-Garvan beaker in ANTIQUES for February 1935. Others of like significance will follow.) In the present discussion, sufficient material is presented to satisfy the requirements of the general reader. Those who are concerned with certain controversial matters relative to Dummer's activities, and who wish to have access to a complete check list of the master's known work, should acquire Mr. Clarke's monograph, *Jeremiah Dummer, Craftsman and Merchant, 1645-1718*, to appear this autumn. — *Ed.*

DURING 1632 some two hundred and fifty persons came from overseas to Massachusetts. Among the thirty-odd passengers arriving in Boston by the ship *Whale*, on May 26 of that year, was Richard Dummer.

At the time he was about thirty-eight years of age. He "furst sat down in Rocksbury" and immediately became active in the affairs of the young colony, then less than two years old. Soon, however, he moved to Boston and thence to Newbury, where he settled in 1636. In due course he became one of the richest and most prominent men in the colony. Following his embroilment in a religious controversy in 1637, he visited England for the better part of a year, returning to the country of his adoption by the ship *Bevis* in 1638. In 1643 or 1644 he married for his second wife Mrs. Frances Burr, widow of the Reverend Jonathan Burr. By her he had five children, of whom the first, Jeremiah, the subject of our study, was born September 14, 1645.

Richard Dummer's farm in Newbury stood on the site of the present Governor Dummer Academy, and here presumably Jeremiah spent his boyhood. Of this period in his life we know nothing except that the substantial character of his father assured the upbringing that was to be reflected in the lad's later years. Shortly before his fourteenth birthday Jeremiah went to Boston as apprentice to John Hull, the silversmith and colonial mint master. In his diary for 1659 John Hull wrote: "1st of 5th I received into my house Jeremie Dummer and Samuel Paddy to serve me as apprentices eight years. The Lord make me faithful in discharge of this new trust committed to me, and let his blessing be to me and them!"

Hull was the first of the long line of New England silversmith artists whose work we know and admire today. (The only silversmith of whom we have record who worked in the colonies earlier than Hull was John Mansfield; but so far as known none of the latter's work is extant.) "A puritan goldsmith in glacial Boston! And not alone in that pursuit. Boston supported a dozen goldsmiths before she was able to find employment for a single lawyer — so uncivilized were the early puritans." (Quoted from *Builders of the Bay Colony*, by Samuel Eliot Morison, *p. 143.*) John Hull was also one of the most successful merchants of his day, and from him Jeremiah Dummer undoubtedly learned the principles of trade that guided him in the successful shipping ventures during his life.

In 1666 he started his own career. The Town of Boston, then in its thirty-sixth year, was a growing and prosperous community. It was the commercial centre of the New England colonies. John Josselyn, a traveler of those days, made several trips to New England and in 1671 wrote of Boston:

The buildings are handsome, joyning one to the other as in London, with many large streets; most of them paved with pebble stone. In the high street towards the Common, there are fair buildings; some of stone; and, at the east end of the Town, one amongst the rest, built by the shore, by Mr. Gibs [Benjamin Gibbs] a merchant, being a stately edifice, which, it is thought, will stand him in little less than 3000 pounds before it is fully finished. The Town is not divided into parishes, yet they have three fair meeting-houses or churches, which hardly suffice to receive the inhabitants and strangers that come in from all parts. . . . The town is rich and populus. On the south there is a small but pleasant Common, where the Gallants, a little before sunset, walk with their Marmalet-madams, as we do in Morefields, till the nine-o'clock bell rings them home to their respective habitations; when presently the Constables walk their rounds to see good order kept, and to take up loose people. (*An Account of Two Voyages to New England*, by John Josselyn, published in London, 1674.)

Late in the year 1672 Jeremiah Dummer married Anna, the eldest child of Joshua and Mary (Blakeman) Atwater. From this union, Dummer's only marriage, nine children were born, of whom two lived to be prominent in their services to the Province of Massachusetts.

Dummer refers to himself, as do the contemporary records, as both "goldsmith" and "merchant." His eight years under the guidance of John Hull taught him alike the art of the goldsmith and the principles of merchandising. As early as 1685, he was interested in shipping, and the archives at the State House in Boston preserve records dated from March 1697 to September 1713 showing that he was a part owner in at least eleven ships.

Jeremiah Dummer's civic activities began in 1675 when he became a constable of Boston, an office which he held for two years. In 1671 he had joined the Artillery Company and in 1679-1680 he was second sergeant, later becoming captain. In April

Fig. 1 — TANKARD BY JEREMIAH DUMMER
An early form with so-called "flat lid," overhanging the body. Purchased about 1676 by the Charlestown, Massachusetts, First Parish Church with proceeds of a bequest from Richard Russell.
From the collection of Henry F. du Pont

1689 the "Council for the Safety of the People and Conservation of the Peace" was formed and Dummer was made a member. Following the adoption of a new charter for the colony, Dummer was elected Selectman of Boston at the Town Meeting held March 9, 1690/1691, and was again elected for 1692. On September 29, 1691, he was also chosen "Comissionr for the Towne of Boston." From 1693 until the date of his death he was a justice of the peace. In 1701 he was made Treasurer of Suffolk County, and in 1702 an overseer of the poor. During the latter part of the seventeenth century he served almost continuously as a member of the Council.

Jeremiah Dummer's wife died September 16, 1715, and, after several years of invalidism, death came to Jeremiah himself, May 24, 1718, at the age of seventy-three years. The span of his life had covered one of the most critical periods in the first century of the New England colonies. His father had been a man of vision and toleration. The son, ably following in his father's footsteps, took an active part in bringing the colonies through the struggle that in their infancy threatened their destruction. Conspicuous in the religious life of the colony, yet tolerant, a man of justice, honesty, and fair dealing, he commanded the confidence of his fellow citizens and served faithfully in public office. A man of rare versatility for the times, he learned and successfully pursued the vocation of silversmith, producing pieces that today win admiration for their dignity, simplicity, and artistic workmanship. He was, too, one of the leaders in the mercantile development of the New England colonies.

Colonial silversmiths drew their inspiration from the styles of the mother country. The Puritan influence in England during the latter part of the reign of Charles I and during the Commonwealth caused the virtual abandonment of ornamentation on English plate (see ANTIQUES, December 1932, *p. 210*). It was the English silver of this conservative period that dominated the earliest designs of the colonial silversmith in New England. The first examples of the Boston silversmith's art were, indeed, even

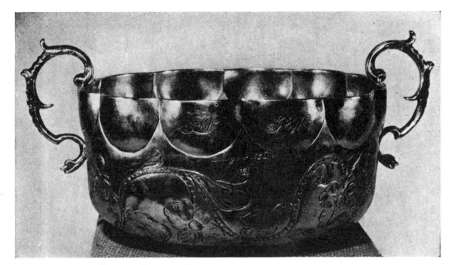

Fig. 2 — DRINKING BOWL BY JEREMIAH DUMMER
Clearly exhibiting Portuguese influence.
From the collection of De Lancey Kountze. Photograph by courtesy of the Gallery of Fine Arts, Yale University

Fig. 3 — BAPTISMAL BASIN BY JEREMIAH DUMMER
Made in 1695. Bequeathed to the Church of Christ, Cambridge, Massachusetts, 1717.
Owned by the First Church, Cambridge

simpler in form and ornament than the English plate of the Commonwealth period. Though after the Restoration in 1660 English silver, responding to the introduction of French and Dutch tastes, became increasingly florid, Dummer and his Boston associates remained conservative in their style and avoided the exaggerations of their English contemporaries. R. T. Haines Halsey pays high tribute to the craftsmanship of these artists in his introduction to the catalogue of *American Silver* exhibited at the Museum of Fine Arts, Boston, during 1906. He says:

The silver is of the period when the ancient geometrical shapes held sway among craftsmen; when purity of form, sense of proportion and perfection of line were preferred to elaborateness of design; when dignity and solidity were considered superior to bulk, and when the beautiful white metal was allowed to take its colors from its surroundings rather than be made the medium for a display of skill by workers in metal. . . . The early American silver, as in the case of our early architecture and furniture, is thoroughly characteristic of the taste and life of the period in America. . . . Social conditions here warranted no attempt to imitate the magnificent baronial silver made in England, illustrations of which are to be found in all English books on plate.

The earliest approximate date to which any piece of silver made by Jeremiah Dummer may be ascribed is about 1676, although there is a beaker extant that has somewhat earlier characteristics. Richard Russell of Charlestown, who died in 1676, bequeathed to the Church of Christ in Charlestown one hundred pounds "to be pd by Exr to the Deacons for the use of the Church." Part of this legacy was expended upon a tankard made by Jeremiah Dummer. Still surviving, this piece is now owned by Henry F. du Pont. It has a plain, straight-sided body and a low, flat-topped cover typical of the period.

The latest examples of Dummer's work whose date may be estimated are three standing cups that came into the possession of the First Church of Boston as a gift from Joseph Bridgham, a local tanner. Bridgham's will, dated January 3, 1708, directed "ye sum of £20 to be paid to ye Deacons of ye sd church and by them Invested in plate for the Service of the Communion." So it is evident that Dummer practiced his craft at least within ten years of his death in 1718.

During forty-odd years Jeremiah Dummer made, and left for the appreciation and enjoyment of succeeding generations, standing cups, caudle cups, beakers, porringers, tankards, and various other objects for sacred and secular use. At least one hundred and nine pieces made by him have been preserved for lovers of beautiful things to admire. Doubtless other pieces have been re-melted or still lie hidden in trunk or cupboard, their quality and value unappreciated by their owners.

Of the one hundred and nine Dummer pieces, fifty-three are now, or have been, in the possession of churches. These were either expressly made or purchased for sacred purposes from gifts or legacies, or were originally devised for domestic use and were bequeathed or presented to the churches. Of the other items, fifty-six were made for secular use

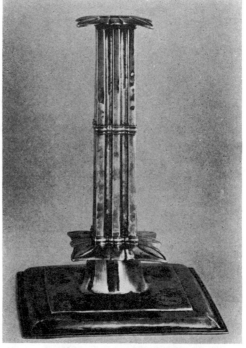

Fig. 4 — SILVER STANDING SALT BY JEREMIAH DUMMER
Bequest to the Boston Museum of Fine Arts from the late Charles H. Tyler

and have been thus employed until, in some cases, they have passed into the possession of museums.

Stylistically Dummer's work underwent fewer changes during his productive career than did that of some of his contemporaries. Virtually all of his pieces follow the simple and dignified lines of the Commonwealth and early Charles II periods. During his later years, however, he adopted certain decorative motives in vogue in England: notably embossing, fluting and gadrooning, and cut-card work, all of which he regarded as secondary to the vigorous and graceful lines of his pieces. Especially was this true in the use of fluting to form a pleasing contrast with the plain surfaces of his standing cups and beakers.

Dummer fashioned fifteen standing cups which are today treasured by several churches in Massachusetts and Connecticut. The First Church of Dorchester owns a pair of standing cups which it acquired by the will of Governor William Stoughton, the legacy reading "To the Church of Dorchester I give two pieces of Plate for yᵉ Communion of six pounds value each." In the same will was a similar legacy bequeathing a like gift to what is now the First Parish Congregational Church of Milton: "Unto the Church of Milton I give one piece of Plate for the Communion of six pounds value."

At least nineteen beakers or cups came from Dummer's workshop. He also made no less than twenty-three caudle cups. This pyriform type of cup with its graceful ogee line was, in its day, very popular in England and was considered almost as indispensable in an English household as the tankard. (This form of cup is often termed "porringer" in

speaking of English plate and must not be confused with the porringer made by American silversmiths. For a fuller explanation of these terms see *History of English Plate*, by Charles James Jackson, Vol. II, *p. 712*.) The caudle cup was used for the serving of warm drinks consisting of thin gruel mixed with sweetened and spiced wine or ale, commonly called caudle, or for posset, which contained hot milk curdled with ale or wine and flavored with sugar and spices. Pepys in his diary mentions in 1659–1660 that he "went to bed and got a caudle made me and slept upon it very well."

Related in form to the caudle cup is the two-handled drinking bowl now owned by De Lancey Kountze, and one of the most remarkable pieces by Dummer in existence. The body of this bowl has straight sides, the upper part divided into twelve lobes or scalloped panels in the manner of Portuguese drinking bowls of the seventeenth century. The lower part of the body is decorated with a flat-chased stylized floral spray, a type of decoration popular in England during the late Stuart period. The cast scrolled handles extend above the lip, and the lower ends terminate in snake's heads. The Portuguese influence observable in this bowl is particularly interesting because Dummer, during his mercantile ventures, was a partner with several English merchants resident in Portugal. It is not improbable that through this association he became conversant with the Portuguese silver of the period.

The tankard was a popular form of drinking vessel in the New England colonies from the date of their founding. The custom of drinking beer and other malt liquors came to the American shores with the colonists. When the *Arbella* arrived in Salem harbor, June 12, 1630, John Winthrop and others of the ship's company went ashore and "supped with a good venison pasty and good beer which probably was not their every day's commons." (Winthrop's *History of New England*, Vol. I, *p. 30*.) Included among the household goods of most families were one or more tankards made of silver, if the owner could afford it, or of pewter or even of wood, as in the early English households of the common folk.

At least nineteen tankards, now extant, came from Dummer's shop. The ability of any craftsman is usually best judged by the workmanship of his more elaborate pieces. To evolve a tankard it was necessary for the silversmith to form, fit, and join together several parts — the bottom, the sides,

Fig. 5 — SILVER CANDLESTICK BY JEREMIAH DUMMER
One of a superb pair. *One of the pair lent to the Boston Museum of Fine Arts by Mr. William A. Jeffries; the other, to the Fogg Art Museum, Harvard University, Cambridge, by Mrs. James H. Means*

the cover, and the handle. A study of Dummer's tankards shows a high degree of skill. His tankards, like those of Coney and of his contemporaries, are generally free from over-ornamentation and depend upon their simplicity and fine proportions for their effect. This simplicity, a reflection of the Puritan influence, contrasts with the profuseness of the tankards made by the silversmiths of the New Netherlands, which reflect the Dutch taste in decoration.

A large silver bowl or basin is treasured by the First Church, Unitarian, of Cambridge, and is now used for the baptismal rite. This historic basin, made by Jeremiah Dummer, was presented by his (Brattle's) pupils in 1695 to the Reverend William Brattle, tutor and fellow at Harvard College from 1707 to 1717. He died February 15 of the latter year. In his will he directs: "I bequeath and present to the Church of Christ in Cambridge for a baptismal basin, my great silver basin, an inscription upon which I leave to the prudence of the Revᵈ President and Rᵈ Mr. Simon Bradstreet." The "Revᵈ President" was John Leverett, then president of Harvard College. Engraved around the wide rim of the basin is this inscription: *A Baptismall Basin consecrated, bequeathᵈ & presented to the Church of Christ in Cambridge, his Dearly beloved Flock, by the Revᵈ Mʳ Wᵐ Brattle Pastʳ of the Sᵈ Church: Who was translated from his Charge to his Crown, Febr 15: 1716/17.*

The two outstanding pieces of Dummer's workmanship which are unique examples of colonial silver are a pair of candlesticks. In form they resemble the columnar candlesticks of silver or pewter made in England during the early years of the Charles II period. Candlesticks made by colonial silversmiths are very rare, and this pair is not only the earliest but one of the most magnificent of its kind. Another object of rare importance from Dummer's workshop is a standing salt bequeathed by the late Charles H. Tyler to the Museum of Fine Arts in Boston.

It may be reasonably assumed that Jeremiah Dummer's most productive period as a silversmith was the last quarter of the seventeenth century. While he probably made some pieces during the decade following the close of his apprenticeship to John Hull, there seems to be no historic evidence of his work until 1676. On the other hand, the forms of his pieces indicate that he made very few after 1700, when changing styles in England led colonial silversmiths to alter their own mode.

Dummer was not prolific either in the variety of the objects that came from his workshop or in the quantity, if we may judge from the number of his pieces extant as compared with those of his contemporaries, like John Coney or Edward Winslow. John

Coney, for instance, is known to have made at least one hundred and fifty-eight pieces compared with Dummer's one hundred and nine. There still remain twenty-eight varieties of articles from Coney's workshop, whereas only fifteen varieties are known to have been made by Dummer. He was versatile, however, as is indicated by the diversity of his porringer handles, and by his use, on occasion, of a form of decoration not found in the work of his contemporaries. His use of line fluctuates to a marked degree, as for instance in his caudle cups, where the student will find sundry treatments of the ogee form. His workmanship was excellent. Joints are well and carefully executed. Simple moldings, usually of the classical type, are used to strengthen and finish the union of separate elements. When occasion required the addition of a casting, such as the handle tip or thumbpiece of a tankard, the molds were carefully made and the castings well finished. Occasionally a casting was used as a distinguishing line between two sections of a piece, as in several of the standing cups where a pleasing casting is placed between stem and base.

As an engraver, Dum-

Fig. 6 — STANDING CUPS BY JEREMIAH DUMMER
(*Left*) Standing cup bequeathed in 1705 or purchased with funds bequeathed in 1705 by Governor Stoughton to the First Church in Dorchester. *Owned by the First Church, Dorchester.*
(*Right*) Communion cup purchased 1708 with funds bequeathed by Joseph Bridgham to the First Church in Boston. *Owned by the First Church, Boston.*
These two exhibit similarities in certain details; but the earlier is the more finely proportioned and the more happily assured and vigorous in workmanship

mer displayed his skill not only in the engraving of the arms and inscriptions that appear on some of the pieces that came from his hand; but he was commissioned to engrave the plates for the Colony of Connecticut when, in 1709, the issue of paper currency was voted. Eleven of his known pieces of silver have coats-of-arms engraved upon them. Like his contemporaries, in the engraving of these heraldic designs Dummer followed English precedent and adopted a mantling of feathery plumes or scrolls.

Jeremiah Dummer indeed enjoyed an abundant life, for his was a finely balanced creative mind possessed of a sense of form and structure as applicable to the organizing of a shipping venture, or the preservation of the political equilibrium of a community, as to the shaping of a silver vessel. Master first of himself, he was fit to be and thus became *magister artium et hominum*.

Four of Dummer's children survived him. William, the eldest, spent several years in England as acting commissioner of the Province of Massachusetts Bay. Returning to Boston, he became Deputy Governor of the Province in 1716, and was acting Governor from 1723 to 1730. Jeremiah, Jr., went to Europe to study theology and remained there for the rest of his life, except for about four years in the colonies. He served as agent for Massachusetts from 1710 to 1721, and also served the Connecticut colony in a similar capacity. Anna married John Powell and died in 1764. The youngest child, Samuel, was successful in several ventures in the British Colony of Jamaica.

JOHN EDWARDS, GOLDSMITH, AND HIS PROGENY

By KATHRYN C. BUHLER

Mrs. Yves Henry Buhler is assistant in silver at the Museum of Fine Arts in Boston. Her book, American Silver, *was recently published in the American Arts Library series.*

A THREE-GENERATION FAMILY of Boston goldsmiths has recently been overlooked in the illustrations of two important publications—after having featured in all the previous ones on American silver—and it seems only just to bring John Edwards, his sons, and grandson back from temporary oblivion. Proof of the first-named's worthiness is offered in a flagon *(Fig. 1)* made in 1712 for the church of

which Edwards was a member, matching one included in *The One Hundred Masterpieces of American Silver* (ANTIQUES, April 1949, p. 283) made in 1713 by Edward Winslow. Both men, apparently, were copying flagons made in 1711 by Nathaniel Morse and John Noyes and the four pieces show a marked similarity in skill.

John Edwards was two years Winslow's junior, born in England in 1671. His father, a chirurgeon, is thought to have come to Boston in about the year 1685 when, presumably, young John was beginning his apprenticeship; the question remains thus far unanswered, was it in Old or New England? In any event, in 1694 he was married in Boston to Sibella Newman, granddaughter of Governor John Winthrop and step-daughter of Zerubabel Endicott. In the 1690's and at the turn of the century he was in partnership with John Allen, using the mark that is found on the early pieces of his independent craftsmanship. This apparently coincided with the last years of the partnership, for a beaker by Edwards alone is dated 1699. Another piece bearing this early mark is a very interesting cup in Christ Church Parish, South Carolina, fashioned even to the cast collar of the stem like those made by Jeremiah Dummer in the first decade of the eighteenth century (ANTIQUES, April 1949). Although no explanation is given in E. Alfred Jones' great tome, *The Old Silver of American Churches*, of how or when the cup arrived there, "missionaries" from Dorchester, Massachusetts, are known to have set out as early as 1695 for South Carolina (Dorchester

FIG. 1—FLAGON by John Edwards *(1712)*. Height, 12 1/16 inches. Inscribed, *This belongs to the Church in Brattle street 1712. Museum of Fine Arts, Boston.*

FIG. 2—MUG by John Edwards *(c. 1700-1710)*. Height, 4 1/4 inches. Inscribed, *S. Russell. Museum of Fine Arts.*

FIG. 3—BEAKER by John Edwards *(1744)*. Height, 5 3/4 inches. Inscribed, *The Gift of Mr John Clough to the Church of Christ in Summer Street of which the Revd Mr Samuel Checkley is Paster 1744. Museum of Fine Arts.*

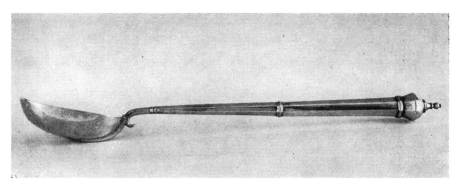

FIG. 4—PUNCH LADLE by John Edwards. Length, 18⅛ inches. *Mr. and Mrs. Mark Bortman.*

FIG. 5—PORRINGER by John Edwards *(1715-1725)*. Length, 7⅞ inches. Inscribed, S. *Franklin 1745. Mrs. Robert C. Terry.*

Antiquarian and Historical Society, 1859). Edwards with his partner shares honors with both Winslow and Dummer in having made, respectively, the three surviving standing salts of colonial fashioning.

Edwards' early mark also appears on an unusual porringer which is again akin to Dummer's work. It is engraved *M: Storer 1724* for his daughter, but both its style and mark indicate that it is probably earlier than the engraving. The mark is here clearly seen on the side of a stalwart mug *(Fig. 2)* from the Philip L. Spalding Collection; its rather delicate terminal mask on the handle is exceptional but not unique on mugs and tankards by Edwards, who more frequently used a

plain or slightly convex disc, or finished the handle by itself as on the Brattle Street Church flagon. This is the first dated piece known to me to bear Edwards' second mark—similar to the first but with jogs at the angles—which apparently was used very briefly. A baptismal basin so marked in the North Church, Portsmouth, New Hampshire, is dated 1714.

A small mark of his initials in a rectangle, as on a ring dated 1710/11 in the Essex Institute, Salem, was used on small pieces for two decades or longer; but Edwards' most frequently found and final mark, appearing at least as early as 1715, is that on a beaker made in 1744 *(Fig. 3)*, matching but slightly larger than a similarly stamped one of 1720.

FIG. 6—CHAFING DISH by Thomas Edwards *(c. 1723)*. One of a pair made for Ebenezer and Mary (Edwards) Storer. Diameter, 5¹⁵⁄₁₆ inches. *Mrs. Hale Sutherland.*

made much domestic plate. Such handsome pieces as the Worcester Art Museum's "spout cup" of 1706 and the Wyllys chafing dish were illustrated on a plate showing a selection of sixteen from the forty-odd pieces by him assembled for the Boston exhibition in 1911. It is perhaps significant of his standing in the craft that he was chosen by the son of Jeremiah Dummer to make, in 1726, the flagon which the Lieutenant-Governor presented to the First Church in Boston, armorially engraved and with a slightly higher cover than on the earlier one, and in 1729 a pair of cups for the Church in Newbury Falls (now Byfield, Massachusetts).

The gifts of flagons by King William and Queen Mary to King's Chapel in 1694 had apparently introduced this very popular church piece to the Colonies; at the same time their Majesties gave a covered cup on a rather cylindrical stem which, with one of the flagons, is now owned by Christ Church, Cambridge. This seems to have served Edwards as the model to make in 1724 the only similarly ecclesiastical cup of New England origin known to me, for another Anglican church— an individual's gift to Christ Church, Boston.

Edwards held his share of public offices in the town of his adoption, and the records of his church disclose that in 1722 "by a Great Majority" he was elected to but declined the office of Deacon. The following year, with his fellow church member and craftsman, John Noyes, he valued a tankard bought of Deacon Draper "out of the Church moneys." Of his church's surviving plate the records tell only of money applied in 1718 "to the further supply the Communion Table with plate." Occasional mention of an allowance is made, as in 1722 when the sexton had forty shillings per annum "for the keeping, cleaning, bringing & carrying the Plate for the Communion Table & washing the Linnen used thereat." But for the church, besides the flagon, he made in 1728 a tankard, which was sold in 1839, and in 1732 a pair of cups from Stephen Minot's bequest of "the sum of Thirty Pounds for a piece of Plate for the use of the Communion Table."

Edwards had two sons who followed his craft, indubitably under his tutelage. His first wife predeceased him, as did his first two children recorded by the town: John who was a bookbinder or seller, and Antipas named for his maternal grandfather. In the church records, John aged five, Elizabeth aged three, and Mary aged one week were baptized on the tenth of March 1700, and Antipas, born in November 1698, does not appear. John Edwards died in 1746 "a Gentleman of a very fair Character and well respected by all that knew him." His widow by a second marriage, three sons, three daughters, and a grandson were mentioned in his will. He left a goodly estate; its total value of £4840/8 "old Tenor" was a not inconsiderable sum in those days.

Edwards' second oldest surviving child was his daughter Mary who, in 1723, married Ebenezer Storer. From her younger brothers, Thomas *(1701/2-1755)* and Samuel *(1705-*

From the early years of its use, it is on a hitherto unpublished porringer *(Fig. 5)* with an added date on its "geometric" handle. The mark is also on a handsome punch ladle *(Fig. 4)* whose extreme neatness in pouring and unique small hook at the back of the bowl indicate its use, though others in similar size are variously called goose, basting, or hash spoons. Again one may cite a comparable piece by Winslow whose "basting spoon" in the Currier Gallery of Art, Manchester, has however fewer moldings on its circular hollow handle.

Aside from a wide range of church pieces, John Edwards

FIG. 9—MRS. JOHN EDWARDS (nee Abigail Fowle, widow of William Smith) by Joseph Badger (1708-1765). *Museum of Fine Arts.*

1762), the Storers commissioned much silver which has descended in various branches of the family. Both brothers used marks akin to their father's last one, and Thomas adopted the fashion of a mark with his initial and surname; both also had small initialed stamps for small pieces. Thomas made cups and chafing dishes *(Fig. 6)* heraldically engraved for his sister and her husband, who seems to have preferred another coat-of-arms than that to which he was entitled—or, at least, than was connected with his surname. Thomas and Samuel both made teapots with the new-fashioned repoussé shoulders; and Thomas advertised after his father's death. "The Goldsmith's Business is carried on at the Shop of the deceased, as usual, by his Son, Thomas Edwards."

Thomas survived his father by less than a decade, during which it seems probable that he was training Zachariah Brigden in his craft; for this skilled silversmith reached his majority in 1755 and married Thomas Edwards' daughter Sarah in the following year. Thomas' estate recorded a house on Cornhill and one in Cambridge and, like his father's, two Negroes. The wrought silver of his inventory was valued at seven shillings fourpence per ounce, whereas the appraisal of "unwrought and Household Plate" was six shillings eightpence—an interesting and seemingly significant estimate of craftsmanship. A child's porringer *(Fig. 7)* of his fashioning for his family has an unusual handle-cutting in the general "keyhole" category.

Samuel is credited with considerably more silver in Mr. Jones' church silver book than is Thomas, perhaps because of the latter's advertised connection with his father's shop; yet both together do not equal their father's pieces recorded there. In the 1911 catalogue seventeen of his thirty exhibited pieces are illustrated. Unillustrated was a charming small plate whose mate, engraved with the arms and name of E. Jackson, was a recent gift to the Museum of Fine Arts *(Fig. 8)*. Equally rare, and anticipating the so-called "Chippendale" trays of great popularity (ANTIQUES, July 1949), are two trays of his fashioning in private possession. Both exemplify, with their

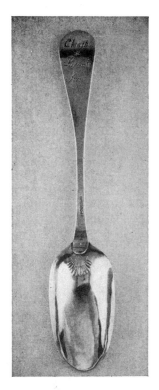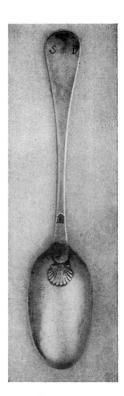

FIG. 11—SPOONS by Samuel Edwards and Joseph Edwards, Jr. *Mr. and Mrs. Mark Bortman and Museum of Fine Arts.*

embryonic shells dividing scalloped moldings, the Edwards' skill and sense of style. He used successively three distinct punches of a similar mark—his initials crowned with a device below—and a small one of his initials in an ellipse.

Samuel married in 1733 Sarah Smith of Charlestown, whose mother, Abigail (Fowle) Smith, seven years later was to become the second wife of John Edwards. The Widow Smith in 1730 had ordered her husband's six funeral rings from John Burt, and as the Widow Edwards was painted by Joseph Badger about 1750 *(Fig. 9)*. Perhaps it is the artist's fault that she seems so uncompromising—but her daughter and son-in-law-stepson received a special bequest "in token of my remembrance of their kindness to me." Her son, Isaac Smith, further confused the family relationships by marrying her second husband's grandchild; and another son, to whose daughter Abigail she bequeathed a gold necklace and gold locket, was to be the grandfather of John Quincy Adams. She left each of her daughters and daughters-in-law a silver porringer, and each of her eleven granddaughters a silver spoon.

Samuel Edwards' small cup *(Fig. 10)* bears, like so many pieces, the adopted arms of the Storer family and is inscribed: *The Gift of Mary Storer to Mary Smith 1758.* This interpreted genealogically is from the craftsman's sister to her step-brother's daughter who was her own grandchild. Mrs. Storer survived her husband by ten years, dying intestate in 1771— an accounting of her estate records "a Negro boy Jack aged 2½ overlooked in the inventory" who had been ever since in the service of her son-in-law! Samuel's niece, Hannah Storer, had a porringer with his mark, engraved with her own and her husband's initials and his crest. Presumably it commemorated their marriage in October 1762, yet in the Boston *Gazette* of April 19, 1762, was reported: "died here after a few Days Illness of a violent Fever, in the 57th Year of his Age, Mr. Samuel Edwards, goldsmith, who, for several Years has been one of the Assessors of the Town; and esteemed as a Man of

FIG. 10—MUG by Samuel Edwards *(1785)*. Inscribed, *The Gift of Mary Storer to Mary Smith 1758.* Height, 3⁷⁄₁₆ inches. *Museum of Fine Arts.*

Integrity; exact and faithful in all his Transactions; His Death is lamented as a publick Loss."

He had no children and to his nephew, Joseph, Jr., son of his youngest brother who was a stationer, he left "a thimble stamp and a swage for tea and large spoons as a token of my respect to him." Joseph, Jr. had undoubtedly been apprenticed to Samuel—for Thomas had died before the youth reached his majority and Samuel's will bespeaks a special regard for this nephew. That it was reciprocated may be inferred from the many proofs that Joseph continued to use the spoons and swage bequeathed him by his uncle. A spoon by each is illustrated *(Fig. 11)*, Joseph's engraved for the church of his forebears; even on his spoons of newer style with backward-bent handles the same shell appears. Samuel's estate had paid a commission for selling plate, yet two years later Joseph, Jr. was offering in the Boston *Gazette* "A Variety of Articles at Apprizement" including "Table and Tea spoons large and small . . ." It is interesting to note the change in nomenclature from the "large spoons" of the will to the "Table spoons" of the advertisement and present-day usage.

The third generation of craftsmen by the name of Edwards is represented solely by this Joseph *(1737-1783)*, whose work is the least known of the family. This might have been because his normally most productive years were war years, or because of the greater number of goldsmiths available. Even in the immediate family, his cousin had married the aforementioned Brigden and three of his step-cousins had married respectively Samuel Burt, scion of another prominent craft family, and two members of the Austin clan working in Connecticut. A third explanation might be the greater enthusiasm for imported plate; in 1772 Benjamin Pickman commissioned a baptismal basin from Joseph Edwards, while his son presented a newly-made pair of London canns to the same North Church in Salem.

In 1765 Edwards debited Joseph Green for sundry items *(Fig. 13)*, and his engraving of the coat-of-arms on the canns *(Fig. 12)* proves his skill in this branch of the craft. His predilection for the "small wares" of the bill is shown by the numbers of buckles, boxes, casters, spoons, and jewelry stolen from him in the same year. These he advertised to recover, setting forth their markings: "Stamp'd I.E." or "Name at length," which was his surname with an initial. These two are the only marks of his known today, the former sometimes confused with but differentiated from his grandfather's by a pellet between the initials.

Fig. 12—Cann made by Joseph Edwards, Jr. for Joshua and Hannah (Storer) Green *(1765)*. Height, 5³⁄₁₆ inches. *Museum of Fine Arts.*

Mr Joshua Green to Joseph Edwards Junr. Dr

April 22, 1765	To pr Pocket Book Clasps	£ 0:7:2
May 11,	To pr Tea Tongs	0:18:8
18,	To 2 Silver Canns	11:18:10
	To 1 Silver Porrenger	3:11:1½
June 3,	To 2 Silver Castors	4:1:7¼
7,	To 6 Do Tea Spoons	1:5:8
17,	To 6 Do Table Spoons	5:9:8
21,	To 1 Do Punch Strainer	2:5:6
July 5	To 2 Do Gravey Spoons	3:6:1½
6	To 1 Do Marrow Spoon	0:11:8
	To Engraving 12 Crests	0:8:–
	To Do 2 Coats of Arms	0:18:8
		£ 35:2

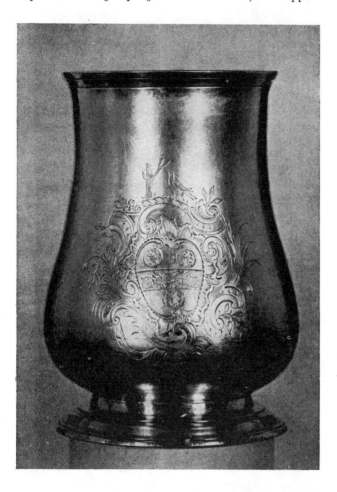

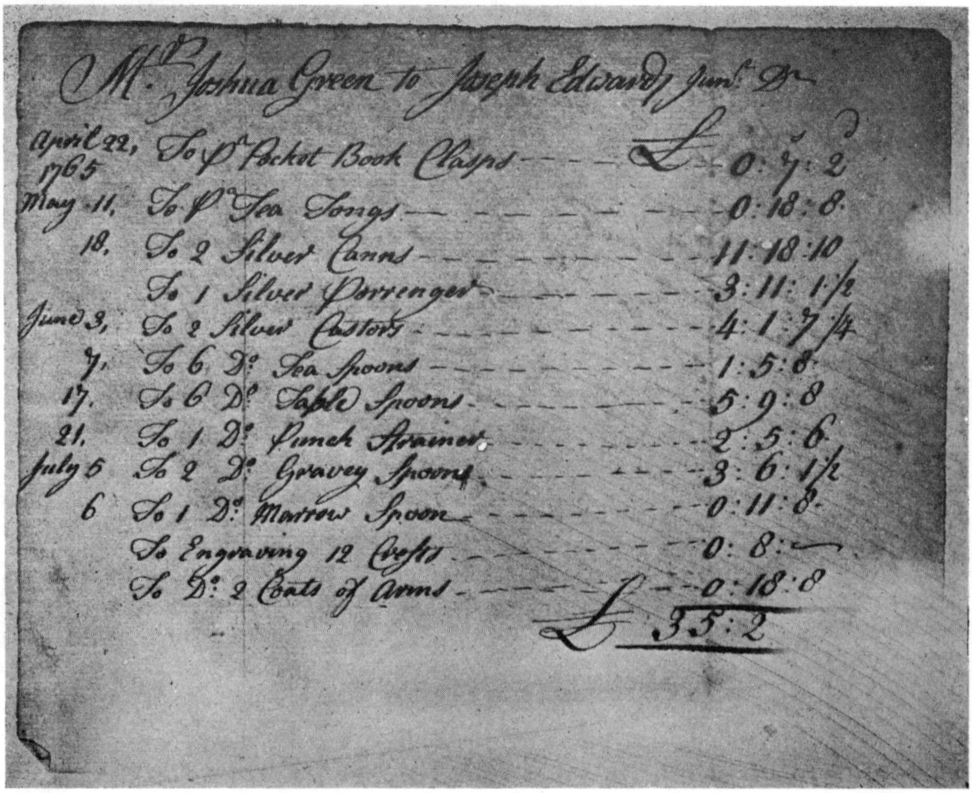

Fig. 13—Bill of Joseph Edwards, Jr., to Joshua Green, which includes the above cann. *Museum of Fine Arts.*

Fig. 1—A plain group, typical examples of Casey's work, all marked S:CASEY. Height of mug, 5½ inches. *From the Marble collection in the Los Angeles County Museum.*

Photographs by Lewis H. Athon.

A Samuel Casey Coffeepot

BY GREGOR NORMAN-WILCOX

IN CHECK LISTS of the colonial silversmiths, many a master craftsman who lived soberly, fathered a dozen fine children, was a deacon in his church and captain of the militia, rates a dull three-line notice. Samuel Casey, whose respectable career came to a scandalous end, is given half a page.

Samuel Casey was born 1723/4 at Newport, Rhode Island. He may have been apprenticed, as Kathryn C. Buhler has suggested, to Jacob Hurd of Boston, for whose daughter Ann he made a spoon dated 1751. Casey was made freeman in 1745 in Exeter, and about 1750 moved to Little Rest (South Kingston) where he was a freeman in 1752. He married in 1753, and from that year worked in partnership with his brother Gideon *(1726-1786)* until in 1762 Gideon moved to Warwick. Arrested in 1770 for counterfeiting, Samuel Casey was tried and convicted, and sentenced to be hanged. But he was delivered from jail by loyal friends, and vanished from sight.

We are not here concerned, however, with Casey's misbehavior. This is to report the discovery of a wonderful coffeepot he made, illustrated in Figure 2 and on the frontispiece*of this issue. Apparently unique in American silverwork, this unpublished and "unknown" example was recently found in England.

What else did Samuel Casey make, alongside which we may set this coffeepot? The group in Figure 1 is representative—workmanly objects of good weight and careful finish, simple in taste but of handsomely judged form. We know of no other large, bell-shaped mug like this one, initialed for Thomas and Mary Vernon who were married in 1766. Notice the robust profile of the cream jug, and its lively stance, when so many another

*see page 74

of this type is thick-throated and wearily sagging. Those tiny, tight-curled scrolls on both the mug and cream-jug handle (the latter with a saucy fishtail) appear often in Casey's work.

For its Rhode Island Tercentenary loan exhibition of portraits, furniture, and silver in 1936, the Rhode Island School of Design gathered 37 examples of Samuel Casey's silver. Greatest in number were five keyhole-handled porringers. (Altogether, we have counted 14 of these by Casey, plus a pair discovered in England, pictured in ANTIQUES for November 1935, p. 215.) There were a pair of hoof-footed sauceboats, and four cream jugs of the type shown here. There were three fine tankards,

Fig. 2—Silver coffeepot made by Samuel Casey of South Kingston, Rhode Island (*c. 1760*). Marked S:CASEY. Height, 10 inches. *From the collection of Mrs. John E. Marble, Los Angeles County Museum.*

April, 1952

SILVER COFFEEPOT BY SAMUEL CASEY

From the collection of Mrs. John E. Marble in the Los Angeles County Museum
See the article on Casey in this issue

including the Garvan piece pictured in ANTIQUES for September 1938, p. 137; one of these was perhaps the tankard sold in November 1929 at Sotheby's in London.

A teapot in the exhibition was one of three quite similar, all with the inverted pyriform body, all valanced with engraving or flat chasing around the lid. The second was seen on page 240 of ANTIQUES for April 1946. The third (made for Sarah S. Gibbs who died in 1756) was No. 574 in the Norvin H. Green sale, December 2, 1950, at the Parke-Bernet Galleries in New York.

A remarkable cream jug, nearly like our Figure 1 but with claw-and-ball feet, was shown on page 251 of ANTIQUES for May 1940. Besides a reversed cipher, it bears a broad band of foliation in very shallow relief, called "the only example of Casey's use of raised ornament." Now our coffeepot robs it of this distinction.

In the 1911 exhibition of *American Church Silver* at the Boston Museum, there were still another tankard. one more cream jug, and a cann with leaf-topped double-scroll handle.

With three bell-shaped small cups, a few casters and salts, tongs, and a good many spoons, this seems to complete the list of Samuel Casey's recorded work. Now we can add this elaborate coffeepot, apparently the only one he made.

English precedent for the form of our pot is found in two London examples of some years earlier, 1737 and 1741 *(Fig. 3)*. Here is a plain George II pot with octagonal spout, low-domed lid, plain handle sockets with a molded drop on the body. Its companion shows the developing fashion for rococo enrichments—a spout and handle sockets quite like Casey's, a double-domed cover the same, relief chasing of massy scrolls and flowers with acanthus frilling.

But the ornament of our pot is its glory. Worked in relief upon a matted ground, and framed with molded C-scrolls, the body shows flower branches and fruit sprays, scallop shells and acanthus. Frilling surrounds the spout, with panels of imbrication below, and large frilled cartouches crowd both sides of the body.

For this, it is not too much to say that Casey's pot numbers among the six or eight most elaborate pieces of pre-Revolutionary American silver. We think of such as Edward Winslow's sugar box or John Coney's great monteith (both shown in ANTIQUES for February 1949, p. 117) or the famous Joseph Richardson kettle (July 1949, p. 42), all in the Garvan collection.

Obviously, such work as George Wickes' *(Fig. 3)* was Casey's model. Casey's coffeepot has a distinctly un-American look, and we can already hear the dissenting cries of skeptics. Is this decoration original, or is it a later addition?

Much early silver was "improved" in the nineteenth century, from Regency through Victorian times. Considered too plain, it was given new-fashioned embellishments in the Rococo Revival manner, sometimes coarse and heavy-handed, sometimes naturalistic and trivial. But comparisons will show that Casey's pot follows mid-eighteenth, not this nineteenth-century taste.

The fact that our pot came to light in England (carried there, presumably, by some royalist who fled America at the time of the Revolution) suggests another possibility. Might the showy decoration have been added by a London engraver? Hardly—for by then, its style would have been some thirty years out of date. For all its Englishness, Casey's pot was surely "born that way" in Rhode Island. Its form and ornament are integral.

An American eagle atop the lid asks us to notice little queernesses in the rich design—awkward or uncertain lapses, such as might betray an engraver working from a pattern book of unfamiliar designs, which he sometimes copied verbatim or again rearranged in rather hesitant fashion. Mrs. Buhler has already shown (in the April 1940 *Bulletin*, Museum of Fine Arts, Boston) that Samuel Casey consulted Sympson's *New Book of Cyphers* (1726). Undoubtedly he used other design books, too.

Lastly, some curious armorial and other engravings offer an interesting suggestion. Within the ornately frilled cartouche on one side of the body *(frontispiece)* is a beautifully rendered coat of arms, its dexter quartering perhaps for Micklethwait, the sinister not yet identified. Jutting from the right of this cartouche, onto a cramped area of plain ground, is a tree trunk with a leafy branch. Evidently this was not a crest. Could it have been an American provincial's way of indicating that his patron belonged to "a branch" of the family whose arms he depicted?

Opposite, the matching cartouche is engraved with the crest of a griffin's head. Above and left of it, an embossed American eagle perches upon a scroll of ornament. And on the field below and to the right, a speckled insect is poorly drawn. An entomologist assures us that no such insect ever flew; it is not the Jacobite moth, but more resembles a butterfly. What is it doing there?

Fig. 3—English coffeepots. *Left*, by John White (*London, 1737*). Height, 9⅛ inches. *Right*, by George Wickes (*London, 1741*). Height, 9¾ inches. *Privately owned in San Marino, California.*

DANIEL GREENOUGH

Early New Hampshire Silversmith

By FRANK O. SPINNEY

IT HAS LONG seemed improbable that Portsmouth, New Hampshire, an early colonial port enriched by the resources of the inner province for which it was the chief outlet, should have produced no craftsmen comparable to those of other sections. Published material, however, yields but scant information concerning workers in wood and metal of this early-settled region.

In the matter of silver, Samuel Vernon, John Burt, Edward Winslow, and other New England craftsmen lived and worked in places hardly more favorable to their success than was this city. Portsmouth was a channel through which were shipped the tall masts and huge spars for the King's Navy, a trade of great importance and productive of great wealth. In unending quantity in colonial times, lesser lumber, shingles, staves, and that forest-clearing by-product, potash, as well as the prodigal yield of the fishing fleets, all went out from the port and contributed to its fortunes. In and around Portsmouth lived Pepperells, Vaughns, Wentworths, Gilmans, and other families whose houses would have been mansions in any contemporary setting and whose strongboxes guarded fabulous stores of plate. Wealth there was in abundance to tempt the artist in precious metals.

If any such vacuum existed, it was soon filled, in the person of Daniel Greenough, the earliest New Hampshire silversmith about whom we have any detailed information.

The first clue to Greenough's existence came from an early collector. Samuel Winkley, a wealthy gentleman of Portsmouth, made a collection of silver in the first part of the eighteenth century. He was justly proud of his display. In it were to be found examples from the hands of Jeremiah Dummer, John Coney, Andrew Tyler, and several pieces created by one Daniel Greenough. Winkley's inclusion of Greenough's work among productions of those others is an impressive recommendation from one who was apparently a discriminating lover of silver. Mr. Winkley, possibly one of our earliest collectors, died in Portsmouth in 1726. Here are excerpts from his will:

> The thirteenth day of November Anno Domini 1726: I Samuel Winkley of Portsmouth. . .Esqr. . .Give and bequeath unto my Son William Winkley. . .a silver Porrenger made by Mr. Dummer, & six silver spoons wth mine & his mothers name on y^m & silver Whistle & two silver Canns wth my Name on them & Made by mr Tyler. . .
> I alsoe give unto my said son Sam^{ll}. . .my Silver Tankard made by m^r Greenough. & six silver spoons made by m^r Cunny. . .
> Item I give unto my Kinswoman Elizabeth Hunking. . .one Silver Spoone made by Dan^{ll} Greenough. . .
> Item I give unto Mary Grant my old Servt a Silver Spoone Made by Dan^{ll} Greenough. . .

It is unusual to find an early will disposing of plate in which the makers of individual pieces are so carefully recorded. The ordinary procedure was simply to name the object. Samuel Winkley was apparently an enthusiast.

Daniel Greenough was born in Rowley, Massachusetts, on February 22, 1685/6, the second son of Robert Greenough and Martha Epps (or Epes) Greenough. Robert Greenough was a man of some substance and prominence. During his term as Town Recorder for Rowley from 1690 to 1693 he placed the names of his two sons, Robert Junior, born in 1682, and Daniel, on the register of births. On a tax list of 1691 containing one hundred and thirty names, only fifteen were assessed higher than was Daniel's father. In addition to this evidence of property, he is known to have been a Falmouth

(Portland, Maine) grantee in 1680, and it is recorded that in 1684 he purchased one hundred acres of land in the township of Wells and Cape "Porpus" (Maine).

Daniel Greenough's mother, Martha Epps, was the daughter of Daniel Epps, an attorney residing in Ipswich, Massachusetts. Her death must have occurred while her son was still an infant, for we know that Robert Greenough Senior was married March 6, 1688, to Sarah Mighill, widow of Stephen Mighill of Rowley. The second wife brought three children of her own to the Greenough household, and two daughters were the issue of her union with Daniel's father. What the early life of Daniel was like in this confusion of brothers, foster-brothers, and half-sisters we can only speculate.

It is reasonable, however, to assume that at a fairly early age he may have left his home to enter an apprenticeship in the silversmithing craft, for by 1708 he was certainly well established in New Castle, New Hampshire, the island adjunct of Portsmouth. In that year took place his marriage to Abigail Elliott. The time necessary for his training, his transfer to and firm settlement in New Castle would have required departure from home in his first teens.

Robert Elliott, Abigail's father, was an important figure. From 1707 to 1715, except for three years, he served as a member of the Council of the Province of New Hampshire. Three other daughters made him father-in-law to Colonel George Vaughn, Captain Timothy Gerrish, and Major Charles Frost, all men from families of wealth and position.

Daniel Greenough's acceptance as a fourth son-in-law argues strongly for his accomplishments and promise. There may have been a previous connection between the Elliotts and Greenoughs; if not, there evidently came to be one. Upon Robert Elliott's death, not only was the son-in-law made a beneficiary, but Elliott bequeathed to Daniel's brother a "Rapier with ye Silver head."

Further proof of Elliott's prosperity is to be found in his will. To his daughter and son-in-law, Robert Elliott bequeathed "my Dwelling house and wharfe and Garden and all my land upon Great Island (New Castle) . . ." and ". . . to Elliott Frost and Daniel Greenough and Abigail Greenough all my land that will fall to my Proportion of ye Comons at Kittery (Maine) . . ." The first Greenough grandchild, Sarah, was given a tract of two hundred acres of land in Falmouth near Cape Elizabeth which was sold in 1734 for the sum of £460. If Robert Elliott dealt as generously with his other sons-in-law and grandchildren, there can be no question but that he was a wealthy person.

Sarah, the granddaughter just mentioned, was one of five children that Abigail bore to Daniel Greenough. The New Castle town records bear eloquent testimony that Daniel was a worthy son of his prolific father. The years 1710, 1712, 1714, and 1718 date the birth of four offspring. The fifth, a daughter Abigail, not recorded in this town list, was mentioned in her father's will.

Abigail Greenough, the mother, "Dyed" in June 1719, and on January 25, 1721, Daniel Greenough married Elizabeth Hatch, widow of Captain Samuel Hatch. The New Castle town records contain the names of three children born of this second marriage. A fourth is listed in the record of baptisms kept by the Reverend Jonathan Cushing (of Dover, New Hampshire), and Daniel's will names three other still younger sons not mentioned elsewhere.

In addition to his marital duties thus duly documented, Daniel Greenough's other activities in New Castle can be traced in some detail between the years 1708 and 1737.

In the *Journals* of the Council and Assembly for the year 1712, the committee for auditing the public accounts of the province is recorded as having allowed "Daniel Greenoe's acct. to be taken out of the 200 lbs. raised to Repaire the fort. allowd 1:17:00." What service he rendered is not described, but a skilled worker in metal could have been employed in a variety of ways.

In that same year, 1715, Daniel Greenough helped in the administration of the estate of Nathaniel Fryer, his wife's grandfather, and there exists a "Bond of Daniel Greenough, Goldsmith. . . as surety in the sum of £40. . ." This is the first written evidence of his craft.

During these years, 1708 to 1737, he was called upon frequently to act as an appraiser for inventory purposes in many estate matters. His name also appears often on documents in this period as a witness to a deed or will. The manner in which he was registered in these papers affords a tantalizingly dim reflection of his life. At odd intervals he signed himself *Daniel Greenough, Goldsmith*. Sometimes it was simply *Daniel Greenough* or *Daniel Greenough of New Castle*. In 1721 he was *Capt. Daniel Greenough*. And for the administration of the estate of his son in 1737, the last of the twenty-eight times that his name occurs in matter of this sort, he listed himself as *Daniel Greenough of New Castle, Gentleman*. . . That he was a man of integrity and of judgment is implied in the number of these occasions. And that he enjoyed a wide reputation is suggested by the fact that his services were sought by men as far apart as William Pepperell, later to become Sir William Pepperell and leader of the Louisburg Expedition, and by one Robert Saunders of Smutty Nose, "Isles Sholes," very likely a fisherman from the rugged islands ten miles out in the Atlantic.

Another reason for his popularity in affairs of this sort may possibly be elucidated by an event which occurred during Greenough's brief term as member for New Castle in the House of Representatives of the province. In May 1720, Lieutenant Governor John Wentworth "was pleased to appoint Mark Hunking and Richard Wibird, Esqrs. to administer the oathes in the case required by the Law" to "Capt. Daniel Greenough." After he had served on two committees during the spring and summer of 1720, a vote of May 16, 1721, was taken to the effect "that Cap. Greenough be Clark of this house till further order." He held this post until it was voted in November to hire a clerk not of house membership, but Greenough was called upon to act in a *pro tem* capacity at least once before the house was dissolved in June 1722.

It seems reasonable to propose that Daniel Greenough's ability as a scribe is the explanation for his frequent appearance in the documents of this period, an era in which many signed themselves with the X of illiteracy. Whether he made a profession of his skill is not determined, but his unusual activity in this sphere is suggestive.

The silversmith was beaten in his attempt at re-election to the House, although he accepted his defeat only after a petition to the Assembly resulted in a vote that his opponent, Jotham Odiorn, Esq. had been legally chosen as representative for New Castle. Only one other essay into politics is recorded. In 1728, Daniel Greenough held the post of Selectman.

From 1730, the story of his life is obscure. Whether this implies a lessening of activity on his part, a move to some other place as yet untraced, or is to be attributed largely to the fragmentary nature of our evidence, cannot be determined. He was still a resident of New Castle in 1737, as noted in connection with his son's estate.

The next record we possess is his will dated March 15, 1745, wherein he speaks of himself as ". . . Daniel Greenough of Bradford in the County of Essex & province of Massachusetts

Bay in New England, Gent. . .'' In this document, preserved in Salem, no clear hint as to the motive for his removal from New Castle is given. Perhaps the reason was the inheritance of a house in Bradford where his father is thought to have moved in later life. In any case, it is certain that in 1745 he owned property in Bradford including a house and blacksmith shop, and that he was aware of approaching death.

His will, composed more than a year in advance of his demise in 1746, reveals him as a man of considerable wealth. To his wife Elizabeth, his sole executrix, he bequeathed ''. . . halfe of my dwelling House in Bradford, as also of the Land about it. . . also my household Goods & plate & my negro servant-maid, Violet.'' He left to ''. . . son Nathaniel & my Daughter, Sarah Robins, & my daughter Abigail Colefax my House at New Castle in New Hampshire (in which I formerly lived) & my pasture Lands there. . .'' and ''. . . to my said Daughter Abigail Colefax, one Looking Glass, an oval Table, one bed & likewise one silver porringer & two silver Spoons, & one iron pott.'' The bequests continue: ''. . . to my Sons, Symon & John, a dwelling House at New Castle. . . where in dwell at present one Sparks & Sparling, with my Land about said House. . . my Lands at Epson in New Hampshire to be equally divided between. . . Symon & John. . . to my son William my Blacksmith shop & all my utensils belonging to said trade & also the other half of my dwelling House in Bradford. . .'' To the younger sons, he gave money, appointing an older brother as trustee until they should be of age.

Unfortunately the inventory and appraisal of the estate, customarily accompanying a will, are in this instance missing. While we do not require the final appraisal to realize that Daniel Greenough was well-to-do, the loss of the inventory deprives us of opportunity to know more details of the plate that was given to his widow. Some gauge of his output and capacity as a silversmith might have been made from this as well as from the list of the tools of his craft.

The mention of the blacksmith shop injects a new and puzzling element into the picture of our silversmith. There exists, however, a deed, dated 1733, and signed by John Greenough of Boston, Blacksmith'' concerning land ''. . . which accrues to me (John Greenough) in Right of My Father Robert Greenough late of Rowley. . .'' This John was, in all probability, Daniel's nephew, the son of Daniel's older brother Robert, who died in his early thirties leaving six children, one of whom was named Robert. It is conceivable that at some time, the nephew came to Bradford, established himself there in his self-confessed trade, and that somehow his property came into the possession of his uncle. Another hypothesis might be that Daniel, after his shift to Bradford, had set up his son William in business and had retained title to the investment until his death. That the silversmith himself doubled in this trade of brawn and muscle is possible, of course, but hardly likely.

The period to Daniel Greenough's life is to be found carved on a tombstone. ''Here lies Buried the Body of Capt Daniel Greenough who died April 20, 1746 in the 61st Year of His Age.'' And on another stone: ''Here Lies Buried the Body of Mrs. Elizabeth Greenough (Relict of Capt. Daniel Greenough) Who Departed This Life Dec yᵉ 3ᵈ 1765 in yᵉ 73 Year of Her Age.'' These inscriptions were published in the Essex *Antiquarian* in 1906. A recent (1941) examination of the old burying ground of Groveland, once the East Parish of Bradford, where the stones were described as standing, revealed that many of the older ones, eroded into illegibility, or broken, had been moved and possibly discarded. A few Greenough stones of later date are preserved, but those commemorating Daniel and his wife were not discoverable.

Little description in this article has been given of the silver coming from Daniel Greenough's hand. The explanation for that deficiency is sadly simple. At the present writing, so far as I have been able to determine, only one example attributed to him is extant. That is a sugar box, on loan at the Boston Museum of Fine Arts, which has been tentatively identified as the New Hampshire silversmith's creation. Samuel Winkley's will, by its mention of a tankard, makes it clear that Greenough was not a mere maker of spoons. The tankard and the sugar box, if we accept the latter's identification, are good evidence that Daniel Greenough was a fully qualified craftsman and one whose name can be justly included in the list containing the names of his better known contemporaries of the early eighteenth century.

Verifying a Hull and Sanderson Porringer

By Mrs. Russel Hastings

A STRANGE little silver porringer with an unusual cast handle came into the marketplace shortly after the depression reached bottom. It bore what appeared to be the genuine marks of John Hull (*1624–1683*) and Robert Sanderson (*1608–1693*) of Boston. The southern city where it emerged from hiding is far from the Boston Museum, and there was no immediate way of comparing it with accepted pieces by the famous partners. Moreover, it was so obviously "wrong," in collector's parlance, that the dealer who bought it dared risk only a small sum on acquiring a mere gamble. The lady of ancient Boston lineage who parted with it had inherited much silver in the 1890's from a series of childless relatives and, misled by the *W. F.* engraved on the porringer's handle, had attributed the piece to her Frothingham great-aunt — though the name is not Frothingham.

Immediately, the little vessel began its hopeful travels, which, though entertaining in the extreme, we cannot recount at length. The piece went to Boston for inspection by a learned jury of experts; it made journeys to New York; it lived long in Philadelphia; but nowhere was it encouraged to abide. No one doubted the genuineness of the marks, but since its ornate cast handle could not be explained, it went into retirement.

I chanced upon it one lovely spring day two years ago. Its owner took it casually from an unlocked cupboard, averring that it was the earliest known porringer by an American maker (which it possibly is). Now such important objects do not ordinarily dwell in unlocked cupboards, and as its owner was a stranger to me, I listened with interest but without particular conviction to her story. But as I browsed among other things in the place, I began to realize that the porringer was clamoring for my attention. In spite of myself, I went back to hold it and turn it about and look at it through a strong glass, with mounting curiosity. At length I asked that it be sent to one of our major museums for more convenient study and comparison.

Soon after, it was heartening to learn that the editor of ANTIQUES had long held an instinctive belief that the little thing was genuine. The point to be decided at the outset was the purely technical one of whether or not its condition was original. Several of the foremost experts, after careful examination, assured me that beyond the letters of the handle and a minor repair in the casting, the porringer was in every way original. Its "fire coat" was intact, though marred by prolonged contact with salted almonds on feminine bridge tables. The solder with which the handle had been attached to the bowl was "heavy," that is, lumpy and crude, showing that no modern blowtorch had ever swept its surface. In so far as could be judged, the piece was precisely as Hull and Sanderson had composed it about 1675. I say "composed," because as yet we have no way of knowing who made the familiar castings so freely used in America at that period. The learned pronouncements removed all possibility that the porringer was spurious.

The next matter for investigation was the pedigree as indicated by the previous owner's records. Now while this owner had a theory regarding the *W. F.* of the handle, she could not explain the early and original letters, *V* over *I*M*. She generously gave me the data used in compiling her pedigree; but among her hundreds of ancestors and those of the Frothinghams of whom I have spoken, there

Fig. 1 — PORRINGER BY HULL AND SANDERSON OF BOSTON (*c. 1670–1680*)
Weight, 3 oz., 14 dwt., 6 gr. *Height*, 1 5/8 inches. *Width over all*, 6 inches. *Diameter of bowl*, 4 5/16 inches. Because of the Continental flavor of the cast handle the genuineness of the piece was at one time questioned. *Privately owned*

Fig. 2 — SIDE VIEW OF THE HULL AND SANDERSON PORRINGER
Showing the rather low position of the handle, which suggests that the porringer was in reality a skillet lid

Fig. 3 — Pricked Initials *V* over *I*M* on Porringer Bowl
The same device appears on a tankard by Sanderson, which is illustrated elsewhere in this issue

Fig. 4 — Marks of Hull and Sanderson on Porringer
Jones' *The Old Silver of American Churches* describes (*p. 162*) a piece dated *1674* with the same marks

was no one with a surname beginning with *V*. When a well-known Boston physician was encountered perched among the outermost branches of her family tree, I began to suspect that we were barking up the wrong one. In more gracious days, beloved medicine men were the recipients of all sorts of treasures from grateful patients. Hence it is no novelty, in tracing the pedigree of a piece of silver, to be halted by a famous doctor standing squarely in the path. These gifts were given and received in a fog of emotions so tender as to preclude questions. In such circumstances, the searcher must tactfully retire and approach his problem from some far-distant point.

Such was my procedure. There were, I discovered, but few couples in all seventeenth-century New England who bore the initials *I* (or *J*) and *M V*. Of these, upon investigation, but one seemed worth considering. Isaac Vergoose (*1637–1710*) married, about 1668, Mary Balston (*1648–1690*) of Boston. It was easily proved, by old deeds and Sewell's *Diary*, that the couple knew John Hull and were his neighbors.

At this juncture another character enters this silver drama. It is a very large tankard by Sanderson alone, done presumably after Hull's death in 1683 and before Mary Vergoose's end in 1690, since it bears the selfsame pricked initials that appear on the porringer. It was owned by a lady of such dignity as only Beacon Hill in Boston knows. It was found, some seventy years ago, in her mother's attic, in a box tightly nailed up — dark as to color and darker still as to its past. No amount of family investigating has ever cleared up its mystery. But in her family tree stands a famous philanthropist, to whom we might impute this second silver waif. His private benefactions were abundant, the encyclopedia

assures us. The tankard may be a gift pressed upon him in a burst of gratitude, but never considered by him as exactly his own possession.

As will be seen, the bowl proper of the porringer is of Cromwellian or Stuart type, with an unaccountably florid cast handle, set a trifle lower than is usual for porringers. For that reason, it may well be considered a skillet lid bereft of its base. In 1701 William Penn brought to America a "caudle cup with 3 leggs & a porringer to cover it." A skillet by William Rous, a seventeenth-century Boston maker of Dutch origin, has been recorded. Another by John Van Newkirke of New York has also been encountered, but like the Rous example has since vanished.

To test the hypothesis that this porringer was a Vergoose heirloom, a skeleton genealogy of the clan was assembled — no mean task, it may be added. Deeds, wills, inventories, and early printed records of the Massachusetts Bay Colony were searched, and as many months were spent in doing this as it will take minutes to tell the outcome. With each step, in which the constant effort was to cast doubt upon the theory, it seemed clearer that I had found the truth. But the most dramatic confirmation of it came through my discovery of two inventories, in each of which both tankard and porringer appear to have been recorded.

Isaac Vergoose and Mary Balston had ten or more children. Shortly after Mary's death, Isaac took to wife a courageous spinster named Elizabeth Foster (*1665–c. 1757*). Elizabeth not only mothered the survivors of Mary's large brood, but produced six or more of her own. One of them, Elizabeth Vergoose, or just as often Goose, married Thomas Fleet (*1685–1758*), a printer from Tislock, White Church Parish,

Fig. 5 — London Porringer (*date letter for 1637*)
Brought to New England about 1640. Belonged to President Henry Dunster of Harvard College and his wife Elizabeth, whose initials appear on the bottom. *Weight with added plate, 5 oz., 10 dwt. Height, c. 1 ½ inches. Width over all, 6 ⅝ inches. Diameter of bowl, 4 ⅞ inches. By courtesy of Harvard University*

Fig. 6 — Front View of Dunster Porringer
Showing extensive patch

Shropshire, who arrived in Boston in 1712. Fleet had learned his trade in Bristol, and was said to have fled the city because of an embroilment in the Jacobite riots at that place. He founded a famous printing house in Boston and a newspaper, which evaporated at the beginning of the Revolution. He was a fellow contributor to the *New England Courant* with young Benjamin Franklin, the proprietor's brother. The Fleet imprints are numerous and to bibliographers the name is very familiar.

One of the routine procedures in tracing the pedigree of an heirloom is the careful scrutiny of wills or inventories, in the hope that some mention of the object of one's regard may be encountered. My search in this direction was twice rewarded. Isaac Vergoose left behind him 169 ounces of plate, of which we are quite safe in assuming that some had been acquired and suitably inscribed in Mary's lifetime. Elizabeth had "one large silver tankard wt 42 oz" and "one silver bason, one cup, and four old spoons weighing 19 oz, 9 dwt." Among the grandchildren of Isaac Goose was Captain William Fleet, a mariner (*1720-1787*), who eventually inherited from unmarried brothers and sisters most of the family belongings. His ample inventory shows "*one large tankard weighing 41 oz, 15 dwt*" and "*one small porringer weighing 3 oz, 16 dwt.*"

On the base of the large tankard recently acquired by the Boston Museum is scratched "41–15"; and to an optimistic eye there appears to be a far earlier "42." The piece weighs today 41 oz., 11 ½ dwt. This represents a suitable loss from two hundred and fifty years of cleaning. The little porringer weighs today 3 oz., 14 dwt., 6 gr., again a suitable diminution in weight. The later letters *W. F.* on the handle obviously indicate the ownership of Captain William Fleet. Hence it cannot be doubted that the evidence points heavily to the Vergooses as the original owners of the porringer by Hull and Sanderson as well as of Sanderson's solo tankard.

The Vergooses, moreover, furnish a logical theory to account for the porringer's very Continental handle. Either it was transplanted from some earlier bowl, brought to this country and perhaps too dilapidated for further use; or else it was cast by Hull and Sanderson from another handle to which they had access. The study of these cast ornaments on early American silver is still in its earliest infancy, but the one in question may hardly fail to prove rare if not unique. I am assured by some eminent London authorities that it is a type found on seventeenth-century brandy bowls from the Low Countries. May it not equally well be a single ear from a French or Flemish écuelle?

An eminent Dutch genealogist now in America says that the Vergoose family was from Goes in Zeeland, on the coast close to the Belgian border. The form of the name indicates that they had not long been absent from their native island. The use of the sea horses on which the *putti* so confidently rest is frequent in Flemish design. Isaac Vergoose's father, Peter, was a ship joiner, and several of his descendants were seafaring men. This was a traditional calling for the foreign refugees of England's East Coast. Isaac had a brother Peter living in Norwich in 1685. The Vergooses had much to do with the French inhabitants of Boston, and had several intermarriages to their credit. It would be strange if, with all these ties with the Continent, some little shreds of its influence had not survived.

Note. A tradition exists that in 1719, Thomas Fleet brought out a volume of the songs which his mother-in-law Elizabeth Vergoose sang to her stepbabies, her own babies, and her grandbabies, inflicting boredom on the printer, it was whispered. The volume was reputedly called *Songs for the Nursery; or, Mother Goose's Melodies for Children.* The tradition is now reliably thought to have been a figment of someone's imagination; but as truth almost never overtakes falsehood, many of the old stock in America believe it. Boston swarms with students throughout the year, and few of them can escape being told that the Granary Burying Ground, on one of the city's busiest streets, enshrines the mortal remains of "Mother Goose." Now the grave thus signalized is not that of Elizabeth, the supposed Mother Goose, but of Mary, her predecessor. To a guide this is a small detail which never gives him a moment's pause. And so our little porringer appears to have been made for the goodwife in the Granary Burying Ground who to millions of Americans goes by the name of "Mother Goose."

If we must relinquish the charming idea that we may stand beside the grave of our childhood's friend, it diverts attention from the pain of loss to contemplate the little "bason" which surely was the purveyor of nourishment for many little Vergooses and Fleets—so many, indeed, that Elizabeth Foster, second wife of Isaac Vergoose, is widely believed to be the original

" . . . old woman who lived in a shoe.
She had so many children she didn't know what to do.
She gave them some broth without any bread,
Then whipped them all soundly and put them to bed."

That the old woman was, according to interpreters of folklore, Old Mother England, and the children her colonies at the time of James I, is another story. Katherine Elwes Thomas, in *The Real Personages of Mother Goose*, discusses the origin of the best-known nursery rhymes, and their roots are far from Boston Common, for their characters are the great personages of English history. These English rhymes have been invented and sung and hawked about in chapbooks for centuries. The crowds around Buckingham Palace during the past year had not abandoned the custom.

Fig. 7 — ENGLISH SKILLET (*date letter for 1665*)
Weight, 22 oz., 18 dwt. *Height 5 ¼ inches. Diameter of bowl*, 5 ½ inches. The placing of the handle on these skillet lids is farther below the rim than is conventional in independent porringers. Hence the question as to whether or not the Hull and Sanderson piece may not be a skillet lid, bereft of its skillet. Compare Figure 2.
From Christie's Catalogue, June 16, 1931

A new form in
American seventeenth-century silver

BY GRAHAM HOOD, *Curator of American art, Detroit Institute of Arts*

SEVENTEENTH-CENTURY SILVER is the area of American art where one least expects an important and hitherto unknown form to emerge. That there are still objects to be found, however, which may slightly change our perspective of the period and our ideas of its forms and its relationships is confirmed by the recent discovery of a covered skillet by the rare Boston maker William Rouse (1639-1705).

The skillet (Fig. 1) has a deep, bowl-shape body with straight sides slightly tapered from the lip to the rounded bottom. It stands on three cast scroll feet, which are lozenge shape at their juncture with the body. It has a squat, hollow handle with serrated, shield-shape terminal; the upper surface of the handle extends over the terminal and is also serrated. The cover is slightly stepped, with a flat top, a shallow applied bezel, and a wide flange with an incised line close to the edge. It also has an applied, hollow, reel-shape handle, with an engraved sunflower radiating from its base.

On this piece Rouse used his elaborate mark of W·R with star and two pellets above and pellet below, in shaped shield; the mark is at the lip of the body to the left of the handle, and on the flange of the cover. Since this was obviously a commissioned piece, he added the Foster arms and crest within an elaborate and finely engraved, scrolled-acanthus cartouche on the front of the body (Fig. 2), and the arms in the shield alone on the top of the reel-shape handle (Fig. 3). Barely discernible is the original record of the weight, *18-3*, scratched on the bottom. The skillet now weighs eighteen ounces.

William Rouse probably came to Boston in the early 1670's either directly from Wesel—his native city, according to the *Journal* of Jaspar Danckaerts (1679-1680)—or via England. He married Sarah Kind, a widow, about 1675 in Boston. Danckaerts refers to "Ross" as a Dutchman, and his wife as an Englishwoman. He was certainly a practicing craftsman by 1678, for the will of Harman Jonson, who died in Boston in that year, designated "Rowse goldsmith" as his executor. In 1692 he helped appraise the estate of his fellow goldsmith Timothy Dwight, and his own tools were appraised, after his death in 1705, by John Coney. In his obituary in the *Boston News-Letter* for January 15-22, 1704/5, his name is spelled Rowse; it also appears in Boston records as Roesz.

Only eleven pieces by Rouse are known at present, and

Fig. 1. Covered skillet by William Rouse (1639-1705), Boston, Massachusetts. Height 4⅜ inches; length 7½ inches; diameter at the lip, 5 5/16 inches. *Collection of Mr. and Mrs. Donald W. Henry, currently on loan to the Yale University Art Gallery.*

Fig. 2. The Rouse skillet; Foster arms engraved on front.

Fig. 3. Cover of the Rouse skillet, engraved with sunflower; the Foster arms engraved on top of handle.

of this small number four were made for the Foster family. The skillet is the most elaborate of these, and is the only one bearing engraved arms. A patch box at Yale, its cover decorated with an engraved sunflower, bears the initials of Lydia (Turell) Foster (ANTIQUES, December 1955, p. 556), and a small cup with the same initials was once lent to the Museum of Fine Arts, Boston. A rare pair of sucket forks was engraved for John and Lydia Foster (ANTIQUES, June 1950, p. 441). In addition, two tankards by Rouse have been published. One is the well-known example in the Mabel Brady Garvan Collection at Yale, to which were later added the initials of William and Elizabeth (Davenport) Dudley, married in 1721. On the cover of this tankard is engraved a sunflower design very similar to that on the cover of the skillet. The second

tankard (now on loan to the Los Angeles County Museum) is the only previously known piece by Rouse embellished with armorial engraving (ANTIQUES, April 1937, pp. 174-175; and January 1954, p. 49). The cover of this tankard is decorated with a sunflower very similar to that engraved on the Yale patch box. Completing this short list of objects by Rouse known today are two beakers, in the First Church, Dorchester, Massachusetts, and the First Congregational Church, Guilford, Connecticut; and two small cups, one in the Detroit Institute of Arts and another which appeared on the art market in 1964.

As was customary in the late seventeenth century, the arms on both skillet and tankard were set within scrolled-acanthus helmeted cartouches. Beautifully executed, they fully attest to Rouse's skill with the graver. The engraving on the skillet is somewhat unusual, for the leaves are broader and do not swirl so vividly as those in the cartouche of the tankard. Nor is there sufficient space on the side of the skillet body for the cartouche to surround the shield completely in the usual manner. A later and less striking version of these arms, in an oval scrolled cartouche, can be seen on a large dish by Edward Winslow which was bequeathed to the Second Church, Boston, in 1711 by Abigail, the second wife, and widow, of John Foster.

Rouse's work certainly reveals the strongest English influences. His tankards are virtually identical to English examples of the 1680's and 1690's, and it is only natural that his skillet should have been closely derived from an English form (Fig. 4). While the claw feet used on the English piece were appropriate to the 1660's, Rouse utilized the scroll bracket form popular in New England around 1700. These feet are identical, for example, to the scroll brackets applied to the tops of the three known American standing salts, all of which were made within the first decade of the eighteenth century. Although the covers of the skillets are different, it is instructive to note that arms in a shield, but without cartouche, are engraved on the cover handle of the English example, as indeed they are on the handle of the Rouse piece. It should be observed, too, that the cover of this English skillet is very similar in form to the earliest type of New England porringer—its sides are straight and appear to be curved to a flat top slightly domed in the center, while its pierced handle is identical to that on the Hull and Sanderson porringer in the Spalding collection, Museum of Fine Arts, Boston.

Another English covered skillet, by James Birkby of Hull (Fig. 5), is inscribed with the date 1650 and has armorial engraving on the front of the body, as Rouse's has, although the mantling is of course in the earlier style. When this example was illustrated in ANTIQUES for June 1958 (p. 550), Mrs. G. E. P. How conjectured "that the single-handled porringer developed from the top of a skillet, which supports the theory that this form was intended for use at the table and not as a bleeding bowl."

Shortly after the Rouse skillet appeared, Kathryn C. Buhler reported that another skillet, excessively battered but nevertheless recognizable as a Hull and Sanderson piece, had turned up in Boston. Thus it appears more likely than ever that the Spalding porringer was originally a skillet cover. In other words, it was not a mere "piece of Puritan plainness," as it has been described, but a part of a much more ambitious piece—a part, moreover, that could serve a dual function as cover and porringer, as in the English prototypes, and in the same way that the covers of the large Coney and Onckelbag seventeenth-century two-handled cups also served as covers and stands.

Another Hull and Sanderson porringer is known, of course, with an identical body and a highly unusual cast, figured handle; it is now in the Henry Francis du Pont Winterthur Museum. It came as a pleasant surprise to me to discover that when this piece was described thirty years ago in ANTIQUES (September 1937, p. 116) the author, Mrs. Russel Hastings, conjectured that it might have been a skillet cover, and went on to state that skillets by Rouse and Jan Van Nieukirke had at one time been recorded, but had subsequently disappeared.

As befits its seventeenth-century origin, the Rouse skillet has a squat and solid appearance. It gives the impression of resting firmly on, rather than rising from, the surface on which it stands, an appearance to which the primarily horizontal curves of the heavy handle contribute. Although this type of hollow handle is used on the earlier English skillets, it is interesting to note that it is not found on American two-handled cups or simple mugs until somewhat later. The engraving undoubtedly adds an elegant touch in the early baroque style; it is finely executed and tightly controlled. Most seventeenth-century New England silver quotes English domestic silver almost verbatim, and this skillet is no exception. But it, and the discoveries related to it, somewhat enlarge our view of the seventeenth-century New England silversmith and his milieu.

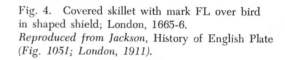

Fig. 4. Covered skillet with mark FL over bird in shaped shield; London, 1665-6. *Reproduced from Jackson,* History of English Plate *(Fig. 1051; London, 1911).*

Fig. 5. Covered skillet by James Birkby; Hull, c. 1650.

LITTLE-KNOWN MASTERPIECES

VII. A Unique Early Colonial Salt

By S. W. Woodhouse, Jr., and Horace H. F. Jayne

So much has already been written about the Colonial silver of New England, its history, its makers, and its excellence, that it would seem almost impossible to unearth any new fact of interest. However, as is true of all mines of historical research, the deeper the student goes, the wider the vein he uncovers, and the greater his chance of finding an important nugget.

Such a nugget came to light at the recent loan exhibition of silver held at the Pennsylvania Museum in Philadelphia. Among a number of pieces of New England silver lent for the occasion by Mr. Nathan Hayward, the remarkable standing salt-cellar shown in the accompanying illustration was discovered. It is a piece of plate which has been in Mr. Hayward's family for many generations,—so long, indeed, that, in the passage of time, its real use had been forgotten, and that which in days gone by had doubtless occupied a prominent position on the family board, had come, of recent years, to serve in the capacity of flower vase. Much surprise was evinced by the owner when he learned that his vase was made originally for salt and not for flowers; and that the four attached scrolls which, quite naturally, he had believed to be legs, were in reality supports projecting from the top to hold a napkin or a plate for the covering of salt contained in the circular depression.

The surpassing interest of this piece to connoisseurs and collectors of American silver lies in the fact that it is the only American made standing salt-cellar known to exist. Hence as an authentic rarity it is quite unparalleled. In fact, the only other salt-cellar of contemporary Colonial ownership is the Glover Salt in the possession of Harvard University. And this was made in England about 1635. English standing salts of the seventeenth century are, themselves, rare and interesting examples of the silver workers' art. How much more interesting and alluring is the only piece of native smithing of its sort yet discovered!

It will be not out of place to give here a brief history of silver salt-cellars, in general. We shall find it, however, to be a story of degeneration; for scarcely any individual piece of table silver has so markedly shrunk in estimation and importance. In mediæval times the "salt" (the shortened form is, for convenience, generally used) was quite the foremost piece of domestic plate. When it is borne in mind that, in earlier days, almost the whole supply of salt was obtained by laboriously evaporating sea-water, it will be realized that the receptacle which held this precious condiment must have been of considerable consequence in the household.

At the high table, where sat the lord and master, was placed the great salt—a large and elaborate piece. The smaller receptacles (if the family owned any) were placed on other parts of the table. Sir Charles Jackson has shown that the salt never served as a definite dividing line between the nobles and the menials, as has been commonly believed. To be sure, since the great salt stood before the host and the important guests sat near him, in order of their rank, it is easy to understand how the impression gained full credence that the salt itself was the determining factor in the banqueter's importance.

"The principle standing salt having been placed before the lord," as Jackson instructs us, "and smaller salts set on other parts of the table, each person helped himself, from the nearest of these receptacles, with his knife, to as much of its contents as he required and placed it on the side of his trencher; into the salt so placed each slice of meat was dipped, and thence conveyed to the mouth."

In the earliest times these great salts were chiefly the property of the nobles, but it was not much later that associations, such as colleges and guilds, had them designed and made to grace their banquet tables. Such ceremonial examples were kept with reverential care, were brought out only for State occasions, and were handed down from generation to generation. Even to this day, many of them are in the possession of the very bodies for which they were made. It is to these pedigreed salts that we turn in order to trace the history of the family in general.

The earliest types of all—those of the fifteenth and six-

1490   1554   1626   1660   1676   1697

THE PASSING GLORY OF THE STANDING SALT
Drawings illustrative of the succession of salt-cellar types from the fifteenth century to the close of the seventeenth.

LITTLE-KNOWN MASTERPIECES

VII. STANDING SALT-CELLAR, OF SILVER (*about 1695, approximately actual size*)

Made by John Edwards and John Allen of Boston.
Only American piece of its kind known. Insert shows makers' marks.
For discussion see following pages.

teenth centuries—were very large and very impressive, and their form varied greatly. In every case the body was tall, shaped often as an hour-glass, often as the pedestal of a column, and sometimes as an animal, such as an elephant, dragon, or dog, or even a human figure. On the upper part of the body occurred the depression for the holding of the precious mineral. In the earliest forms this depression was covered by a close-fitting lid, always kept on when the salt was not in actual use. Later the lid came to be supported upon balls or scrolls, some distance above the salt, so that the diner could reach under it with his knife and help himself without removing the unwieldy cover.

Since the great salt was one of the most prominent pieces of plate on the table, the silversmith naturally expended much effort in making it beautiful and creditable to his craft. Hence all which have come down to us are richly decorated and beautifully chased with ornamental devices or with scenes of various kinds; and their covers are usually surmounted with delicately sculptured figure finials. Some are set with cut crystal or ivory, and many are gilded. Early examples of these great salts are owned by New College, Oxford, Christ College, Cambridge, Ironmongers Hall, the Vintners Company, and the Norwich Corporation. Still others are shown among the Royal plate in the Tower of London.

This elaborate type of salt, in an infinity of variations, remained popular until the middle of the seventeenth century, when we discover a marked tendency toward simpler forms, directly reflecting the shrinkage of the salt's importance at the banquet. With the Restoration came the omission of the cover; but the scrolls or supports which had served to hold it in place remained and were used to hold a napkin or a covering plate. Hence the origin of the supposed "legs" on our American piece. Toward the end of the seventeenth century, even these scrolls were dropped, and the whole salt diminished, scarcely a hint of its former grandeur left, until it had dwindled to the comparatively insignificant piece that we know and use today.

Mr. Hayward's Colonial standing salt was made by John Edwards and John Allen, of Boston, about 1695, and in the centre of the circular depression we find their marks, IE and IA, in two quatrefoils with a pellet between.

These two silversmiths were partners in the craft, and we have record of their joint workmanship in 1699. They were also brothers-in-law, Edwards' sister, Elizabeth, being John Allen's wife. John Edwards was the elder by a year, having been born in England in 1670, son of John Edwards, chirurgeon of Limehouse, London, who came to the colonies shortly before 1688. During his life Edwards, junior, was not only a preëminent silversmith, but a worthy citizen of Boston. He held a number of public offices in the town, including the position of Fourth Sergeant of the Artillery Company in 1704. He died in 1746, leaving an estate amounting to nearly five thousand pounds. Two sons and one grandson survived him and continued to ply the trade of silversmith.

John Allen was an American, born in Boston in 1671. His step-uncle was Jeremiah Dummer, one of the earliest and best-known New England silversmiths. It seems highly probable that Allen was apprenticed to Dummer, and from him became skilled in the craft, which he followed until the time of his death in 1760. The partnership between Allen and Edwards dates from the time when Allen married Elizabeth Edwards, but it did not last after the beginning of the eighteenth century; for we have authenticated pieces of plate made by each of the two men, separately, after 1700.

As an example of early silversmithing, the salt is creditable; the joints between the successive steps are well fashioned, the scroll uprights are neatly cast and are finished by hand; time and wear have dulled the cutting of the gadrooned borders, but the metal itself, of excellent quality, still possesses that indefinable "fire", which is so hard to describe, but which is so characteristic of all Colonial silver. Still, not even the most enthusiastic collector would deem it a piece of great beauty. It has much antique charm, to be sure, but further than this we cannot honestly go.

Its original owner was Soloman Stoddart, and it is engraved on the upper border $_{SE}^{S}$, block letters, standing for Soloman Stoddart and his wife Esther. Stoddart was born in America, probably in Boston, in 1643, and was a student at Harvard, from which he was graduated about 1660. He then entered the ministry. In 1672 he moved to North Hampton, Massachusetts, and about the same time, we suppose, he married a widow, Esther (Wareham) Mather, whose first husband was a descendant of Cotton Mather. She, herself, was the daughter of John Wareham, the first minister of Windsor, Connecticut. Soloman and Esther, we may venture to guess, received the salt after they had been married twenty-five years, or upon the twenty-fifth anniversary of Mr. Stoddart's pastorate, as a present from his grateful parishoners. That they had it made for themselves seems scarcely probable, for the family tradition tells us that Stoddart was a man of very small means, who would have been reluctant to allow himself such a distinct luxury as a standing salt. Esther and Soloman had twelve children, eight of whom lived to marry and have children of their own. One of the daughters, Esther, was the wife of the Rev. Timothy Edwards of Windsor, and the mother of the famous Jonathan Edwards.

Perhaps we may be excused if we seem to have written less about the salt than about its makers and its history. After all, apart from its peculiar rarity, it is the traditions which have clung to it through the centuries, the wide span of its reverend years, and the stories, meagre though they be, of the hands that fashioned it and the hands that prized it and passed it from generation to generation, that give to this venerable salt its grace and elegance in our eyes, and its elusive charm.

The nine colonial sugar boxes

BY KATHRYN BUHLER, *Assistant curator of decorative arts, Museum of Fine Arts, Boston*

Fig. 1. Sugar box by John Coney (1656-1722). Inscribed *The Gift Grandmother Norton to Anna Quincy, born 1719;* according to family records, the date was added after 1837. Names of four subsequent owners, the eldest daughter in each generation, may have all been added at once; the latest is dated 1900. Stamped several times with the maker's fleur-de-lis mark. *Museum of Fine Arts, Boston.*

Fig. 2. Sugar box by Coney with "pibling" (an obsolete term for pebbling, or matting) on the lid. *Currier Gallery of Art.*

IN THE LITERATURE on English plate of the early seventeenth century no one seems to have concerned himself overmuch with distinguishing between the spice box and the sugar box. Contemporary inventories apparently did not use the term sweetmeat box, which we find in much of this century's British writing; in early days this word was evidently reserved for shallow dishes and flatwares.

In the inventory of Elizabeth I there appears "Item oone Spice box fationed like a Cofer of silver guilt with a lidde . . . and within the same a litell guilt Spone having a boy upon the toppe of the steele of the same being a Spice box poiz xxx oz." Other spice boxes therein listed were of weights appropriate to pomanders or were specified as having "Romes" (*i.e.,* compartments, presumably to separate spices from each other). Elizabeth's "comfett box . . . fashioned like a Tortoise with a little folding spoon" is as near as the listing comes to a reference to sugar. The *Oxford English Dictionary* lists from the Unton inventory of 1620 "A sugar boxe, . . . one sugar boxe spoone" and in 1639 "I Scollup Suger boxe." Could the latter refer to the scallop-shell form of the surviving boxes fashioned in the late 1500's and the first quarter of the 1600's and called in our own day spice boxes? Only one is recorded, by Bernard and Therle Hughes (*English Domestic Silver*, Pl. 34), as a "shell-shaped sugar-box, London 1616—formerly the property of Samuel Pepys." Half a century after this box was made Pepys wrote: "1664 Dec. 30. To several places to pay away money, to clear myself in all the world, and, among others, . . . paid . . . the silversmith 22£ 18s for spoons, forks and sugar box."

The list of plate brought to this country in 1638 by the widow of the Reverend Jose Glover (he died on the voyage) is a matter of record because it was subse-

The sugar box, perhaps the most sumptuous form in early American silver, was discussed by Homer Eaton Keyes in a gallery note in our issue of December 1937 (p. 309); at that time only six examples (Figs. 1, 3, 6, 7, 8 here) had been recorded. In the intervening years we have had notes on sugar boxes in ANTIQUES for August 1939 (p. 88), June 1942 (p. 371), November 1943 (p. 237), March 1946 (p. 178), and February 1949 (p. 117). When Colonial Williamsburg acquired the most recently discovered example, the handsome Coney box illustrated in Figure 4, we asked Mrs. Buhler to bring our readers down to date by giving the background of the form (according to John Marshall Phillips it became popular in England toward the end of Charles II's reign) and illustrating and describing the nine American boxes now known.

quently involved in estate litigation. Her servants remembered "a great silver trunke with 4 knop to sta[n]d on the table and with sugar." This most nearly suggests the Elizabethan coffer; the elliptical form known in American plate seems not to have appeared even in London until the mid-century.

When a plain, straight-sided box made in London in 1661/62, probably by Andrew Moore, was given to the Boston Museum of Fine Arts in 1933, we had but recently been requested to use the contemporary term sugar box in relation to the earliest American one now known (Fig. 1). Therefore the English one was so recorded until its donor wrote hastily to the effect that the dealer had called it a sweetmeat box and so should we. But the Victoria and Albert Museum now calls its chinoiserie example of 1683 a sugar box, and we find ample support for the use of that term.

In the Colonies, the earliest receptacle for sugar which I have found mentioned, aside from Mistress Glover's, belonged to the widow Mary Truesdale and was inventoried at her death in 1674 as a "sugr dish." In 1690 John Clarke, chirurgeon, had "2 sugar dishes" in a collection of plate with a total weight of one hundred and seventy-seven ounces, valued at £57.10s.6d. In 1693, in a similar grouping of silver, James Lloyd had "2 sugar boxes," and a "sugar dish" was listed in John Saffin's inventory in 1710; but since no weights are given for these they may have been the shallow small-handled sweetmeat dishes unknown today in American plate. In the eighteenth century the term sugar box was usual, with occasionally an individual weight, though the 1760 inventory of Harvard tutor Henry Flynt lists a "Sugar Pot 22 oz. 14 dwt." which to judge by its weight may have belonged to this group.

Although Mistress Glover's "great silver trunke" was brought here in the year that Robert Sanderson arrived and John Hull inventoried Mary Truesdale's silver, the earliest American goldsmith known to have fashioned these boxes is John Coney (1656-1722), Boston's most versatile goldsmith. There are four examples of his work in this form known to be extant (Figs. 1, 2, 3, 4).

An entry in the Boston Museum's 1911 silver exhibition catalogue reads: "Box with hinged cover. L. 8⅜ in. W. 6¾ in. Copy of an English box. Oval with four twisted feet, repoussé with acanthus border on cover, and snake handle. The gift of Grandmother Norton to Anna Quincy, born 1719. Lent by Mrs. J. R. Churchill." Two years later the lender and her daughter, namesake of Anna Quincy, presented the sugar box (Fig. 1) to the museum.

In 1911 Sir Charles J. Jackson (*Illustrated History of English Plate*, p. 832) published Lord Llangattock's "sweetmeat box" (Jackson's term) of 1676 which, except that it has sixteen lobes on the body as well as on the cover, is startlingly akin to Coney's. The latter's snake handle on the slightly domed lid is far bolder than the London one, as are his almost corkscrew feet; the London box has a more elaborate hasp.

A very similar box by Coney, with the same wide-awake snake somewhat differently coiled, is shown in Figure 2. Its past history is unknown. Its hasp, pierced with hearts and commas (or perhaps tadpoles, to carry out the naturalistic motif of the handle), is more elaborate than the Norton one.

A third box by Coney (Fig. 3) has strangely flat-chased pad feet and curved sides with sixteen flat

Fig. 3. Sugar box by Coney; 1700-1710. Inscribed on hasp *S G*, probably for Captain Samuel Gardner of Salem: a sugar box of approximately the same weight as this one was mentioned in the 1769 inventory of a Gardner grandson who was also the captain's namesake. *Museum of Fine Arts.*

Fig. 4. Sugar box by Coney, with maker's early fleur-de-lis mark. Owners' initials *L/IE* inscribed on hasp in the triangular form used for a husband and wife. *Colonial Williamsburg.*

Fig. 5. Sugar box attributed to Daniel Greenough of New Castle, New Hampshire (1685-1746). Initials on the bottom are those of Robert and Sarah Elliott of New Castle, whose daughter Abigail was Greenough's first wife; the sugar box descended in their family. Weight, *22 oz, 12 dwt,* is also inscribed on the bottom. *Metropolitan Museum of Art.*

Fig. 6. Sugar box by Edward Winslow (1669-1753). Inscribed *Ex dono/ Sarah Middlecott/ N England/ to MM/ 1702.* Fleur-de-lis mark occurs flanking the hinge and twice just above on the rim of the cover. *Collection of Mrs. Edsel B. Ford.*

ellipses, each framed in reeding; embossed trefoils fill the interstices. Its cover is molded and more highly domed than those of the earlier boxes, with a midband of reeding and an ellipse of gadrooning around its coiled serpent handle; the serpent itself has no scales. The shaped hasp, with comma cutting surrounding a fleur-de-lis, is engraved *S G,* undoubtedly for Captain Samuel Gardner of Salem: a sugar box of approximately its weight is mentioned in the 1769 inventory of a Gardner grandchild who was also the captain's namesake. The cover shows no sign of ever having had a bezel.

Coney's most recently discovered sugar box (Fig. 4), which was found in England in 1961, also bears his early mark. The snake handle on the cover trails its tongue across the upper of two matching bands of reeding. The acanthus of the seventeenth-century boxes appears again but on the body this time, giving direction to the swirling deep gadroons outlining a boss on each of its four sides.

The only piece of plate attributed to Daniel Greenough (1685-1746) of New Hampshire is a sugar box made for his father- and mother-in-law (Fig. 5; see ANTIQUES, June 1942, p. 371). It has an engraved coiled snake for a handle and a wide band of gadrooning on the molded and domed cover and on the curve of the elliptical body. Above the latter is a band of matting, and the feet could almost have been cast from Coney's mold. The hasp is very elaborate.

Four boxes by Edward Winslow (1669-1753) are also known. One was illustrated by Jackson on the same plate (opp. p. 832) with the aforementioned London box owned by Lord Llangattock. Two of Winslow's are dated, and the four bear more relation to one another than do Coney's. All are somewhat akin to the Coney one at Williamsburg, with similar cast feet and acanthus motifs embossed on the body against a granulated ground; all are encircled at the base of the gadroons by a band of reeding. On all but one, punched decoration tops the gadroons; the covers are high domed and molded. One has a snake handle, the others have symmetrical and leafy scrolls forming a rather large loop with only a little variety in their tooling. The flanges of all the covers have stamped molding on their edges.

The box illustrated in Jackson (Fig. 6 here) is inscribed on the bottom: *Ex dono/ Sarah Middlecott/ N England/ to MM/ 1702* and has the Winslow family arms and crest chased and embossed within acanthus leaves on a circular hasp with serrated edge. Richard Middlecott was the third husband of the silversmith's aunt Sarah Winslow. The inclusion of *N England* in the legend suggests that the box may have gone immediately to England, where it eventually came into the possession of Jackson (the *10 March* for *to MM* in his caption is a typographical error). In the ellipse beneath the coiled-snake handle of the Middlecott box, in high relief on each side, is an attenuated winged and robed figure bearing branches. Narrow gadrooning and a band of leaf tips frame these and are in turn framed by reeding within rising moldings. The bosses at the back and in the ends show a sword-wielding horseman against a matted ground.

For his own use, by family tradition, is another Winslow box (Fig. 7) on which the three bosses have dragons identifying the equestrian figures as representations of St. George. Its scalloped circular hasp has an

Fig. 7. Sugar box by Winslow;
dated 1702.
*Yale University Art Gallery,
Garvan Collection.*

embossed acanthus cartouche for an unadorned heraldic shield. The domed cover has a single band of reeding and a very much wider rayed foliate band surrounding similar winged figures with somewhat cherubic faces, flanking the scroll handle. Although Edward Winslow had decreed that his plate was to be sold to meet expenses and legacies, members of his family apparently availed themselves of an enviable opportunity, for several pieces are known to have been until recently in the possession of his descendants; this was acquired from one of them.

Another Winslow box dated 1702 (Fig. 8) was taken to England by the famous Tory Oliver family. This was identified in ANTIQUES for March 1946 (p. 178) as the gift of Lieutenant Governor William Partridge to Daniel and Elizabeth (Belcher) Oliver, all of whose initials it bears. On its hasp as well as on the bosses is an equestrian figure brandishing the familiar sword and holding an oval shield chased with scrolls and a mask. Its lid has a band of reeding and a wide area of foliate design with a central wreath. It, too, is marked on both sides of the hinge, as was Winslow's own, but it is smaller than the others by this maker.

The simplest of Winslow's boxes (Fig. 9) has a running foliate design on the lid instead of the rayed leaves of the others, its bosses are unornamented, and its hasp is missing, but it bears four marks, as does the Middlecott box. A lug on the front boss proves the erstwhile existence of a hasp, but the hasp must have hidden the owners' initials. Its hinge is also lacking, and a very irregularly applied bezel seems to be an early compensation for these missing parts. Connecticut Governor Gurdon Saltonstall's third wife was Mary Withington, widow of William Clarke, whose great basin by John Coney she bequeathed to the Old South Church in Boston. Mary survived her second husband, and in 1729/30 she left, in her three hundred and twenty-nine ounces, four pennyweight of silver, "1 sugar box & spoon" to prove that sugar as well as spice boxes sometimes had a spoon—even though we cannot identify these today.

Fig. 8. Sugar box by Winslow;
engraved on botton *O/ D.E/ Donum W.P 1702* in block and semiscript letters. *Henry F. du Pont Winterthur Museum.*

Fig. 9. Sugar box by Winslow.
Inscribed *S/ G M* for Gurdon and Mary Saltonstall.
Museum of Fine Arts.

III New York State: The Mingling of Traditions

New Netherlands was reputed to be the most poorly governed colony in America, and there seems to be some justification for this claim. Like Virginia, New York was settled with an eye to profit—the fur trade along the Hudson promised instant prosperity. The presence of settlers simply insured that Dutch claims in the New World would be recognized. Fort Orange, now Albany, was first established as a fur trading outpost. New Amsterdam, now known as New York, followed quickly.

Immigrants were a mix of Dutch, French Huguenot, Spanish, and English whose religious backgrounds were as diverse as their nationalitites. This variety gave New Amsterdam a cosmopolitan air and created a luxury-loving society which counted on trade—legitimate and illegitimate—for its livelihood. Hundreds of taverns and an air of prosperity enlivened the city. Even after the bloodless English takeover in 1664, a relaxed but decidedly mercantile atmosphere and Dutch character lingered in the city.

New York silver, like the brick or stone homes built in the colony, was sturdy and straightforward in form. This solidarity was emphasized by the ornament lavished on most pieces. The same principles applied to New York furniture. Flat surfaces were there to decorate. The immense *Kas* found in most households were covered with painted designs, and pendant fruit and floral swags which often graced these *Kas* appear in the engraved cartouches and applied cast ornament added to New York silver.

The first two articles in this section define and characterize early New York workmanship and its allure for the collector. C. Louise Avery (pp. 96-99) provides some particularly useful illustrations which simplify the comparison of forms. This approach makes it easier to trace the French, Dutch, and English influences in the work of craftsmen like Benjamin Wynkoop (1675-1728), Peter van Dyck (1684-1751), Peter de Reimer (1738-1814), and Daniel Christian Fueter II (worked c. 1754-76).

Mrs. Russel Hastings (pp. 100-103) describes one of the most spectacular pieces of early American silver—a large beaker by Cornelius Vanderburgh, with strapwork engraving at the rim and a series of allegorical figures engraved on the midsection and base. Mrs. Hastings traces the sources for these allegorical motifs which had been subject to previous misinterpretation. In subsequent articles (pp. 104-118), she includes Dutch genre scenes, touchmarks, and discussions of individual smiths to illuminate the general social milieu in which New York silver was made and used. Some biographical dates given in these articles should be adjusted: Benjamin Wynkoop (1675-1728), Jacobus Van der Spiegel (1668-1708), Bartholomew Schaats (c. 1670-1758), and Peter Van Dyck (1684-1751).

Albany seems to have retained its Dutch heritage long after New York took on an English cast. Robert G. Wheeler (pp. 119-121) describes this continuing influence in Albany silver through the first two decades of the 19th century, while John D. Kernan, Jr., (pp. 121-123) and George Barton Cutten (pp. 124-128) emphasize particular silversmiths of the area. Kernan's tentative attribution of the demi-horse mark to Kiliaen Van Rensselaer III remains an exciting possibility. Cutten provides a detailed picture of two generations of the Albany Ten Eyck family. He also cites fascinating excerpts from the ordinances of Albany, some of which demonstrate the persistence of medieval traditions in the colonial crafts and in society at large.

Throughout this section a number of illustrations of early tankards provide a good review of the interpretation of this form in New York. Most show high base moldings with applied foliated bands. Meander or wriggle wire, applied to the base or rim, flat lids, and the "corkscrew"-curled thumbpiece are other features characteristic of New York work. Tankard handles generally have cast ornament applied along the topside of the grip, and tousled cherub masks (as opposed to the less windblown New England putti) gracing the handle terminal. All these motifs can be found singly and in combination on tankards of other areas, but few silversmiths in other regions applied them so liberally or with such verve.

Other forms, like the two-handled "grace" cups discussed by Louise C. Belden (pp. 129-131) are also New York variations on a theme. When two-handled cups are mentioned, one thinks first of the Boston products of Edward Winslow and John Coney. Belden shows that New York craftsmen were more than able to interpret this impressive form. The paneled, or lobate, bowl, on the other hand, was a unique product of New York silversmiths. Two articles by John N. Pearce (pp. 132-138) follow the development of the form from its Renaissance beginnings to its later use in the Netherlands. Immigrant silversmiths brought the form to New York, where it developed its own personality. Two dates in Pearce's checklist (pp. 135-136) should be revised: Jacob Bohlen lived c. 1654 to 1722, and Jacob Ten Eyck's birth year should read 1705.

By the middle of the 18th century, the exuberance of the rococo had overpowered most Dutch influences in New York silver. Pattern books were in demand and arrived in America within months of their European publication. New Yorkers translated these designs into full-bodied, capacious serving pieces and drinking vessels whose proportions recalled the earlier work. The vigorous rococo ornament and elaborate cartouches undoubtedly appealed to these New York craftsmen, raised as they were in a tradition of comfort and worldliness.

THE DISTINCTIVE QUALITY OF EARLY
NEW YORK SILVER

An Editorial Note

*Illustrations, with the exception of Figure 9, from loans to
the recent exhibition of New York silver sponsored by the
Women's Committee of the Museum of the City of New York*

EARLY New York silver has for some years past been more highly prized by collectors than have corresponding wares of like period turned out by the craftsmen of other colonial communities. To be sure, striking exceptions to the rule may be cited. In no public sale has the price of any piece of American silver surpassed that brought by John Coney's New England monteith. Again, it would be hard to find a New York item of greater money value than the Edward Winslow Boston sugar box recently retrieved from long hiding in Scotland (ANTIQUES for March 1937, *p. 140*, and December 1937, *p. 309*). But these and perhaps a few other instances aside, the preliminary observation will hold. To explain its whys and wherefores is another matter. Relative scarcity may have something to do with the situation, but a conclusive test of any such hypothesis would involve a complicated statistical investigation. Perhaps it would be safest to say that, in general, New York silver — at least that made prior to 1750 — exercises a greater measure of appeal than does silver made elsewhere.

So sweeping a statement obviously invites trouble. Are articles of New York manufacture of better quality in design, material, or method of fabrication than those items produced in New England and in the neighborhood of Philadelphia? Probably not. Philadelphia, we may recall, was later than New York in attaining full stride in silversmithing. So that city suffers something of a handicap as concerns the early period. New England, on the contrary, does not. Furthermore, from the standpoint of refinement and delicacy the silver of New England perhaps outranks the New York wares.

Why then talk about "appeal"? Unfortunately, so subtle an attribute is virtually beyond verbal analysis. To employ the familiar vernacular, a thing "gets you," or it does not. Early New York silver "gets you," and therewith analysis and argument come to an ignominious end. Yet it may justly be remarked that articles of handcraftsmanship are highly susceptible to the temperament of the craftsman, and in their turn possess for all time an occult power of radiating his personal vibrations. Thus an aura of puritan austerity and restraint seems almost always to encircle even the finest of old New England work in furniture, silver, and the like. To contemplate these manifestations is to experience a feeling of admiration and of æsthetic satisfaction. Seldom, however, are these reactions accompanied by that life-enhancing thrill which is conveyed by things in whose conceiving and fashioning the maker has yielded to an intense creative joy.

Confessions of enjoyment are not native to the puritan tradition, nor is the frank expression of pleasure a puritan trait. New Englanders have always inclined to keep a tight rein on their enthusiasms. In New York and in the neighborhood of Philadelphia, where the infusion of Continental blood and Continental ideas was strong, life was more abundantly savored, imagination more lively, and actual repression less dominant. When we stop to realize that the silversmiths of old New York were prevailingly of Continental stock — perhaps chiefly Dutch, to some extent French, to some extent we are not sure what — we are in a position to understand why surviving examples of their work seem so incomparably robust, so heartily and humanly inviting, so generously outspeaking of compatibility and substantial fellowship.

FIG. 1 — TANKARD
By Gerrit Onkelbag (*working 1698–1732*). Like other early New York tankards, this has a flat lid in two stages, fairly wide overhang of lip, serrated or scalloped in front. The thumbpiece is characteristically of corkscrew form, and a band of foliation surrounds the bottom. Also characteristic, the heavily mantled pseudo-armorial device, a rose in a field, is a kind of pictorial pun. *From the collection of Mrs. James Roosevelt*

FIG. 2 — TANKARD
Ascribed to Jacob Marius Groen (*working 1701–1750*). The lid inset with a medal is elaborately engraved. The richly ornamented cast handle terminates in a boss.
From the collection of LeGrand B. Cannon

FIG. 4 (*above*) — TEAPOT

Ascribed to Stephen Bourdett (*working 1730*). A strikingly original interpretation, displaying a boldness of conception and vigor of execution characteristic of early New York examples.

Anonymous ownership

FIG. 3 (*top of page*) — TEAPOT

By Peter Van Dyck (*1684–1750*). Strongly Dutch in character, even to the handsomely engraved cypher. This pear shape, as opposed to the inverted-pear shape, suggests a date in the neighborhood of 1715.

From the collection of Miss Elizabeth M. Bates

FIG. 6 (*right*) — MUG

By Benjamin Wynkoop (*working 1698*). Relatively simple in form and decoration except for the richly mantled cypher. The mass and sweep of its handle are superb. The supporting feet are most unusual.

Anonymous ownership

FIG. 5 (*above, centre*) — TEASET

By Peter de Riemer (*working 1769*). A complete three-piece tea service at so early a period is excessively rare. This service is said to be the earliest in the category of New York silver. The skill with which the maker has maintained harmony in form and decoration without exact duplication should be noted. The handle of the creamer is delightfully individual. No Dutch influence is evident in this set.

From the collection of the late Francis P. Garvan and Mrs. Garvan

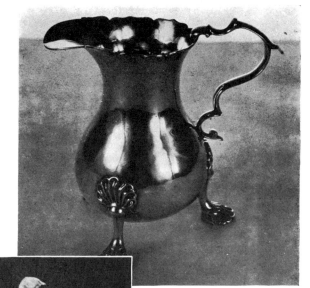

FIG. 7 (*above*) — CREAMERS
Left, by Adrian Bancker (*working 1731*). A sturdy design, in which Dutch feeling pervades an English form.
From the collection of Mrs. Arthur Lenssen
Right, by Daniel Christian Fueter (*working 1756*).
From the collection of Mrs. J. Ramsay Hunt

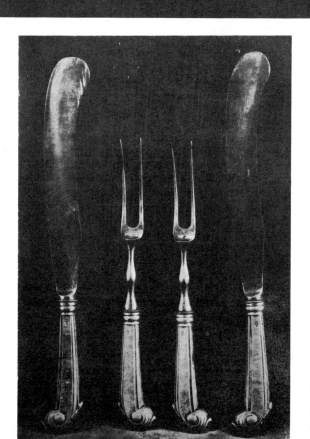

FIG. 8 (*left*) — TWO-HANDLED BOWL WITH COVER
Attributed to Jacob Boelen (*1654-1729*). Closely similar to a bowl by Gerrit Onkelbag illustrated in ANTIQUES for December 1936, *p. 284*. Of the two bowls the Boelen item shows the better treatment of foliation around the base.
From the collection of Arthur Iselin

And so, likewise, we may understand that our liking for these articles is due to the fact that their lusty vibrations induce a sympathetic response in our own centres of emotion.

As for the particular features that distinguish the silver of early New York from that of other colonial centres, they are adequately summarized in Luke Vincent Lockwood's excellent preface to the catalogue of silver by New York makers published in connection with a loan exhibition held early in 1938 at the Museum of the City of New York. Mr. Lockwood calls attention to the foliated border common to the base of tankards and other hollow ware, the wire ornament on the lip of tankards and mugs, the accompanying corkscrew thumbpiece, and the cast handles often richly adorned with reliefs. New York beakers, again, incline to be tall, and in form and decoration to emulate Dutch examples. Porringers, though in the bowls resembling other colonial vessels of the kind, exhibit handles whose complicated piercings are peculiar to themselves. Teapots made prior to 1750 are invitingly bulbous and comfortably Dutch in character. Cream jugs differ from those made elsewhere mainly in their

sturdier contours. So Dutch and English modes meet and mingle in New York silver to create a distinctive style, which after the mid-century gradually yielded to English fashions until its individuality was virtually lost. In New York silver of the late 1700's and early 1800's the romantic eye may perceive a surviving fondness for the amplitudes of an earlier period. With the advent of the 1830's, no trace of local flavor remained. Thenceforth New York silversmiths adopted the gaudy elegancies which, though we call them Victorian, represented a worldwide epidemic of bombastic ostentation.

— *H. E. K.*

FIG. 9 (*left*) — SILVER-HANDLED KNIVES AND FORKS
From a full set; handles marked I L in an ellipse, for John Le Roux, working 1723 and for some years thereafter. In *Early American Silver* Miss Avery observes that the mid-eighteenth century saw many pistol-handled knives and forks, and names the New York smiths John Le Roux, John Hastier (*working 1725–1791*), and William Anderson (*working 1746 and later*) as making these articles. Joseph Richardson of Philadelphia (*1711–1784*) is included in Miss Avery's list.
Formerly in the collection of the late W. Lanier Washington

Early New York Silver

By C. Louise Avery

Illustrations by courtesy of E. Alfred Jones, Esq., London, and the Metropolitan Museum of Art, New York

TWENTY–FIVE years ago the average American collector, if you had questioned him about the silver used in the Colonies, would doubtless have looked a bit bewildered and would finally have dismissed the matter by telling you that most of it was probably imported from abroad. He was handicapped much more than we are now, for in that quarter of a century so many pieces, then tucked away in attic chests, in storehouses and church vaults and known only to their immediate guardians, have come to light that today we can see in a single museum about nine hundred examples of American silver made prior to 1825, half of them dating from the Colonial period.

What, then, has piped these treasures from their hiding-places? First of all, the persuasive tones of a collector's voice and the jingle of his gold. Some twenty years ago a few men, keen enough to recognize the excellence of this American handicraft and to appreciate its charm, began to hunt down early examples, and, though the search was difficult and they had only their own taste and judgment to guide them, their persistence and their enthusiasm enabled them to build up collections of high rank before the general public knew that anything had happened. Among these pioneers were W. L. Andrews, R. T. H. Halsey, T. S. Woolsey, and A. T. Clearwater. When, like Mr. Halsey and Judge Clearwater, eager to share their delights with others, they have lent their collections to museums for indefinite periods, they have helped immeasurably in spreading a knowledge and appreciation of this early American art.

The vision of museum officials in plan-

Fig. 1 — DUTCH MARRIAGE-BOX (*Haarlem, 1620–30*)
Engraved ornament and mouldings similar to designs in New Netherland silver. *Metropolitan Museum of Art.*

ning, from time to time, great loan exhibitions of Colonial silver has also increased the general interest and has brought to light many rare and historic pieces. At the instigation of F. H. Bigelow, an ardent student and collector, the Boston Museum, in 1906 and again in 1911, held such exhibitions, drawing from New England churches and private collections a wealth of plate, the very cream of Boston silversmithing. This array of flagons, tankards, cups, beakers, porringers, and teapots gave New Englanders an opportunity to see what skilful craftsmen their ancestors were.

The Metropolitan Museum, in 1907, in 1909 in connection with the Hudson-Fulton Celebration, and in 1911, with the aid of the Colonial Dames, organized notable exhibitions in which the work of the silversmiths of New York and vicinity was especially featured. At other times similar exhibitions of early American silver were held at the museums in Jamestown, Providence, Philadelphia, Hartford, and Baltimore. Such occasions have brought to public view for a brief interval many charming pieces which, immediately afterward, have retired again to the seclusion of private collections and church storehouses. There must still be much silver, unknown and undiscovered, which, when it does eventually come to our notice, may add as much to our knowledge as these earlier exhibitions have thus far contributed. This possibility lends much fascination to the pursuit of Colonial silver.

Whenever an enthusiastic student has had time to gather information, a new publication has appeared. The earliest, J. H.

Fig. 2 — DUTCH BEAKERS MADE IN HAARLEM (*1638 and 1645*)
Shape and engraved ornament both characteristic. *Collegiate Church, New York (founded 1628).*

Fig. 3 — TYPICAL EARLY NEW YORK BEAKERS
With figures of Faith, Hope and Charity. Made by Jacob Boelen (*c. 1654–1729*). *New Utrecht Reformed Church, Brooklyn.*

Buck's volume on *Old Plate* which appeared in 1888, has now been largely superseded by more comprehensive studies. Mr. Halsey wrote extremely interesting and informing accounts of the Boston and New York silversmiths and their work as introductions to the Boston (1906) and Metropolitan Museum (1911) catalogues. E. A. Jones prepared for the Colonial Dames a handsomely printed and illustrated volume on *Old Silver of American Churches*, a work as valuable as it is expensive and difficult to procure.* *A List of American Silversmiths and Their Marks*, compiled by Hollis French under the auspices of the Walpole Society, is practically the only record of its kind, and very useful. *Philadelphia Silversmiths* have been listed by Maurice Brix. *Early Silver of Connecticut and Its Makers*, by G. M. Curtis, *Historic Silver of the American Colonies and Its Makers*, by F. H. Bigelow, and *American Silver of the XVII and XVIII Centuries*, *A Study Based on the Clearwater Collection*, published by the Metropolitan Museum, complete our shelf of books.

It is to be hoped that, some day, the achievements of various leading silversmiths may be made the subject each of a special monograph: there exist enough examples of their handiwork to make it possible for us to discover the individualities of style of at least a score of these men. The task, however, is not to be lightly undertaken, as it entails a vast amount of research through old records and genealogies, a search sometimes fruitful, sometimes most unprofitable and discouraging.

Already enough silver has been brought together to enable us to distinguish certain types: (1) the great group of New England silver, patterned after contemporary English styles; (2) the New York silver of the late seventeenth century and of the eighteenth century, which never loses the marks of its Dutch ancestry; and (3) the Pennsylvania silver of the eighteenth century, which developed certain distinctive features of its own.

It is with the silver made in New York prior to 1750 that we are now most concerned: what were its chief characteristics and how shall we recognize them?

New York silver is, first of all, based upon Dutch silver of the seventeenth and early eighteenth centuries, both in its general form and in the details of its decoration. Many pieces of Dutch silver illustrate just those features which we have come to recognize as the earmarks of early New York silverwork. This is perfectly natural. New Netherland might be rechristened New York, but men whose names were Van Dyck, Boelen, Van der Spiegel, Wynkoop, Ten Eyck, and Onclebagh did not speedily forget their national traditions. They modeled their silver after the styles they knew so well. They were sturdy, energetic, practical men, and their handiwork is correspondingly massive, rugged, forceful and, despite the use of a considerable amount of ornament, it is simple and never fussy. The New Netherland silversmith loved to engrave and emboss his pieces, but he always subordinated such ornament to the general form, and never forgot the medium in which he was working. Consequently he modeled shapes that were suitable to the metal and to the use for which he designed them; their strength of line and beauty of proportion are never obscured but are rather emphasized by their ornament.

Though we do not know just when the first silversmith began to ply his trade in New Netherland, it was certainly prior to 1664. But unfortunately the earliest

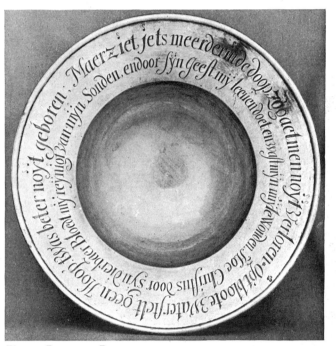

Fig. 5—Baptismal Basin
By Jacobus Van der Spiegel, purchased by the congregation of the South Reformed Church, New York, in 1694 at a cost of 63 Holland guilders. The inscribed verse composed by Dominie Selyns explains the inner meaning of baptism.

Fig. 6—Baptismal Basin by Jacob Boelen
Presented by Frederick Phillipse to the Reformed Church of Tarrytown N. Y. Foot added later.

*Of this notable work some dozen copies remain unsold. They may be purchased at $50 each through the medium of ANTIQUES.

examples of which we have definite record appear to have been made after this date, and even pieces made before 1680 are very rare. The earliest are naturally the most purely Dutch in style, as yet untouched by foreign influences. Dutch conservatism clung tenaciously to its native types long after the English took possession of the colony; and, during the eighteenth century, New York silver retained its distinguishing characteristics, though increasingly modified by the use of English ornament and of English shapes.

Fig. 7 — TYPICAL SERIES OF NEW YORK TANKARDS
By Jacobus Van der Spiegel, Benjamin Wynkoop, Peter Van Dyck, and H. & M. *Halsey and Pruyn Collection.*

Fig. 8 — TANKARDS
By Jacobus Van der Spiegel (with de Peyster arms) and P. V. B. Each silversmith has developed his own foliate border design at the base. *de Peyster and Garvan Collections.*

To study New Netherland types, then, we should turn to the earliest pieces. These we find to be, as a group, the beakers. These tall tapering cups had long been popular in Holland—used at first as domestic cups and, after the Reformation, adopted by the Protestant churches for their communion. Similar customs obtained in New Netherland. Doubtless there were many beakers used in the homes of the seventeenth century Dutch Colonists, but almost all of them have been lost; a few of those presented to the Reformed churches have, however, been preserved. Seven of them, made in Holland and later presented to the Colonial churches, show us the patterns which the New Netherland silversmiths followed. Mr. Jones has described and illustrated these imported beakers and also eleven others fashioned by New York makers. In one instance, the Colonial example is a copy of a Dutch beaker belonging to the same church; in all of them we see the same general style, the tall, tapering, rather heavily-wrought body, the strong base mouldings, the very typical engraved bands of strapwork, floral scrolls, birds, and symbolic figures, which, in these communion beakers appropriately represent Faith, Hope, and Charity.

They illustrate the Dutch artist's love of engraved ornament; though the drawing is often crude, it is wrought with sincerity and appealing naïveté. In a beaker of rather later date (*Fig. 4*) Adrian Bancker has shown his preference for sturdiness and simplicity unadorned, yet so ably has he fashioned this piece that it is as charming as those with embellishment. One needs to see these beakers to appreciate the texture of their deftly-hammered surfaces, the color and mellowness of the silver.

In the Dutch Reformed churches the beaker was used almost exclusively as the communion cup; practically the only other object coming from these old churches is the baptismal basin, of which Figures 5 and 6 are historic examples. The little gray stone church, still standing on the Albany Post Road north of Tarrytown, was built in 1699

Fig. 9 — LID OF TANKARD BY WYNKOOP (*Working 1698–1740*)
Showing characteristic engraved decoration. Wynkoop's mark shows clearly in upper portion. *Pruyn Collection.*

Figs. 10, 11, 12 — Mugs

Fig. 10 — Mug by Koenraet Ten Eyck (freeman, 1716), showing use of mid-band, spiral wire, and beaded rat-tail ornament on handle. *Halsey Collection.*

Fig. 11 — Mug by Simeon Soumaine showing mid-band and leaf-border at base. *Garvan Collection.*

Fig. 12 — Mug by J. Ten Eyck, an early example showing slight curve in outline. *Metropolitan Museum of Art.*

by Frederick Phillipse, lord of the manor, and his wife Catharine, daughter of Oloff Stevenson van Cortlandt, "the right honorable, God-fearing, very wise and prudent my lady Catharine Phillipse . . . who has promoted service here in the highest praiseworthy manner." By making it the centre of his *Legend of Sleepy Hollow*, Washington Irving has woven a further spell about this old church.

While the beaker was probably the earliest form of cup in New Netherland, it can hardly have been so popular as the tankard, for, though we find only a few beakers today, we find quantities of tankards. The latter were probably never used in the Reformed churches here; in fact, it seems probable that the general form was derived from English tankards of the second half of the seventeenth century, though the ornamental details are distinctly of Dutch origin. At all events, these early New York tankards, designed for beer and good fellowship, must have suited well the tastes of the Colonists; the number in our collections today and their generous proportions would indicate that beer, rum, cider, and ale flowed very freely indeed and, as the old records show, upon all occasions. Mr. Halsey has discovered that one New England village of forty families

*Fig. 13—*Cup

Originally with one handle, made by Peter Van Dyck. *Presbyterian Church, Setauket, L. I.*

in 1721 stored away as its winter supply three thousand barrels of cider, and there is no reason to suppose that New York held second place in the quantity or variety of "strong liquors" consumed.

Our illustrations show the typical New York style of tankard: the large and slightly tapering body, the flat lid, the so-called "corkscrew" thumb-piece, the applied border of leaf design above the moulded base. The other ornamental details are equally characteristic and show the Dutch love of ornament, engraved, cast or repoussé. The lids of these early tankards were seldom left plain; more often they were enriched with engraved designs of Dutch inspiration (*Fig. 9*), with repoussé decoration (the one on the Cover is an unusually elaborate example) or with inserted coins or medals. Applied ornaments on the handles served to strengthen the grip of a sometimes unsteady hand; while coins, cherub heads, masks, and more elaborate designs were used to finish the tips. The last tankard on the right in Figure 7 shows another style of thumb-piece and a double scroll handle, features which indicate the adoption of English styles of the second half of the eighteenth century. When the owner of a tankard had the right to bear arms, he proudly displayed them engraved in a bold and flowing manner with scrolled mantling, swags of fruit, and other typically Dutch embellishments. (*Fig. 8.*)

Mugs are similar in form to tankards but are smaller and without lids. When straight-sided they are often girdled by moulded bands and spiral wire, giving them a solidity and sturdiness which reflect the temper of the Dutch Colonists. Later eighteenth century styles tended toward more delicacy and refinement, expressed chiefly by the use of curved lines, a development which can readily be traced in the increasingly curved outlines of the mugs.

With beakers and baptismal basins to suggest their devotion to church and dominie, and tankards and mugs to remind us of their lighter and more convivial hours, we have caught a glimpse of the life of the Dutch Colonists in New York and of the tasks they set their silversmiths. What other things they used, designed in the "genteelest Taste and newest Fashion," we shall discover later.

The Sanders-Garvan Beaker by Cornelis VanderBurch

By Mrs. Russel Hastings

IN SOME respects the most impressive piece of early American silver in the Mabel Brady Garvan Collection in the Gallery of Fine Arts at Yale University is the so-called "ceremonial beaker," which, until its recent acquisition by Mr. Garvan, had been handed down through eight generations of the Sanders family of Albany and Schenectady (whose name has been shortened from the earlier Dutch form, Sandersen). This beaker is slightly taller than any of the other large beakers of New York origin or association that betray Dutch influence. Its workmanship is excellent. Its reputed history is plausible. The man now generally accepted as its maker was Cornelis VanderBurch (c. 1653–1699), the earliest native New York silversmith thus far recorded. The really arresting feature of this masterpiece, however, is the series of cryptic decorations that adorn its surface.

In an earlier number of ANTIQUES (May 1929, pp. 388–390) was published an interesting article concerning the Sanders beaker and the alluring patina of tradition which it had accumulated during its long sojourn with the descendants of the original owner. Yet, though interesting, the account is not altogether satisfying. In the minds of the curious it prompts more questions than it answers. So it came about that I was drawn into a deeper study of the piece, particularly of its engraved decorations, and of the smith who stamped his mark upon the finished work. The results of the search have been dramatic in the extreme. To be sure, they have all but completely eliminated the overlay of tradition which enshrouded the piece; but the facts now revealed are far more captivating than the legend.

Tradition vs. History

According to the article in ANTIQUES previously referred to, the beaker in question was presented to Robbert Sandersen in 1685 by Indian tribesmen, in token of gratitude for services rendered by the recipient as interpreter and intermediary during sundry negotiations between the savages and their white neighbors. The story is an attractive one. But is it true? Is it even likely?

Sandersen was well liked by the Indians and enjoyed their confidence. Had this not been the case, he could hardly have brought his diplomatic undertakings to a successful conclusion. We may further credit some of the tradition of Sandersen's popularity to the fact that later generations may have confused him with another ancestor, the well-known Major Glen of Schenectady County, whose wife was beloved by the savages because she

Fig. 1 — THE SANDERS-GARVAN SILVER BEAKER (*1685*)
Originally a gift to Robbert Sandersen, and for generations owned by his descendants, who shortened the name to Sanders. Recently acquired by Francis P. Garvan and added to the Mabel Brady Garvan Collection at Yale University. First published in ANTIQUES for May 1929, where its making was credited to Carol Van Brugh of New York. It is now ascribed to Cornelis VanderBurch, more usually spelled Cornelius Vanderburgh.
Height, 8 inches. *Weight*, 18 ounces

"had been kind to French prisoners," and whose home and family were, in consequence, spared in the Schenectady fire and massacre of 1690. But without indubitable evidence to support the tradition, are we justified in believing that the silent children of the forest would have sent to Manhattan and ordered a silver beaker for bestowal upon their paleface friend? Such a performance, in 1685 or in 1935, would seem singularly at variance with Indian character and conceptions of propriety. Since, as a matter of fact, not an atom of evidence in its favor is available, let us examine a more plausible theory as to the beaker's reason for being.

It is a matter of record that, on August 10, 1685, a deed conveying certain lands from the Indians to the ownership of that canny Scot, Robert Livingston, was duly signed. Livingston was long Commissioner of Indian affairs and used the opportunities afforded by his office to obtain from the natives part of the domain constituting Livingston Manor. The tract affected by the deed of 1685 consisted of the six hundred acres, known as Tachkanick (modernly Taconic), lying east of the present Germantown-on-the-Hudson. It is to be particularly observed that the document referred to names Robbert Sandersen as "interpreter," a rather ingenuous title for the diplomat who beguiled the Indians into exchanging their territory for what today seems a scanty mess of pottage. In later years it was testified that Livingston, in accumulating the acreage of his manor, "was at great charge, trouble and expense in purchasing the same from the native Indians, and particularly that part thereof which is contiguous and adjoining to the colony of the Massachusetts Bay, called and known by the name of Tackanack."

The outcome of the bargain between Livingston and the Indians, with Sandersen acting as interpreter, was a small principality for the Scot and a handful of miscellaneous loot for the savage parties to the contract. If a special donation to memorialize the *coup* was in order, the obligation for its bestowal clearly rested upon the new potentate. That under the circumstances the gift should take the form of a handsome silver beaker would be quite in keeping. Livingston was in a position to obtain such an object and to ensure its correct inscribing. The Indians were not.

So, briefly presented, the historical likelihoods confront the figments of tradition. In default of demonstrable proof one way or another, the reader is at liberty to take his stand on whichever side he prefers.

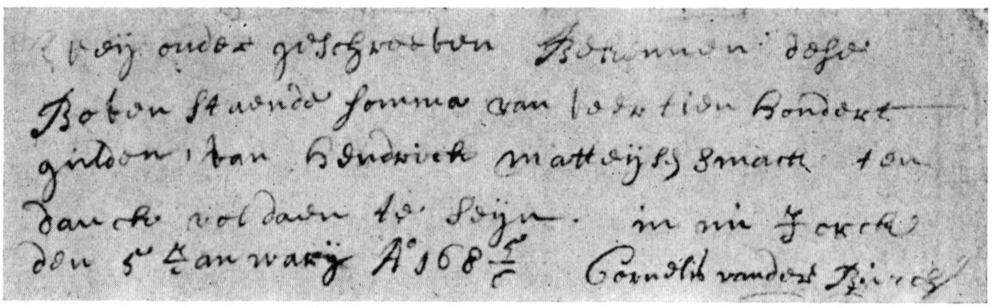

Fig. 2 — CORNELIS VANDERBURCH'S PENMANSHIP
From an autograph document. The script is that of a reasonably well-educated man. The resemblance of the writer's numerals, and certain of his letters, to those engraved on the beaker suggests, though by no means proves, that the same hand which penned the document executed the silver designs

aphoristic fables and reflections, presented variously in Dutch, French, German, Greek, Latin, Italian, Spanish, or English, as befitted the author's wide scholarship and his somewhat polyglot audience, were in their day the most popular secular literature in Holland, second only to the Bible. Usually illustrated with engravings after designs by the artist Adriaen vander Venne (*1589–1662*), the poems were first issued, at irregular intervals, in slender volumes. Calculated to appeal to old and young alike, these little books found their way into the homes of all classes in Holland, where their author came to be affectionately spoken of as "Father Cats." We have knowledge of the fascination which these books held for young folk. As a boy, Sir Joshua Reynolds owned a copy of *Proteus*, Cats' early work in Emblem Book form. It had made its appearance

Fig. 3 (above) — Vase of Flowers on the Sanders-Garvan Beaker
Of this design no exact prototype has been discovered, though the general motive is frequently encountered in seventeenth- and eighteenth-century books of engravings

The Beaker's Engraved Medallions
As will be observed in the accompanying illustrations, the Sanders beaker is elaborately engraved. Its lip is bordered by strapwork panels enclosing floral scrolls. Below, at each of three equally spaced points on the cylindrical sides, occurs a wreath-enframed medallion: one portraying a spray of blossoms in a vase; another, an apparently dead or sleeping animal surrounded by a low earthwork; another, a group of feeding geese. Between the medallions, and rising above the scalloped ornamentation about the base, we descry the engraved figure of a lizard pursuing a spider and, in turn, being devoured by a stork whose leg is entwined by the coils of a serpent; a figure of death mounted on a crocodile; and a representation of an eagle, with a tortoise in its talons, flying above a sharp upheaval of rock.

Obviously symbolic in meaning, these curious designs have been variously interpreted (see Antiques, as above). But the correct elucidation of their source and intent has waited upon a discovery made only after long and diligent search. It may now perhaps be best approached by a somewhat circuitous detour.

One of the lights of learning in seventeenth-century Holland was Jacobus Cats, who was born in Brouwershaven, Zeeland, November 10, 1577, and, after a long and active life, died not far from the Hague in September of 1660. Educated in Leyden, Orleans, and Paris, by profession a lawyer, twice an emissary to England, where he was knighted by King Charles I, Cats is chiefly remembered as a didactic poet. His profuse writings consisted of allegories, moral dissertations, idyls, and what not else.

Cats' allegories, which appeared in the form of short

Fig. 5 — Cypher on the Base of the Beaker
Below this cryptic symbol occurs the silversmith's mark of Cornelius Vanderburgh (originally Cornelis Luycasse VanderBurch), the initials *C.V.B.* in a heart

Fig. 4 (above and left) — The Ermine and the Ring of Mud (*Integrity*)
Showing the original illustration for *Veldt-Teycken* in the Jacobus Cats folio volume of 1658 and the derivative silver engraving on the Sanders-Garvan beaker. *Abstract of the accompanying poem:* The ermine, when surrounded by mud, prefers death to soiling his precious coat, so starves to death rather than venture forth. Joseph, hero of the poem, flees from a beautiful woman who offers him not only love but riches and power. Some persons laugh at the Josephs of the world, but he who in his youth thus conquers the flesh is indeed blessed

in 1618, and had been brought to England by Joshua's Dutch great-grandmother. Its weird illustrations enthralled the future Royal Academician, who spent many hours in making drawings from them. To this exercise, indeed, has been ascribed the artist's subsequent occasional excursions into the horrible.

In 1655 the printer and publisher Jan Jacobus Schipper of Amsterdam conceived the ambitious plan of issuing the collected works of Cats in one volume with text and illustrations complete. Pessimists assured the foolhardy printer that the cost of the undertaking would land him in bankruptcy. Nevertheless he persevered, and was rewarded for his enterprise by sales that presently exhausted the first printing of the book and within three years justified the issuance of a second edition in a thick Royal Folio.

These collections are known today as the "Second Bible of the Dutch," and examples of them were almost certainly carried across the ocean to New Amsterdam by emigrants from Holland. Here they were doubtless even more eagerly thumbed than they had been in the homeland and became familiar sources of manifold inspiration. Two copies, at least, of the amazing 1658 volume are today preserved in the United States, one in the Folger Shakespeare Library in Washington, the other in the New York Public Library. To the copy in the Shakespeare Library must go the credit for solving the riddle of the engravings on the Sanders

that direction is futile. Perhaps the volume from which these careful transcripts were made may turn up with annotations that will settle the question.

We may now return to a more detailed consideration of the designs on the beaker of our concern. These are here reproduced side by side with the pictures from which they were taken. Since an accompanying caption explains the implication of each symbol, it is not necessary to repeat that information in the present text. The representation of Death astride a crocodile occurs in the Emblem Book *Proteus*. In the earlier editions of this work the crocodile proceeds from right to left; in later appearances he reverses his direction — testimony to reëngraving of the subject. The other symbols are to be found in the *Spiegel* (Mirror of the Past and Present) and the *Self-Strijt* (Inner Strife, or Self-Discipline). The sixth design, a plant flowering

Fig. 6 — Lazy Fox and Feeding Geese (*Industry*)
Original illustration and derivative silver engraving. *Abstract of accompanying poem:* It has been decreed by Adam that those who would eat must work. The lazy fox keeps his feet dry and therefore must endure an empty belly. Those who will not labor may not count on sympathy. . . . The silver version omits the fox and arranges the geese in a more compact composition. From *Spiegel van den Voorleden*

beaker, and thus happily terminating a long and arduous quest. For it was during an examination of this ponderous tome that, one after another, Vander Venne's illustrations for Cats' effusions were revealed as the unmistakable source whence he who ornamented the beaker directly borrowed not only his symbolic ideas but the forms in which to clothe them.

It might, of course, be contended that the New York silversmith Cornelis VanderBurch probably copied both the shape and the decoration of his masterpiece from an earlier beaker brought from Holland or the east coast of England, where Dutch styles in silver were prevalent. Such an hypothesis seems far-fetched. It is more reasonable to believe that, with a copy of Father Cats at hand, the craftsman made his own selection from the book's rich store of poetry and picture. Whether he was furnished the volume by his client, or owned a copy himself, or borrowed one from his rascally, scholarly stepfather (who had come out from Holland in 1669, presumably with a library of sorts) is of no particular moment. Some fellow craftsman may have executed the engravings on the beaker, but conjecture in

from an urn, does not occur in the Cats folio; but, in sundry variations, it is frequently encountered in Emblem Books, particularly those of the German botanist, Doctor Joachim Camerarius. The beaker version of the motive may well be an improvisation on the part of the engraver.

The Sanders Device

The device on the bottom of the Sanders beaker lets down the bars to yet another succulent pasture. From time to time marks based on the Latin cross, particularly that form which, by the addition of an hypotenuse to either upper angle, becomes a "4" or its reverse, have appeared in the America of the seventeenth and eighteenth centuries. Such mysterious figures have been vaguely known as "merchants' marks," "house marks," and so on. A small collection of leaden bale seals thus impressed is preserved in the Numismatic Society's rooms in New York City. The *Bulletin* of the New York Historical Society for January 1931 prints an article by William L. Calver on similar bale seals found among Revolutionary relics. Other examples have, from time to time, been recorded in the *New York Genealogical and*

Fig. 7 — The Strong and the Weak (*Magnanimity*)
Original illustration and derivative engraving. *Abstract of accompanying poem:* The spider eats the fly, the lizard eats the spider and is seized by the stork, which, even before it can fly aloft with its prey, is seized by the serpent. Likewise the dragon gobbles up the snake and the peasant slays the dragon. Thus, no matter how powerful a man may be, there is always someone of still greater power. Remember that whatsoever you do to the weak will be visited upon you by those stronger than yourself. The law of the woods holds also for the world outside. From *Spiegel van den Voorleden*

102

Biographical Record. Pieces of glass exhibiting like mysterious devices have been unearthed by excavators during the restoration of Williamsburg, Virginia, and have likewise been found on old Virginia tobacco casks. Wilberforce Eames, that seasoned and inspiring antiquarian, when shown a photograph of the cypher on the base of the Sanders beaker, suggested its possible kinship with the printers' marks of the Renaissance. Following this hint, search has revealed hundreds of examples of the Latin cross thus used in a diversity of forms from the Renaissance onward for some three centuries. Harold Bayley, in his recently published volume, *New Light on the Renaissance as displayed in Contemporary Emblems*, propounds the theory that these printers' marks and watermarks on paper, particularly those employing the sacred numeral "4," were a means of secret communication between heretical printers who

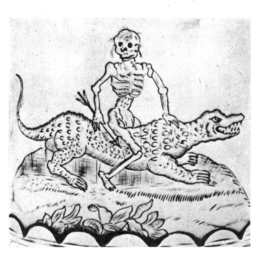

were trying to outwit the Church and its restrictions. No doubt the germ of ancient magic abides in these curious symbols, though its particular potency may have been forgotten even when the symbols themselves were in common use. The cypher on the beaker of our interest may justly be viewed as a personal mark, and there seems little doubt that it was the "merchant's mark" of Robbert Sandersen.

Emblem Books

Concerning the books of the kind that afforded models for the pictorial engravings on the Sanders beaker, a separate essay might be written. Particularly interesting is the vast subject of Emblem Books, to which Shakespeare was deeply indebted. They were collections of short, illustrated moral poems, and were prevalent on the Continent though but little known to English readers of today. Study of their countless illustrations could not but assist us in determining the provenance of our early designs in architecture, gardens, costume, furniture, and household implements. No better depiction of the varied activities, social and commercial, of olden times may be found than is spread before us in these delightful volumes. The Cats folio gives a more than photographically vivid portrayal of Dutch life in the seventeenth century. In consequence, it brings us likewise into closer touch with the time and temper of New Amsterdam than any surviving record made on this side of the water.

The Emblem Books, furthermore, may have

Fig. 8 — Death and the Crocodile *(Faithfulness)*
Original illustration and engraved derivative. *Abstract of accompanying poem:* The crocodile continues to increase in size so long as he lives. Even when Death bears down upon him, he continues to expand. So it is with true love. Those who cherish ambition or greed in their hearts never find the greatest happiness. From the *Proteus*

been the source of some of the perplexing heraldic decorations seen on early New York silver. For example, may not the roses surrounded by mantling on President Roosevelt's well-known early tankard, long accepted as coat armor, be a floral emblem taken direct from one of the books, or a pun on the family name similar to that implied in the mantled wine cask of Wynkoop's massive tankard? One would not be so graceless as to suggest this if the entirely different arms in use in Holland by certain Roosevelts had not been recorded by William J. Hoffman in the *New York Genealogical and Biographical Record (Vol. 64, p. 139).*

Note. For the suggestion that the Emblem Books might be the source of the designs discussed in these notes, thanks are due to the personnel of the Print Room in the Metropolitan Museum of New York. The photographs of the beaker are by courtesy of the Museum of Fine Arts, Yale University. Those from the illustrations in the collected works of Jacobus Cats are by courtesy of the Folger Shakespeare Library, Washington, D. C.   *— K. B. H.*

Fig. 9 — The Eagle and the Tortoise *(Humility)*
Original illustration and engraved derivative. *Abstract of accompanying poem:* The eagle, bearing the tortoise in his talons, soars to dizzy heights to show his passenger the world. The tortoise thinks himself an honored cosmopolite; but he is mistaken. Presently he is dropped upon a sharp rock and his hard shell broken into fragments, so that he may the more easily be devoured by the eagle. How many at court suffer a like fate! He who climbs too high with too many airs is a candidate for destruction. From the *Spiegel van den Voorleden*

Cornelius Vanderburgh—
Silversmith of New York

Part II

By Mrs. Russel Hastings

IN A previous issue of An-TIQUES (January 1936) we contemplated the harassed childhood of one Cornelis Luycaszen Vanderburgh, son of a tapster-soldier, and stepson of the first officially recognized Lutheran minister of New York. Thus far no indication of his calling has presented itself. He is a shadowy person who, only with great difficulty, has been summoned forth from the void. He will never stand clearly defined against the background of his day unless more illuminating records are discovered.

But now a Cornelius Vanderburgh, known to be a silversmith, appears on the scene. He was granted a piece of land in High (or Stone or Duke) Street, near Coentie's Alley, and back of the Stadthuys, in 1687. While I confess unblushingly that there is no irrefutable proof that he is one and the same person as the innkeeper's son, I shall state my reasons for being certain that he is. Shreds of the Lutheran's background cling to him too convincingly to permit any other hypothesis. When Sergeant Luycas Dircksz' son Cornelis was baptized in 1653, his godmother was one Marritje Cornelis, an intimate of the family, who was quite possibly a sister of the baby's mother, Annetje Cornelis, just as Jan Cornelis from Flensborg may have been her brother. There are evidences of such close ties through subsequent years. Most significant of these is the appointing of Lucas as the guardian of Marritje's children when the mother decided to remarry. Her first husband was Hans Christiansen Kettel, born in Holstein on the Danish border of Germany; her second was Representative Cornelis Beekman, born in Bremen; her third husband was Luycas Meyers.

When a widow with children remarried, the Orphan Masters stepped in and appointed two overseers to protect the young folk against any misappropriation of their birthright by their mother and their new stepfather. So the published records of the Orphan Masters tell us that Lucas and another were to be responsible for the two Kettel children's welfare, after Cornelis Beekman took their mother to wife. Marritje and Cornelis Beekman had one child at least, and twenty years later Cornelis vanderBurch was supervising the affairs of Marritje's enlarged family just as Lucas Dircksz' had done on a previous occasion. The example of Cornelis' penmanship reproduced in ANTIQUES for February 1935 is a receipt of 1685 for certain moneys due his wards from the sale of New Utrecht, Long Island, lands. Since a guardian was usually the most responsible next of kin, it seems evident that the Vanderburghs, father and son, were considered the most suitable persons to supervise the fruits of Marritje's successive marriages.

Cornelius Vanderburgh, the silversmith, avoided the Dutch Church adherents as carefully as did the son of Luycas Dircksz'. He moved in the same general atmosphere; he was seemingly of the same age; his surviving daughter, whom we shall presently meet, was of suitable years. In short, it is inconceivable that two Cornelius Vanderburghs, who dovetail so perfectly, could have been other than one and the same person. For this reason, I am emboldened to proclaim Cornelius the silversmith as identical with the Cornelius who was baptized in 1653, and hence the earliest native New York silversmith whose works have thus far been discovered and recorded.

The hard-won history of our earliest silversmith of New York birth consists of trifles not pertinent to craftsmanship, but demanding to be rehearsed in order that the outlines of the man may be at least roughly sketched. Among his Lutheran friends was Jacob de Lange, surgeon, whose wife Haduina Van Horen may have been a relative. When the surgeon died in 1685, he entrusted to his good friends John deBruyn and Cornelius Vanderburgh, without the obligation for an accounting, the care of the little fortune bequeathed to his daughters. John deBruyn was once mayor of New York. Some years later, the two guardians jointly purchased a mortgage upon lands on the Hackensack River, possibly on behalf of their wards. Cornelius' sister, it will be remembered, was living in Hackensack, which may explain the silversmith's interest in that neighborhood, besides arousing a hope that

Fig. 1 — Interior of a Holland Goldsmith's Shop (*seventeenth century*)
From a painting by Cornelis Beelt of Haarlem. Sold at Sotheby's in June 1931. Present whereabouts unrecorded. This portrayal of a goldsmith and his apprentices, with the wife serving as saleswoman, is of the period when New York's first native goldsmith was working in a city essentially Dutch in character and in its customs dominated by Dutch tradition. Hence it is not improbable that a New Amsterdam shop of the 1600's was much like the Haarlem establishment illustrated. *Photograph by courtesy of the Frick Art Reference Library*

hiding somewhere in New Jersey is more silver marked c.v.b.

The date on the Sanders-Garvan beaker indicates that the piece was made at about this time. The next year, 1686, its maker was elected to care for one of the public wells, which were customarily dug, of all places, in the centre of certain streets. This seems a rather fantastic honor, but one which was likewise granted to a fellow silversmith, Ahasuerus Hendricks. Presumably the two were counted fastidious persons, likely to insist upon cleanliness.

When, in 1685, New York became a Royal Province, its new charter gave it title to all the vacant lands in and about the city. These properties were speedily applied for. Among them were what were known as the "Burnt Lands." For one such "Slip or toft" Cornelius Vanderburgh applied in February 1686/7. Two months later, the record informs us, "Cornelius VanerBurge of New York City, silversmith" was granted the coveted land, which lay "within the City in High Street to the east of the house and lot of the said Cornelius VanerBurge, to the west of Geertruy Hibbons, to the north of the ground belonging to the City Hall." This is the first statement as to Cornelius' calling that I have found. It also indicates that he already had a house and lot in High Street, where conceivably the beaker of our interest was fashioned. The record is hidden away in the Comptroller's Office.

The early land records of New York abound in *lacunæ*, dramatically filled in from time to time when some family decides to add its muniments to public collections. The early conveyance of property in High Street to Cornelius Vanderburgh is, alas, among the missing; but a compensatory document was found for me by a kind friend in the manuscript division of the New York Public Library. It is a deed dated 1714 conveying this approximate parcel, from John White and his wife Cornelia. It contains the revealing statement that the real estate was "left unto them by their late father, Cornelius Vanderburgh, silversmith, of New York." This is, roughly speaking, the land at 36 Stone Street. The ancient thoroughfare winds narrowly toward the river, between low buildings. Some feet from Cornelius' messuage lay Coentie's Alley, a tiny slit between dwellings. Back of its former site, with a tablet, now stands the house that replaces the ancient Stadthuys or City Hall. Near by is Coentie's Slip in the East River, and not far away the elevated railroad makes crooked patterns against the sky.

In the next block lay the ample holdings of Carel Van Brugge, otherwise Charles Bridges the Englishman, who was taxed in 1677 for a place "where the silversmith lived." Doubt as to the identity of that haunting silversmith seems to have led early investigators to the erroneous conclusion that the landlord himself was the man. Somewhere along the same street in early days lived Hendrick Ahasuerus, the innkeeper, whose service as appraiser of silver and jewels I have already referred to. To the rear of Cornelius' abode was that of the Van Horn lady, who,

Fig. 2 — TANKARD BY CORNELIUS VANDERBURGH
Bearing the arms of Verdrich Filipse, later Anglicized to Frederick Philipse. The spout, of course, is an unfortunate addition. Philipse may actually have been of noble Polish birth, as tradition asserts. He married that domineering feminine shipping merchant, Margaret Hardenbrook, widow of Rudolph de Vries, whose daughter Eve he adopted. Eve married Jacobus Van Cortlandt in 1691. This probably accounts for the initials on the salt illustrated in Figure 4. *Weight*, 27 ounces, 5 cwt.; *height*, 6 inches

after her marriage, gave birth to Garret Onclebagh, the silversmith. Apparently finding superior artisans to her taste, she subsequently espoused Ahasuerus Hendricks, likewise a fashioner of silver. We may in time establish the fact that, in the late 1600's, this quarter of the city was for some reason considered the advantageous location for silversmiths.

In the spring of 1686/7 Annetje Cornelis' sons were active in acquiring lands. Dirck and Hendrick were busily annexing properties in Delaware. Their purchases, coupled with that of their brother, the silversmith, may imply sudden affluence consequent to their mother's recent death. Having perhaps proved himself an efficient supervisor of the well, Cornelius was the recipient of further public honors. Living in the very back garden of the jail, he was from time to time elevated to the post of High Constable. He witnessed wills for his neighbors. In the French church near by he stood sponsor for a baby with the absurd name of Muckhaylle de Mackaillys. He made a charming salt, from an English model, for the newly married Van Cortlandts. In 1693, he was handed 20 ounces of gold to the value of £106 to make a presentation cup for Governor Fletcher. The money, be it said, represented revenues from the Brooklyn Ferry. This must have been the outstanding event of Cornelius' career; but his masterpiece doubtless saw the melting pot soon after its recipient reached home.

In 1694 it was decided to standardize the weights and measures in the Province of New York, and a distinguished commission was appointed to deliberate upon this all-important project. A Governor's council meeting held July 12, 1694, agreed to the appointment of an "officer for the regulation of weights and seales for Curr't Gold and Silver." In the upshot a committee consisting of the mayor and aldermen of the City of New York, John Barberie and Robert Lurting, merchants, and Cornelius VanderBurgh and Jacob Boelen, silversmiths, was appointed to make a selection. In due course they reported that they "presume to recommend unto your Excellency Cornelius Vanderburgh & Jacob Boelen Silversmiths as Persons of Good Reputation and very fitt to be appointed by your Excellency for the keeping of the Standard of Silver & Gold Weights and marking all such as shall be used in this Citty & Province and that there shall be allowed for the Marking of a Ballance . . . 18° 17° 16° 15° & 14° weights one shilling whi . . . most humbly submitted by," etc.

In spite of Cornelius' apparent standing as a citizen, his homestead in High Street was depreciating in value on the tax lists, while that of his neighbors was rising. He owned not only the High Street house, but an "estate" in the West Ward, whatever that may mean. Such "estates" were always taxed at about £5. This land to the westward was near the land previously owned by Cornelius' father in Broadway. It may, indeed, have been a portion of that property, although another son, Dirck, seems to have inherited most of the tavern parcel. Perhaps Cornelius was drifting into invalidism, for his death in 1699, in his late forties, was untimely.

In 1699 the Stadthuys, having been abandoned in favor of a newer City Hall at the head of Broad Street, had so far deteriorated that it was offered for sale. John Rodman, a prosperous merchant of the day, acquired it for £920. A deed, dated September 20, 1699, and still registered in the Comptroller's office, clearly defines the bounds of the property. Not only does this document record a transfer of land; it likewise establishes the fact that all of Cornelius Vanderburgh's silver is of the seventeenth century. For one significant sentence recites the fact that the recorded area is bounded on the north by the house and ground of Barent Hebon, and that *late of Cornelius Vanderburgh*. As Cornelius' house in this, the Dock Ward, was valued at £20 in the tax list of July 15, 1699, we are amply justified in stating that our silversmith died later in the summer of that year.

A few days after the passing of the Rodman deed, a marriage license was granted to John White, joiner, and Cornelia Vanderburgh, in so far as known the silversmith's only daughter. They held the High Street house for some fifteen years before disposing of it. Meanwhile, the name of the thoroughfare had been changed to Duke Street, sometimes corrupted to Duck Street. A daughter of this pair, Anna, was baptized in the Lutheran Church in 1710; but the subsequent history of the family was engulfed when the Church records disappeared.

For some years the only known piece of silver marked c.v.b. was the famous Sanders-Garvan beaker. (See ANTIQUES for May 1929 and February 1935.) Not long after first publication of this piece, a similar but unpedigreed beaker, dated *1686* and marked c.v.b. in a different manner, came into the open market. It was acquired by Mr. Garvan, and is described by Miss Avery on pages

Fig. 3 — ANOTHER VIEW OF FREDERICK PHILIPSE'S TANKARD
The circles punched in ornamental design on the thumbpiece occur also on the previously published Vanderburgh tankard (ANTIQUES for January 1936). This decorative device is probably unique in seventeenth-century New York silver. Both tankards were used when their owners lived at the Van Cortlandt Manor House, now a museum in the park of the same name

134 and 161 of her *Early American Silver*. The beaker is now believed to be a European piece, probably Dutch, of the seventeenth century, and not by Cornelius Vanderburgh.

After the present study was begun, the assistance of indulgent friends and correspondents, who would doubtless prefer to be anonymous, brought to light three superb pieces by Vanderburgh. An eminent Dutch authority informs me that the Sanders-Garvan beaker is not characteristically Dutch. The two tankards illustrated in Parts I and II of this article display features which are entirely new to students of New York silver. To reveal their roots we may be obliged to delve in Scandinavian or German soil. But this involves labor too arduous for present undertaking. So much of the literature of art in all its forms is in the Germanic or the Icelandic tongues as to debar most Americans from any very thorough explorations therein.

The distinguished family that has inherited the Vanderburgh tankards has among its treasures a caudle cup of English make, upon whose hall marks Cornelius Vanderburgh has superimposed his own maker's mark, probably to indicate that he repaired or engraved the piece. This caudle cup is inscribed on one side with the large initials *V.F.*, with feather mantling, and on the other $\begin{smallmatrix} C. \\ I*E \end{smallmatrix}$ These insignia would seem to indicate an original ownership by Verdrich Filipse and a later one by his step- and adopted daughter, Eve deVries-Philipse, upon her marriage to Jacobus Van Cortlandt (*Fig. 4*).

Cornelius Vanderburgh used two types of mark. The tankards and salt show an identical punch, while the beaker and restamped caudle cup bear the other. A diagram used in ANTIQUES for July 1933 (*p. 8*) was designed merely as an example of a certain type of mark, and must not be taken as an exact portrayal of the stamp of Cornelius Vanderburgh, silversmith of New York.

Note. The small pictures that accompany Parts I and II of the present article are reproduced from Schipper's 1658 edition of Jacobus Cats' collected works. At the top of pages 10 and 11, in ANTIQUES for January 1936, are portrayed, respectively, a woman making sausages and a mother playing with her child. It is not unreasonable to assume that counterparts of these and of the outdoor scene depicted here might have been observed in the predominantly Dutch New Amsterdam of the seventeenth century. It will be remembered that the engravings on the Sanders-Garvan beaker were adapted from Vander Venne's illustrations for the same work. (See ANTIQUES for February 1935, *p. 52*.)

Fig. 4 — OCTAGONAL SALT BY CORNELIUS VANDERBURGH
Owned by descendants of Jacobus and Eve Van Cortlandt, whose initials appear on the sides. At left is shown the underside of the salt, with the maker's mark. *Weight,* 3 ½ ounces

The New York Silver Mark PVB

By Mrs. Russel Hastings

IN 1917 Francis P. Garvan acquired from a lady in Schenectady a superb example of early New York silver — amply displayed in the illustrations accompanying this article. It is a tankard wrought in that highly individual, florid yet dignified, style which to connoisseurs is the unique and unmistakable token of those vaguely Dutch-German-French-Walloon-Danish-Swedish-Norwegian-English silversmiths who practiced their craft on Manhattan Island during the seventeenth and early eighteenth centuries.

The maker's stamp on this tankard is a rectangle, whose somewhat curious conjunction of initials has hitherto been generally accepted as a rendering of the letters *P V B*. This, however, is its actual aspect: **PVB**.

More recently a second piece of early New York silver — this time a porringer — exhibiting a mark closely resembling that on the tankard, came into Mr. Garvan's possession. Tankard and porringer now repose together in the Mabel Brady Garvan collection at Yale University. But the identity of the man who made them, and clearly marked them in the belief that an admiring world would always associate his name with his handiwork, has hitherto eluded the search of antiquaries and historians.

Perhaps the difficulties the research worker must normally encounter have, in the present instance, been intensified by certain discrepancies between the date implied by the stylistic features of these two pieces and that indicated by the date engraved upon one of them. Under the circumstances, it may be well to give them the benefit of a brief restudy, though ever since their discovery they have enjoyed the lively attention of experts.

The tankard, quite evidently, has not been immune against the improving hand. On its lid, however, the handsome cypher within a foliated frame is unquestionably contemporary with the piece that it adorns. Probably it designates the young married pair in whose honor the skill of our mysterious smith was invoked. Of them more anon. Time and much polishing have not sufficed to erase the engraver's keenly incised lines or to dim the elegance of his boldly elaborate volutes, amid whose rich leafage flits a winged cherub mask and two long-tailed birds of paradise.

Far different in every respect is the armorial decoration engraved on the tankard's front. A

Fig. 1 — SILVER TANKARD
Profile view. Characteristically sturdy form enlivened by passages of quite luscious ornament — both cast and engraved — to which the New York silversmiths and their patrons seem to have been specially partial

Fig. 2 — PUNCH MARKS ON THE TANKARD OF FIGURE I
The maker of the tankard had no yearning for the anonymity that he nearly achieved. The punch marks illustrated occur, in the order shown, on the tankard lid; on the body to the left of the handle; on the body to the right of the handle. Initials in rectangle

Fig. 3 — INITIALS ON TANKARD HANDLE
These letters are a recutting of earlier ones, the upper having been *HP* or *HB* (joined); the lower, *IB* or *IC*

Dutch scholar now in New York, who is keenly interested in the coat armor used by our early Dutch settlers, has examined photographs of this detail and has expressed the opinion that it is inferior in workmanship to that on the lid; that it is quite possibly not contemporaneous with the latter; and that, instead of having any heraldic significance, it may well be only a crude bit of improvisation. Another foreign authority, who is conversant with the silver of all times and all nations, has likewise confessed himself mystified by this decoration.

[Were the quoted authorities better acquainted with American capabilities in various directions, they would waste neither time nor thought over the silly symbols of this shield, which could be either the emblem of some small-town young men's sporting club of the late 1800's, or merely a rather witless hoax. Most of the elements of the mantling of the shield, it may be observed, have been derived from armorial devices on well-known New York tankards. *Ed.*]

Again, to at least one expert, the initials at the curve of the handle seem to be later in date than the tankard itself. Obviously they have nothing in common stylistically with the cypher on the lid; yet they are certainly earlier and more credible than the frontal engraving. Perhaps some day the pedigree of this piece may be learned and the meaning of its various inscriptions convincingly revealed. It is probably needless to remind readers of ANTIQUES that three initials on a piece of old-time silver almost invariably indicate a married pair.

The maker's mark on this tankard, as already observed, varies in slight details from that on the porringer. It is smaller; no edge of the enclosing rectangle is serrated; its letters are somewhat differently shaped. Nevertheless, the variant direction of the two arms of the *V*, and the peculiarity whereby one shank of the letter is plain while the other is "crossed," are significantly the same in both pieces.

All in all, we are quite safe in placing the date of this tankard about 1725, and, furthermore, in largely ignoring the later lettering on its handle.

The porringer, alas, affords less easy sailing. As will be seen in the illustrations, its handle is of a type otherwise found only in the work of certain New York silversmiths of the early eighteenth century. The rectangular mark with a serrated edge came into use in America during the eighteenth century. And the punch itself is evidently that of the same man who made the above-described tankard, admittedly of the 1725 vintage, and a rat-tail spoon of about 1735, remembered by a well-known expert, though the spoon is not officially recorded.

In other words, on the basis of its style, almost any sound student would place the porringer in the same period-category with the tankard. By way of contradicting such internal evidence, however, the piece bears the neatly engraved but exceedingly illiterate inscription, *1668 wunn att hanpsted plaines, march 25.*

Now it is a byword among antiquaries that few persons can bring themselves to question the accuracy of statements either made by very aged relatives, or declared in inscriptions. Accordingly, on the basis of its inscription, this porringer has been widely accepted as the earliest of American racing trophies and, concurrently, as the product of a craftsman who was working in 1668. The New York *Sun* for January 24, 1931, published a long and entertaining account of the adventures of this piece, which, if we accept it *in toto* at face value, forces us to some of the following conclusions.

1. The porringer handle was originated by a smith working in 1668, but was not thereafter used until the beginning of the eighteenth century, when half a dozen craftsmen adopted it.

2. The tankard and the porringer, although bearing what appears to be the mark of the same maker, are probably by different makers.

Fig. 4 — Rear View of Tankard

3. The porringer, as it stands today, is of the eighteenth century, but reworked from an earlier trophy bowl whose inscription was preserved by some miracle of dexterity on the part of the hammerman.

I need not point out that, when we hang up these conclusions side by side for close examination, we find them exhaling a faint aroma of absurdity. There are apparently unbridged gaps in the published pedigree of the porringer. Likewise we have need to know whether the inscription on that utensil conforms in style and arrangement as well as in spelling with the usage of the 1660's. Sporting gentlemen of the colonies who were offering silver trophies for horse racing would, we may be sure, have been sticklers for maintaining the same proprieties that were observed in the conduct of turf events at home. All things considered, a heavy burden of proof rests on those who would insist that this porringer is other than a specimen of early eighteenth-century silversmithing contemporary with the similarly marked tankard and by the same **PVB**.

At the same time, we must respect the known history of the piece as well as the lifelong memory of it cherished by the late Howard Sill. As a hypothesis that would reconcile all the conflicting evidence, I suggest the likelihood that the porringer today represents a complete refashioning in the eighteenth century of a demoded piece of the seventeenth, whose inscription, however, was copied *verbatim et literatim* on the new vessel. Objections to this theory will, of course, be many; yet we find a somewhat analogous case cited

Fig. 5 — Doubt and Assurance
Left: Pseudoarmorial device engraved on tankard front. On analysis the mantling is discovered to be made up of shreds and patches borrowed from other items of New York silver, but with the casque sprouting Prince of Wales feathers by way of variety. The devices in the four quarters of the shield might be those of a boys' athletic club — or bare fabrication. The pinched

form of the scrolls and the weak and hesitant character of the cut line, in conjunction with the absurd heraldic implications, suggest the rather recent work of an unskilled hand directed by a none too intelligent head.
Right: Engraving of tankard lid. The cypher I (or J) H B may stand for Jan and Hannah Bogaert (married 1716). The workmanship, clear and vigorous, is evidently of the period of the tankard

in the *History of the Church in Burlington, New Jersey.* In 1745 the Parish had received a piece of silver presented by Mrs. Katherine Pierce. In 1816, Elias Boudinot, LL.D., added the gift of a baptismal bowl. Some twenty years later, in 1839, to be exact, permission having been obtained, the two donations of silver were melted down by Fletcher and Bennett of Philadelphia and converted into two alms basins, one of which was duly inscribed, for the confusion of future generations: *This plate given to the Rev'd. Mr. Campbell by Mrs. Katherine Pierce, for the use of St. Mary's Church in Burlington, 1745;* and the other: *Presented by Elias Boudinot, LL.D. for the use of St. Mary's Church in Burlington, 1816.*

As for the identity of our smith, the *Sun* article, above referred to, quotes me as suggesting Peter Van Brugh, Pieter van Bresteed, Paulus Van der Beeck, some member of the Van Beeck or Van Beek family — or none of the lot. That was two years ago. Now, after twenty-four months of further search, I am confident that my last surmise is the correct one. No one of those whom I previously named should be credited with being a silversmith. The probable maker of these pieces has hitherto been overlooked by antiquaries and by historians of early New York silver and the men who fashioned it.

Hitherto it has not seemed necessary to emphasize one peculiarity common to the **Pℬ** marks, that makes the latter inapplicable to any of the above New York names. This peculiarity is the distinct horizontal line drawn across the first member of the letter *V*. We may not dismiss this line as merely a decorative embellishment of the letter. Were it such a thing, we might properly expect to find a similar adornment on some others among the numerous *V*'s that are wedged into old New York punch marks. We do, however, frequently find a crossing line distinguishing the capital *I*.

We are, of course, quite safe in accepting, without much argument, the initial *P* as standing for *Peter.* The ligature evidently indicates a surname. One of the curiosities of the fascinating subject of American silversmiths' marks is the fact that certain of the New York craftsmen not only employed their actual initials, but introduced an extra letter for the last division of the name. Thus we find Garret Onclebag (*1670–1732*) indicated by *G O B;* Benjamin Wynkoop (*1675–17?*) by *B W K;* John Brevoort (*1715–1775*) by *I B V;* Jacobus Vanderspiegel (*1668–c.1716*) by *I V S;* Cornelius Vanderburgh by *C V B;* and so on. Under the circumstances are we not justified in expanding the cypher of our unknown to read *V I B,* and the complete mark as *P V I B,* standing for a freshly discovered New York smith, one Peter Van Inburgh, born 1689; died 1740?

That name stands forth in clear, vigorous script, appended

Fig. 6 — Silver Porringer
This piece carries contradictory indications of date. Its punch mark, shown below, and the type of its handle point to the eighteenth century. On the contrary, its engraved inscription, also shown below, carries the date *March 25, 1668.* The mantled pellet on the side is that of a married pair, accepted as Francis and Maria Salisbury (married 1693), ancestors of the porringer's former owner

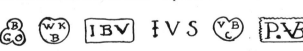

Fig. 7 — New York Silversmiths' Marks
Garret Onclebag, Benjamin Wynkoop, John Brevoort, Jacobus Vanderspiegel, Cornelius Vanderburgh, and the subject of the present study

to an indenture in whose text the signer identifies himself as *goldsmith.* Enough of this document to indicate its drift and purpose:

This Indenture Made the Thirtieth day of October in the thirteenth year of the reign of our Sovereign Lord George the Second . . . And in the year of our Lord Christ One thousand Seven hundred and thirty nine Between Peter Van Inburgh of the City of New York GoldSmith of the one part and Andrew Brested of the Same City Joiner and Carpenter of the other part Witnesseth that . . . the Said Peter Doth hereby . . . Bargain & Sell unto the Said Andrew Breste One full and Equal third part . . . of Eleven Lotts or parcels of Ground and a Street that runs through the Said Lotts Scituate Lying & being within the City of New York, in the Westward of the Same City on the West Side of the Broadway (which Said Lotts & Street are part of Sixteen Lotts lately laid and Surveyed and heretofore belonging to Peter Janse Mesier deceased Grandfather of the Said Peter) . . . In Witness Whereof the partie first above named hath hereunto Sett his Hand and Seal the day and year first above Written.

Peter Van Inburgh (Seal)

Sealed and Delivered
In the presence of
Stephen Bourdett
S. Johnson.

It will be noted that in the course of this long screed Van Inburgh mentions Peter Janse Mesier as his grandfather. With these bare elements to start with, the initiated will be able to reconstruct a family background sufficient to justify an acceptance of Van Inburgh as a personage of some standing in Manhattan and a goldsmith quite capable of making the tankard and the porringer whose initials have so disturbed us. Of the man's career, however, we have no colorful details; nor do we find him mentioned as a goldsmith save in the above-quoted indenture.

We really know more of Peter Van Inburgh's ancestors — or more that is humanly appealing — than of Peter himself, for he came into a vivid family circle, reverberating with historic lore and doubtless glittering with masterpieces of silversmithing. His paternal grandfather was Meester (*i.e.,* surgeon) Gysbert Van Imbroch, merchant, barber-surgeon, scholar, representative from Wiltwyck (alias Esopus, or Kingston in its later days) to the General Assembly, something of a swaggering person as he looms at times almost fantastically through the hazy ancient records.

Gysbert, it would appear, was twice married. We know of his first matrimonial venture only by its fruit, a son Johannis, baptized in 1654. For his second mate, Gysbert chose a lady of quality, Rachel De La Montagne, daughter of the well-known Huguenot physician Jean De La Montagne and his wife Rachel De Forest, whose father Jesse was the Walloon first settler of Manhattan.

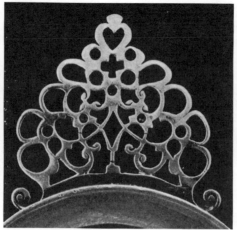

Fig. 8 — Porringer Handles
Left to right: by Peter Van Dyck (*1684–c. 1750*); by Bartholomew Schaets (*c. 1683–1758*); probably by Peter Van Inburgh (*1689–1740*)

Rachel De La Montagne, gently born and gently bred, was perhaps ill prepared for the rigors that she was called upon to endure throughout the brief span of her wedded life. While her eldest child, Elizabeth, was still a tiny girl, Rachel was captured by the Indians at the Esopus Massacre and carried into the forest, whence she escaped only with greatest difficulty. Something over a year later, six weeks after giving birth to Gysbert II, she yielded her weary spirit to eternity. Within another twelvemonth the bereaved husband followed, leaving three orphans to be placed in the care of their aunt and uncle, Maria and Jacob Kip of New York, whom Providence had already generously endowed with eleven offspring of their own.

In this family association, life had ever a silver lining. Not only was Jacob's son Benjamin a silversmith, but a daughter and another son married Kierstedes, uncle and aunt of Cornelius Kierstede, the silversmith, whose work was highly individual. Moreover, a cousin of the Imbroch children, Jacob Verdon, was connected by marriage with the son of Jurian Blanck, the earliest New York silversmith of record. Silver links were further multiplied when, in 1687, the eldest Van Imbroch boy, who had come to be known as Dr. Johannis Van *Emburgh* of Hackensack, New Jersey, married Margaret Van Schaick, sister of Mrs. Garret Onclebag. And yet more of the precious metal: the sisters Van Schaick were related by marriage to the great silversmithing Boelen family, and to Cornelius Kierstede. Jacob Kip's niece, Femmetie Vanderheul, married the goldsmith Benjamin Wynkoop, a member of a Kingston family.

For some reason goldsmithing was a predominant interest among these folk — that and schoolteaching and medicine-surgery. The goldsmiths of the seventeenth century had much the same influence in New York as the bankers of but yesterday.

Nevertheless, when Gysbert II grew into manhood, calling himself Gysbert Van Inburgh, we find him engaged in the then lucrative and far from humble vocation of baker, in which he was admitted to New York freemanship. In 1686 he was joined to the Dutch Church, and, two years later, married Jannetje Messier, daughter of Pieter Janse Messier, miller. Messier père owned a famous windmill near the present Cortlandt Street and adjacent to the Hudson River. To the young married couple was born in 1689 a son, duly christened Peter, no doubt in honor of his maternal grandfather. The family was thrifty, prosperous, and influential. Gysbert the baker was elected in 1702 to the board of deacons governing the school of the Dutch Church. His name figures in sundry real estate transactions. He had at least six children. Is it permissible to surmise that baker Gysbert, brought up as he was among silversmiths, had cherished a secret yearning to become a craftsman in noble metals for exacting patrons, rather than a wielder of dough for the multitude? In any case, it is significant that his first-born son became a silversmith.

Under the seductive influence of Peter's tankard, one might be tempted to imagine a romantic biography for its maker. But, alas! nothing in the least exciting has been discovered about this quiet individual. With his sisters Maria and Johanna, he was admitted to the Dutch Church of New York, February 26, 1717. He was elected Constable of the South Ward in 1717, and Collector of the same ward, 1719. He served as witness at three baptisms, 1709, 1710, and 1720, and died, apparently, a bachelor. According to the records of the New York Church, he was buried August 28, 1740, the day immediately succeeding that of his death.

Peter Van Inburgh had vast numbers of cousins, and I hold a humble theory that the cypher *I H B* on the lid of his tankard may be associated with the marriage of one of them, Hannah Peek of New York, to Jan Bogaert, in 1716, from whom descend many substantial persons in the vicinity of Schenectady and Albany, whence the tankard came into Mr. Garvan's hands.

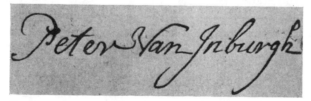

Fig. 9 — Signatures of Witnesses and of Peter Van Inburgh
From a deed of property. Van Inburgh's signature actual size. Stephen Bourdett, above, was a goldsmith (*1698–after 1752*)

Figures 1–5 and the inscription and mark shown in Figure 6 are reproduced by courtesy of the Gallery of Fine Arts, Yale University. The porringer, Figure 6, is illustrated by courtesy of Mrs. Howard Sill.

Figs. 1 and 2 — CHAFING DISH NUMBER 1 BY PETER VAN DYCK OF NEW YORK (*1684–1750*)
French influence is apparent. The central grill is held firmly in place by means of a screw, which emerges through the bottom, and is easily removed for cleaning. *Weight, including handle*, 12 oz., 16 dwt. Height, 3⅜ inches over all. *Diameter of bowl*, 5⅛ inches. *Diameter of base*, 3¾ inches. Marked four times on base, P V D. No inscription. Owned by Jacobus Van Cortlandt or his son Frederick in the early eighteenth century. Figure 2 shows marks and construction. *Private ownership*

Two Chafing Dishes by Peter Van Dyck

By MRS. RUSSEL HASTINGS

O F ALL the objects known to students of early American silver, none exercises a more mysterious allure than the little pierced chafing dishes, which fortunately survive in considerable numbers. In this year of grace, no less than twenty-four examples, mostly by Boston makers, are of record. Chafing dishes, functioning with the aid either of charcoal or of spirit lamps, were generally five inches or more in diameter, and were usually, but not invariably, equipped with wooden handles. Doubtless of Continental origin, these convenient utensils were readily adopted by the English, who in turn no doubt conveyed their ideas to New England silversmiths. Very little mention of the chafing dish occurs in books on English silver, and Wenham, commenting on the paucity of examples in England today, suggests that the American chafing dish or "brazier" may have been directly copied from French models.

But in their day brazier and chafing dish were never confused either in Europe or in America. The brazier was a huge, open receptacle for live coals. Planted on the stone floor of a dwelling, its purpose was to yield a modicum of generalized warmth. It was often supplemented by smaller, variously named heating devices for hands or feet. One variety, indeed, was specifically designed for the altars of churches to warm the hands of the officiating priests and to prevent the sacramental wine from freezing.

The chafing dish, on the other hand, was a diminutive portable stove for cooking or warming foods. Its French name, *réchaud*, sufficiently indicates its purpose. The chafing dishes recorded in early New York inventories were of copper, brass, pewter, iron, and silver. They seem to have been quite numerous.

Though primarily intended for reheating foods already cooked, the chafing dish was also indispensable in preparing foods, sauces, and beverages in whose concocting the egg played an important rôle and which, therefore, were sure to curdle if heated beyond exact limits of time and temperature. One of the most popular of such mixtures was the caudle, according to the dictionary "a warm, nourishing drink of wine, eggs, etc., spiced and sweetened, for the sick and their visitors." The chafer was also a handy utensil for brewing, in silver tankards, the "burnt wine" of Pepys' *Diary*, and for keeping the punchbowl hot. That it was employed in making sweetmeats and macaroons is amply proved by early English cookery books. Again, it served as a smoker's companion. The tiny silver tongs that appear from time to time in the market may have been specifically designed for transferring glowing coals from silver vessel to pipe bowl. In the dressing room the chafing dish functioned in warming the water for the toilet and in imparting ardor to the lady's curling tongs.

The auctioneer's term for the chafing dish, both in America and in England today, is "brazier." That so grandiloquent a

Fig. 3 — CHAFING DISH NUMBER 2 BY PETER VAN DYCK
Slightly smaller than the other dish here shown. *Diameter of bowl*, 5 inches. *Diameter of base*, 3½ inches. *Weight with handle*, 12 oz., 2.5 dwt. Marked three times on base; same punch used. Engraved inscription on base, $I*S$ over S. Bowl lifted higher from table than Number 1 by straightening of supporting bands. *From the Metropolitan Museum of Art*

misnomer should have crept into the language is not strange. The popular Victorian saucepan with its attached spirit lamp was called a chafing dish regardless of the fact that the true chafer was merely an arrangement for heating, and never included a saucepan. So effectively does commerce have its way, alas, that even scholarly writers, here and there, have accepted its nomenclature, and many a museum labels the little silver dishes as "braziers."

Writers on American silver have observed that, while chafing dishes by other makers are fairly abundant, no example by a New York smith has hitherto come to light. It is gratifying, therefore, to report the recent discovery of two almost identical examples by Peter Van Dyck of New York. Thus in 1934, I was privileged to examine what European archæologists would term a "Treasure." It consists of many hitherto unrecorded pieces of family plate used by early Philipses, Jays, and Van Cortlandts. Next in importance to its Vanderburgh tankards (Antiques, January and February 1936), should be ranked the larger of the two chafing dishes here illustrated. A few months later, an almost identical dish, also with an excellent family history, was taken by its owner to the Metropolitan Museum, where it is now to be seen in the American Wing. So similar are the two pieces in size and design that it was necessary to bring them together for an exhaustive comparison. But, as will be learned from the notes accompanying the illustrations, these two Peter Van Dyck silver chafing dishes are not identical twins.

Peter Van Dyck (1684-1750) was born in New York and died there, to judge solely by the Dutch Church records. His father was Dirck Franszen (Van Dyck), a skipper who was drowned off the lower New Jersey shore of the Hudson River when Peter was but seven years old. The lad's mother, Urseltje Schepmoes, had influential family ties, and lived out her long widowhood in a comfortable house next to Jacob Boelen's in the Heere Gracht, today known as Broad Street. Peter was thus early exposed to the influence of one of our great silversmiths, no matter who was his eventual master.

Peter's paternal grandfather was a schoolmaster, Meester Frans Claesen, who brought his wife and three sons from Amsterdam to the new world. Peter Van Dyck's grandson, the Reverend Henry Van Dyck, was a graduate of King's College and one of the first Episcopal clergymen to be ordained in America after the Revolution. Peter was twice married. His first helpmeet was Rachel, daughter of Bartholomew Le Roux, the French goldsmith; his second was Cornelia Van Varick, a glittering heiress of her day, the daughter of the Reverend Rudolphus Van Varick. These details are presented as further evidence that our early gold- and silversmiths were of an educated class and occupied much the same position in society as the mediaeval goldsmiths, who were the only artisans admitted to the inner court circles.

Peter Van Dyck's chafing dishes are quite unlike the previous American examples recorded by Avery, Bigelow, Ensko, and Antiques (May 1932 and September 1933). They are heavier and less "open to the day," as the French say, and they have no delicate silver flying buttresses to support them. Pierced with the fleur-de-lis of France, their bowls are sturdily elevated from the table by extremely simple strap supports. So similar are they to an early seventeenth-century French dish in copper here pictured that we may unhesitatingly admit their French inspiration. Peter must have seen many an old or new French chafing dish in the homes of the Huguenot refugees who entered New York in his childhood. Whether the

Fig. 4 — Réchaud in Red Copper, French, Louis XIII (*1610-1643*)
A masterpiece from the Decloux collection. Put together with rivets and small bolts. The handle fits easily over a square metal spike. Elaborately pierced with heart and fleur-de-lis. Construction of supports resembles that of Peter Van Dyck's chafing dishes. *Diameter of bowl at widest part of hexagon,* 9 inches.
From the Cooper Union Museum

Fig. 5 — Silver Chafing Dish, with Spirit Lamp, Both by Joseph Ward of London (*1705/6*)
Two of three removable prongs by Robert Garrard of London, nineteenth century. *Weight, not including handle and pin,* 17 oz., 18 dwt. William Penn brought three of these new-style spirit chafing dishes of silver when he came to America in 1701.
From the collection of Mrs. Stanley Resor

Fig. 6 — Evolution of the Chafing Dish or Réchaud, from "Larousse Illustré"
1. Roman (brass); *2.* chafing dish on wheels, thirteenth century (wrought iron); *3.* seventeenth century (brass); *4.* eighteenth century (silver); *5.* table type for alcohol, reversible (nickel); *6.* table type, for charcoal; *7.* for alcohol, with a reservoir; *8.* Arabian

prototype of his two creations was made of silver or of baser metal is immaterial.

The uses of the chafing dish in England and America are so obscure that we are obliged to cross the Channel in our search for literature on the subject. Henry Havard's great work, *Dictionnaire de l'Ameublement et de la Décoration*, is so enlightening that we shall do well to translate his article on the *réchaud*.

"A household utensil," wrote Savary [*Dict. Univ. de Commerce, 1742*] "used for applying fire for cooking or reheating foods which had grown cold. They were made of iron, copper and sometimes silver." . . . Chafing dishes in our country are of very ancient lineage. In the beginning they were called *chauffoirs* or *chauffouers*. In the *Silver Demanded by the Crown from the Heirs of Louis I of Anjou (1385)*, we notice "a *chauffoère* of white silver, with three feet, with the arms of the Dauphin on the lid, weighing five *marcs* and a half." In the *Inventory of the Château of Ménitré (1471)* we also glean, "Three small basins and three *chaffouers* for washing the hands." In the succeeding century these little articles took the name of *chaufferettes*. . . . It was not until the end of the sixteenth century that the word *réchaud* appeared. *The Delivery to the Duke of Epernon of the Effects of the Brothers of Foix-Candalle (1598)* mentions "two more silver *réchauds*, with ebony handles." *The Inventory of Gabrielle d'Estrées (1599)* lists "Item, a *réchaud* of white silver weighing three *marcs*, six *onces*, six *gros*."

All the *réchauds* that we have cited were made of precious metals; but, as Savary explains, along with these chafing dishes of considerable value, one meets, in humbler homes, an infinity of more modest examples in iron or in copper. Of this number certainly was that of which Pierre de l'Estoile spoke: "Thursday, the eighth of January, 1608, the chalice froze in St. André-des-Ars, and it was necessary to go to the pastry shop for a *réchaud* to melt it" (*Journal*, Vol. IX, p. 41). So likewise we meet with: "Two *réchauds* in copper worth together sixteen sous" (*Inventory of Marie Criquet, wife of Pierre Croizet, counsellor to Parliament*; Paris, 1625) . . . "two *réchaud*" (*Inventory of Jean Thomas*, Paris, 1631). . . . Hardly a kitchen was not then thus provided. The prices of these modest utensils were, moreover, very low. . . . We may add that these useful objects in the base metals were often fashioned with skill. The Cluny Museum has a few of these small copper chafing dishes with handles which are of pleasing shape and amusing decoration. Another, of iron, Flemish of the seventeenth century, should also be seen.

All these chafing dishes are made after the primitive formula of the *chaufferettes* or *chauffoires* of the Middle Ages and the Renaissance. Until

Fig. 7 — "The Sick Grey Beard, or January and May" by J. H. Steen (*1626–1679*)
A chafing dish of coals on the floor of the invalid's bedchamber has been used in an effort to tempt his appetite. A jug of broth and an omelet appear to have been the result. The chafing dish or *komfoor* for cookery is here shown in close proximity to the footwarmer or *stoof*. In the background a maid is warming the bed with a closed pan of coals.
Figures 7 and 8 courtesy of the Frick Art Reference Library

Fig. 8 — Detail from "A Terrace Scene" by C. W. E. Dietrich (*1712–1774*)
A chafing dish, perhaps of silver, rests on the table, and a coffee or chocolate pot with accompanying cups stands beside it

the closing years of the seventeenth century, there seemed to be no escape from this hoary model. "A good chafing dish," wrote Richelet, "is made of steel, and consists of a body, three feet, a grill, a base, a socket, and a handle." In these receptacles were placed burning coals which, besides the discomfort due to their fumes, were attended with considerable risk to the dishes of silver and particularly those of pewter which were used upon them. . . . At the end of the seventeenth century, this defect was remedied by the substitution of an alcohol lamp for the doubly dangerous charcoal. Chafing dishes of this sort, then a novelty, first figured in the *General Inventory of the Furnishings of the Royal Household*, April 22, 1697. They are listed as "Two chafing dishes for spirit lamps, on the feet of which are carved in relief three old men's heads, weighing with their chains and tongs, 16 *marcs*, 5 *onzes*, 6 *gros*." [The *marc* was 8 ounces.]

Henceforth, all chafing dishes of any value were made in this way, whether they were single and without any definite purpose, like the gold vessel delivered to M. Duflot in 1750, by Lazare Duvaux, for 285 *livres*, or the small one of silver which the same merchant sold in 1753 to Mme. de Pompadour; or whether they were, on the contrary, part of an ensemble, like the "coffeepot and its spirit lamp, with engraved supports, and a chafing dish of bronzed and gilded steel," bought by Louis XV from this same Duvaux for 1,950 *livres* (*Livre Journal*, Vol. II, *pp. 53, 178, 194, etc.*), or like the "chafing dish with a spirit lamp, turned, and its lamp with two covers, one with five wicks, the other with three," which François-Thomas Germain delivered January 27, 1754, to Versailles to serve the king, and which was accompanied by two vessels for serving soup; or, lastly, like the "gold coffeepot with its two cups, its chafing dish and a spirit lamp, all enclosed in a shagreen case," listed in the *Inventory of Marie-Josèphe de Saxe, Dauphine of France*. . . .

In the eighteenth century, Granchez, jeweler to Marie Antoinette, placed on sale a new chafing dish, "with three circles and a spirit lamp in silvered copper, which could hold dishes of all sizes." "This model," added Granchez, in the advertisement published in the *Mercure (January 1776)* "is copied from the English." . . . We do not know whether the innovation of the celebrated jeweler was relished by the public of his era. In our day it has been revived and perfected. . . .

For the sake of completeness, mention must be made of the *réchauds-cassolettes* which were also in vogue in the eighteenth century, and also *réchauds* of pottery. The *réchauds-cassolettes* were used for evaporating liquid perfumes, like toilet waters, or pastilles of different sorts, or incense. Some of these little *réchauds* had a genuine artistic value. . . . This same purveyor [Duvaux] manufactured . . .

in 1758 "two silver *réchauds* for pastilles"; then in 1757 he sold to the Prince of Francavilla "a *cassolette* made of a Saxony figurine and a dog, the vase and the *réchaud* in silver" for the sum of 168 *livres*. (*Livre Journal*, Vol. II, *pp. 236, 336, 365*.) Lastly, at the *Sale of Mme. de Pompadour* (April 28, 1766), there were knocked down "two little *réchauds* for scents, in porcelain mounted in silver."

These last items bring us to the subject of *réchauds* in pottery, which seem in the beginning to have been part of the most luxurious furnishings. In the *Inventory of Catherine de Medicis (1589)* we find the first mention of these utensils, consisting of a "*réchaud* of blue earthenware" [*terre bleue*]. In the *Inventory of the Château de Nérac (1598)*, we find "Nine saucers of *terre de Venise*, painted in the same colors. Two *réchauds* with pillars and figures painted like the above." Héroard in his *Journal* (Vol. I, *p. 175*) on February 21, 1606, sets down the following note: "My wife took to the Dauphin a little chafing dish and a little *écuelle* in faïence." These almost august beginnings are a strong contrast to the miserable end of the poor *réchauds*, which after the seventeenth century were banished not only from luxurious homes but even from middle-class tables.

It is impossible to study the American silver chafing dishes without developing considerable curiosity as to their daily uses. Such utensils are almost invariably referred to as a "chafing dish of coals" in old English cookery books. A volume of the early sixteenth century offers a recipe for crabmeat, cooked in butter with cinnamon, sugar, and vinegar added, to be done on a "chafying dysche of coles"; another for a tart of prunes, the initial boiling of which with red wine is done on a chafer; another for a dessert of egg yolks poached in sweetened rosewater, and served with cinnamon and sugar.

An excellent "tea caudle" may be prepared on a chafing dish of coals after a Chinese recipe, brought back to England by a traveler in 1664. A pint of tea infusion is made in the usual manner. To this are added two beaten egg yolks, sweetened, in a silver saucepan on a chafing dish of coals. When the mixture is hot and slightly thickened, it is drunk from two caudle cups, and, strange as it may sound, it is indeed a pleasant stimulant at the end of the day's labors. The flavor of the tea is brought out in uncanny Oriental fashion by this long-popular beverage.

Henry Howard (*1708*) has a recipe for macaroons made of ground almonds, rosewater, flour, and a grain of musk, laid out longish on buttered paper and iced over with loaf sugar. For the making of comfits, he directs the cook to provide a pan of brass or tin to a good depth, made with ears to hang over a chafing dish of coals, with ladle and slice of the same metal.

What ancient silver utensils may be most successfully used with a chafing dish of coals it is hard to say. Almost all of the silver warmers exhibit a special type of supporting bracket above the bowl, as if to accommodate a specially fitted plate, or grill, or some type of vessel that has since disappeared. The

Fig. 9 — "Woman at Her Toilet" by Adrien P. van der Venne (*1589–1662*)

The chafing dish has been used for warming water and heating curling tongs.

Courtesy of the Frick Art Reference Library

average teakettle, tankard, punchbowl, or saucepan is in peril of slipping earthward if placed upon these supports. Furthermore, the charcoal seldom burns successfully until covered by a metal plate or basin. The Cromwellian three-legged skillet with a porringer lid may well have been designed for better security on a chafing dish.

The inquisitive possessor of a chafing dish who wishes to use the utensil is counseled to break up the charcoal into bits the size of a hazelnut, place the fuel on the upper grill, moisten it with medicinal alcohol, light it, place a large metal plate or basin upon the upstanding prongs, and fan or blow the fire from below until the coals are well kindled. The plate and the superimposed vessel will soon be hot enough to use. Spirit lamps should be filled to one third of their capacity, with medicinal alcohol.

Fire, carefully used, can have not the slightest ill effect upon old silver. The fusing point of pure silver is 962° centigrade, that of copper is 1082°, while that of less sturdy aluminum is 655°. (The boiling point by the centigrade thermometer is 100° as against 212° by the Fahrenheit scale.) As a hard silver solder is composed of 4 parts silver to 1 of copper, the solder melts at a rather higher temperature than does silver. The collector's precious pieces, therefore, are suited to the warmest use and may be enjoyed in homely ways. They should never be allowed to become red hot, of course.

It is useful in obscure cases, when marks have been all but obliterated, to know that, in 1679, a law in France made it obligatory to mark all silver according to rule. Chafing dishes were to bear the mark and countermark on body and base, whether the base be of the plate or bowl variety. The maker's mark must be placed on the grill, the handle socket, and the supports (Havard, *Dictionnaire*, Vol. III, *p. 1115*).

It is by such inconsiderable crumbs of knowledge that false attributions are avoided. A certain French chafing dish that I have seen, for example, might easily be attributed to any of the Boston makers, were it not that on its scrolled supports there still survive some almost obliterated maker's marks, which definitely transfer its place of origin to the other side of the Atlantic. A similar French chafing dish, of silver, is at present on loan at the Metropolitan Museum. The provenance of these portable stoves indicates a strong undercurrent of Continental tradition in the British Colonies of North America.

Note. I take this opportunity of acknowledging constant and long-continued kindness on the part of Miss C. Louise Avery and Marshall Davidson of the Metropolitan Museum, New York; Mrs. Yves Henry Buhler of the Boston Museum of Fine Arts; Stephen G. C. Ensko, Willoughby Farr, and Richard M. Gipson, all of New York; E. Alfred Jones of London; Miss V. Isabelle Miller of the Museum of the City of New York; John Marshall Phillips, curator of the Garvan collection at Yale University; and Dr. J. Hall Pleasants of Baltimore; all of whom have expert knowledge of early American silver and inexhaustible generosity in sharing it.
— *K. B. H.*

Peter Van Dyck of New York, Goldsmith, 1684-1750

Part II

By Mrs. Russel Hastings

Fig. 12 — MUSTARD POT

Weight, 5 oz. 3 dwt. *Height*, 5 in. Maker's trefoil mark. No inscription. No history. English books usually assure us that silver mustard pots date from 1720-1750 onward, so we are mystified by the frequent mention of them in New York inventories before and after 1700. The Dutch in New York copied their silver largely from English models, but their foods were presumably as Dutch as their speech, far into the eighteenth century. This vessel raises a nice point for someone to settle regarding the uses of the popular mustard pot by the early Dutch settlers.

From the Mabel Brady Garvan collection, Gallery of Fine Arts, Yale University

Fig. 13 — SNUFFBOX

Weight, 1 oz. 11 dwt. *Length*, 2 ⅞ in. *Width*, 2 ¼ in. *Depth*, ⅝ in. Maker's trefoil mark. Inscribed on inner side of tortoise-shell *M. B: P. M: I. W.* Of tortoise-shell and silver. Engraved on outside of shell: Adam and Eve; on opposite side, a lady and gentleman of quality, in early eighteenth-century costumes. No history. Formerly in the Luke Vincent Lockwood collection.

From the Mabel Brady Garvan collection, Gallery of Fine Arts, Yale University

WITHIN a year after their marriage, Peter Van Dyck and Rachel Le Roux had a daughter, Rachel, born in 1712. The young mother must have died soon after. Three years later Peter Van Dyck married a really great heiress. She was Cornelia Van Varick of Flatbush, the widow of Barent de Kleyn, and the mother of a small boy just little Rachel's age. His name was Leonard de Kleyn. We know that Cornelia Van Varick was an heiress, because of the extraordinary inventory of her mother's estate, which gives us by far our clearest picture of the belongings of a Dutch lady voluntarily exiled in the new world in the year 1695. This inventory, most interestingly described in the New York *Sun* for April 6, 1935, is likewise referred to in Esther Singleton's *Furniture of Our Forefathers.*

Cornelia's father was the Reverend Rudolphus Van Varick, who in 1686 came from Holland with much ecclesiastical trumpeting to take charge of the opulent Flatbush congregation. When he landed, the Flatbush church officials wrote to him, "We learn that you, together with your dearest, and your children, have arrived in New York." His salary was to be 900 florins, free fuel, and a new stone house to harbor his "dearest" and her glittering possessions. This lady was born Margaretta Visboom, and, as nearly as we can interpret the confused records and traditions, she was the widow of a rich Dutch governor stationed in Malacca in the East Indies, by whom she had at least one daughter, named Cornelia Hesther. In his younger days Parson Van Varick, having fared forth to Malacca to supervise colonial souls, besides doing a bit of missionary work among the heathen, met and married the well-en-

dowed widow. After a five-year sojourn in the Far East (1673-1678) Van Varick, accompanied by his wife, went to Hem, North Holland, where their daughter Joanna was born. The advent of a son, appropriately named Marinus, occurred during the voyage to America. A daughter, Cornelia, and in 1690 a son, Rudolphus, were subsequent contributions to the population of the new world. It is said by the eminent genealogist DeBoer that other children came, who did not survive.

The ship that bore the parson and his wife to America must have been well laden with the portraits, jewels, "pictures," garments, and fine furnishings appertaining to the former wife of a rich Dutch governor. Would that some enthusiast who reads these notes might be moved to devote his remaining lifetime to reproducing the Dominie's stone house and furnishing it, piece by piece, as Margaretta Visboom left it!

Restless in his Flatbush parish, Van Varick frequently begged to be recalled, but to no avail. During the Leisler troubles, he was imprisoned. Later he fled to Newcastle on the South River to join the Dutch colony there. His wife presently followed him, it is said, with all her worldly goods. In view of the extent of the lady's belongings this is hard to believe. Doubtless the Beekmans and Stryckers and other pillars of the Flatbush Church guarded such things as the oversize kas, "too large to be moved," of the inventory. The

Fig. 14 — GOLD NECKLACE AND CLASP

52 small, 25 large beads. *Length*, 25 in. *Length of clasp*, 1 in. *Width of clasp*, ⅝ in. Maker's oval mark. Inscribed on clasp, *M. I.* Engraving on clasp, bird with spread wings. No history. Formerly in the Maurice Brix collection.

From the Mabel Brady Garvan collection, Gallery of Fine Arts, Yale University

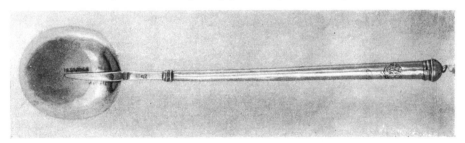

Fig. 15 — LARGE SPOON OR LADLE, WHOSE PARTICULAR USES WE MAY ONLY CONJECTURE

Weight, 7 oz. *Length*, 17 ⅛ in. Maker's trefoil mark. Inscribed *G*R.*, and a cypher which may be *H. B. S.* or its reverse. No history. Formerly in the Luke Vincent Lockwood collection.

From the Mabel Brady Garvan collection, Gallery of Fine Arts, Yale University

Fig. 16 — "Sauce Cup," According to the Inventory of John Cannon (1762), Its Presumptive Owner

Weight, 13 oz. 10 dwt. Scratched on bottom, $\frac{oz\ pw.}{13\ 2:2}$. *Width over all,* 7 ¾ in. *Height over all,* 4 ¾ in. Marked twice on base with maker's oval mark (no pellets). Inscribed in small letters on lip at point of junction with handle *C* over *I∗I*, obviously the initials of John Cannon (*1703–1762*) and his first wife Jerusha Sands (*?–1757*), whom he married before 1725, ancestors of the present owner. In a list of the family plate distributed after John Cannon's death, this "sauce cup," weighing 13 ½ oz., is valued at £6/1/6, and is thus referred to three times. This adds a new term to the nomenclature of eighteenth-century silver.
Courtesy of Le Grand B. Cannon and the Museum of the City of New York

parson in due time returned, with hordes of others, from exile. Not long after, in 1694, he died, and was buried one night in the presence of Governor Fletcher and all the other high officials of the colony. Juffrouw Margaretta Visboom Hesther Van Varick died at the Flatbush (alias Midwout) parsonage the next year. A few discriminating members of the community were designated to inventory her estate. They did a superb piece of cataloguing, covering twenty-odd pages. Juffrouw Van Varick had touchingly wrapped in napkins the trinkets apportioned to each child. Cornelia's allotment — she was then only a little girl — was this:

1 bundle of silver plate rings and jewels that are made up each in a napkin and sealed — my second finest turkey worke carpett & 2 pictures with fine glass before them — other glass case with what stands upon it, that cabinett with the silver hinges, the picture of my daughter Cornelia Hesther dec'd, the picture of a flowr-pott, 2 white china cupps with covers and one china cup bound with silver and the biggest looking glasse with an

Fig. 18 — Teapot, Showing French Influence

Weight, 30 oz. 6 dwt. *Height over all,* 7 ½ in. *Width over all,* 9 ⅝ in. Marked on each side of handle at top with maker's trefoil mark. Heavily engraved with mantling of later date than the teapot. Inscribed on bottom in modern script: *Catharine Van Brugh 1710. Wm and Susan Livingston 1745. John and Sarah Jay 1789. Maria Banyar 1829. John C. Jay 1856. Pierre Jay 1891,* apparently indicating the line of descent.

ebony frame. . . . 2 gold pieces to wear above their ears called in Dutch *glissen.* . . . My negro girl to stay with my daughter Cornelia until she be 14 years of age.

The inventory thus amplifies the list devised in the mother's will:

In a great chist lockt up by the said executors . . . for Cornelia Van Varick bound up in another napkin, one silver wrought East India trunk, one silver saltseller, one silver wrought East India box, twenty eight silver playthings or Toyes, twenty pieces silver monny, all weighing Sixty-eight ounces, a small mother of pearl small box, one comb typt with gold, one bible the clasps typt with gold, a small bundel leafe gold, a pair diamond pendants, two gold chaines, two gold Rings with each one diamand, two small gold rings, a pair Christall pendants edged with gold, one Arabyan duccate, and two gold *stiftens.* . . . In the said Chist for . . . the said Cornelia, the second finist turkey worke carpet, two picters with glasses before them, the one broke, a callico night gowne, a hair brush and one Chint flowered Carpett. . . . Item loose for said Cornelia a small black cabinet with silver hinges, the picture of Cornelia hester deceased, the picture of a flower pott, one china cupp bound with silver, one large looking glasse with an Ebony frame, one fether bedd covered with checkerd linnen, one boulster, three old kussions fild with watten [?], one fether kussion and one small ditto old; one quilt worne and one homespun blancoate; Item more two glaasen Caases [?] bequeathed to Johanna & Cornelia with thirty nine pieces of small China ware and eleven Indian babyes which are pact & nayld up in a half barrel — for Johanna and Cornelia each of them, six small and six larger China dishes. . . . Item more bequeathed to Cornelia Van Varick two white China cupps with covers. . . .

There then follows the inventory of goods "in the shop," showing that yet another of our early *grandes dames* was a merchant on her own account.

Peter Van Dyck and the richly endowed Cornelia Van Varick had at least ten children. Cornelia died in 1733 and was honored by an obituary in the *New York Gazette* (January 14, 1733), a hitherto unheard-of tribute for a woman:

On Sunday the 6th Inst. a Gentlewoman (the Wife of Mr. *Van Dyke,* Silver-smith) of this City, being very much disorder'd by Sickness, the Doctor was sent for, who appointed her a portion of Physick; after the receiving of which, she fell to vomiting to such a degree, that notwithstanding all possible Endeavours used to prevent the same, it continued till Tuesday Evening following, when she died; she was very much lamented by all that knew her, especially by the Number of Motherless Children which she left behind. And was decently inter'd on Friday Evening last.

In 1750 Peter Van Dyck followed his better half into the shadows. His will adequately accounts for his surviving progeny. They were his son Richard, the engraver-goldsmith; his grandchildren Daniel and Rachel Shatford, "children of my late daughter Rachel Shatford"; his daughters Hannah and Cornelia, to each of whom he left a "silver mugg"; his daughter Lena, to whom he left a silver teapot; his daughter Sarah, to whom he left his smallest silver tankard; his daughter Mary, to whom he left

Fig. 17 — Large Caster, Presumably for Sugar

Weight, 9 oz. 16 dwt. *Height,* 7 ½ in. *Base diameter,* 2 15/16 in. Scratched on bottom, *10 o.* Marked once on bottom and twice on slip sleeve of pierced cap with maker's oval mark. Inscribed in script *H. C. R.* Believed to have belonged to Hendrick Rutgers (*1712–1779*) and Catherine De Peyster (*1711– living 1775*), married January 9, 1732, at Kingston, New York.
Courtesy of Henry Rutgers Beekman and the Museum of the City of New York

Scratched on bottom, *21 ½-6 [sic]*, probably record of weight of the pot before the original wooden handle was added. The present handle, finial, and insulating rings are not contemporary. One of the maker's most charming efforts and probably one of his earliest. Catharine Van Brugh (*1689–1756*) married in 1707 Philip Livingston (*1686–1749*) of Albany and was mother of Governor William Livingston, the next owner of the teapot.
Courtesy of Pierre Jay and the Metropolitan Museum of Art

Fig. 19 (left and right) — LIVINGSTON-GARVAN TANKARD

Weight, 39 oz. 12 dwt. Height, 7 ½ in. Scratched on base, *42-⅛ oz*, which raises some interesting questions. Maker's oval mark appears twice to the left of the handle. Inscribed on bottom in contemporary script *L* over *P✳C*. Engraved with the erroneous form of the Livingston arms assumed by Robert, 1st Lord of the Manor, in accordance with instructions sent from Scotland in 1698 (see *Livingstons of Callendar, p. 650*). The crest and motto originated with the 1st Lord. Said to have descended from Philip and Catharine Van Brugh Livingston, married 1707, through Edward Livingston, one of their descendants. Catharine Van Brugh's mother, Catherine Cuyler, was a cousin of Peter Van Dyck

Fig. 20 (*below*) — TANKARD

Weight, 22 oz. 15 dwt. Height, 6 ¾ in. Maker's oval mark with pellets. Inscribed on bottom *S* over *P✳E*. No history. *Figures 19, 20 from the Mabel Brady Garvan collection, Gallery of Fine Arts, Yale University*

his largest silver tankard; and his son Rudolphus, who was to share the residue with the other living children.

Peter had seen his daughter Rachel marry a schoolmaster in 1735, one Daniel Shatford. Likewise he had seen his son Richard marry Elizabeth Strang of Rye, and become a famous goldsmith-engraver-importer of Hanover Square, New York. Richard Van Dyck was commissioned to engrave bills of credit to be used in raising £40,000 by tax for the expedition against Canada in 1746. Again he was recompensed in 1756 for boarding French prisoners of war. In 1750 the Lloyds of Long Island ordered some silver spoons from him. In 1753, he advertised fresh importations to be had at his store in Hanover Square, of wrought plate, looking-glasses, sconces, pictures, and best "French oyl." His advertisements were frequent and verbose. Silver bearing the initials of Richard Van Dyck is so infrequently met that we must infer that commercial concerns rather crowded his art to the wall.

Peter Van Dyck stood sponsor to one grandson, Peter Van Dyck, son of Richard, and doubtless saw and admired the child's brother, Henry, who was to graduate from King's College in 1761 and become successively rector of seven churches in Connecticut, New York, New Jersey, and Long Island. The Reverend Henry Van Dyck has many descendants.

Peter Van Dyck had another son, Rudolphus, a shipping merchant who helped to establish the Moravian Church in New

Fig. 21 — COMMUNION MUG

One of a pair belonging to the Southampton Church. *Weight*, 18 oz. 19 dwt. *Height over all*, 5 13/16 in. *Width over all*, 7 ¾ in. Twice marked with maker's oval mark to the left of the handle. On bottom in a circle in script is the phonetically spelled inscription *For the church*

York. Some of his business letters, now in the New York Historical Society's collection, show him to have been thoroughly educated. His three sisters, as well as his aunt Ann Van Dyck, appear to have been shopkeepers, evidence that gentlewomen in small trade are not the novelty we assume them to be in New York.

Four unmarried daughters remained to solace Peter Van Dyck after Cornelia's death; for Sarah did not marry Hendrick Oudenarde until her father had been long deceased. Oudenarde was a merchant, and Sarah herself seems to have been as able a woman of business as her sisters, for she administered the estates of all the others after the Peace permitted the resumption of business in New York. She had at least four children.

By dint of much patience we are able to resurrect our silversmiths in so far as concerns their family and official lives. Of their art we find virtually no written record, and probably never shall. Many of these men are but once mentioned with a specific reference to their calling. When we find initials that might be theirs upon a piece of silver, we assume their authorship for the work, provided its style accords with the fashions of their life span. Unqualified evidence to support our assumption we have, with few exceptions, none. Benvenuto Cellini, the Florentine master of metals, left a voluminous and perennially delightful account of his life and work. Would that one of our craftsmen had been sufficiently

of Sought hamtun 6 Decembr. 1739. The mate to this mug is taller, and slightly different in detail. It is engraved in script on the bottom in a straight line: *Sought Hamptown Church.* It weighs 19 oz. 12 dwt. Perhaps later in date than the mate illustrated.
From the Metropolitan Museum of Art

Fig. 22 — Teapot

Weight, 22 oz. Scratched on bottom, *21-16; also, 21. Height over all, 7 ½ in. Width over all with present handle*, 9 in. Marked once at left of handle with maker's oval mark. Inscribed on bottom *E∗L*. Recently engraved crest of the Maitland family on side: a lion séjant affronté gules, ducally crowned, in dexter paw a sword proper, in sinister a fleur-de-lis azure. This teapot traditionally belonged to the present owner's ancestress, Elizabeth Sproat Lenox (*1785–1864*), who married Robert Maitland 1814. The early initials inscribed on bottom, however, point to an earlier owner, perhaps Elizabeth Loutit (*1732–after 1750*) great-aunt of Elizabeth Sproat Lenox, of the half blood. Elizabeth Loutit's mother was Elizabeth Van Dyck, daughter of Frans Van Dyck, a first cousin of Peter Van Dyck, maker of the pot. Elizabeth Van Dyck's first husband was Ichabod Loutit, but it is more likely that the pot was a christening gift to little Elizabeth Loutit than a possession of her mother, who had the same initials from 1726 to 1734, when Ichabod died.

From the collection of Maitland Dwight

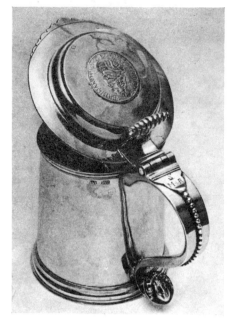

Fig. 23 — Tankard (*c. 1715*)

Weight, 27 oz. 15 dwt. Scratched on bottom, recently, *28 oz. Height over all, 6 ½ in. Width over all*, 7 ⅞ in. Marked twice at left of handle with maker's oval mark. Inscribed at top of handle *S* over *M∗R* in contemporary initials. Traditionally belonged to Captain Myndert Schuyler (*?–1755*) and his wife, Rachel Cuyler (*?–1747*), whom he married in 1693. Rachel Cuyler was a first cousin of Peter Van Dyck. Their daughter married Johannis De Peyster, and was the ancestress of the present owner. Coin identified by the Numismatic Society as a thaler of the Holy Roman Emperor, struck during the reign of Emperor Ferdinand III for Carinthia in Austria; dated *1649;* not especially rare. *From the collection of John D. W. Peltz*

respectful of his calling to indite a similar record! John Hull of Boston kept a *Diary*, but it tells us nothing of his art. Peter Van Dyck was stirred repeatedly by the joy of creating with brain and hand, but, so far as we know, he penned no word describing the experience. If at this late date we may accord him some small measure of the praise he so richly deserves, our effort will not have been in vain.

Notes. Peter Dirckszen Van Dyck, son of Dirck Franszen Van Dyck and Urseltje Jans Schepmoes, was baptized August 17, 1684, according to the records of the New York Dutch Church. He was buried December 1, 1750, according to the same documents, which also record his marriage October 27, 1711, to Rachel Le Roux, and July 22, 1715, to Cornelia [Van Varick, widow of Barent] De Kleyn.

In addition to the pieces illustrated with the two parts of this article, the following items by Peter Van Dyck are recorded by the Mabel Brady Garvan Institute at Yale University:

1. Tankard. Lent by Mrs. Fritz to the Metropolitan Museum of Art, New York.
2. Tankard. Lent by Dr. Howard Townsend to the Museum of the City of New York.
3. Tankard. Formerly owned by Mrs. Elihu Chauncey. Present whereabouts unknown.
4. Tankard. Owned by the First Congregational Church of Bridgeport, Connecticut. Illustrated in E. A. Jones, *Old Silver of American Churches*, Pl. XXXIV (*1*).
5. Tankard. Owned by the Minneapolis Museum. Formerly in the Garvan collection.
6. Pintard-Stout Tankard. Sold at the American Art Association Anderson Galleries, February 8, 1936.
7. Beekman Tankard. Exhibited at the Hudson

Fulton Celebration and described in the catalogue of that notable collection.

8. Porringer. Given by Miss Annie Clarkson to the Metropolitan Museum of Art.
9. Porringer. Owned by Mrs. Horace Binney Hare, Philadelphia, 1921.
10. Mug. In the Metropolitan Museum of Art.
11 and 12. Two bell-shaped mugs with two handles. Owned by the Presbyterian Church of Setauket, Long Island. Illustrated in E. A. Jones, *Old Silver of American Churches*, Pl. CXXVIII (*1*).
13. Eight-inch spoon. In the Mabel Brady Garvan collection, Yale University.
14 and 15. Two tablespoons. In the Stanley B. Ineson collection.
16. Chafing dish. Owned by Miss Charlotte Van Cortlandt. Illustrated and discussed in Antiques, October 1936, *p. 152.*
17. Chafing dish. Owned by the Metropolitan Museum of Art. Illustrated and discussed in Antiques, October 1936, *p. 152.*

Undoubtedly other pieces by Peter Van Dyck exist in two outstanding collections which are not available for study.

William J. Hoffman has just reported the important discovery that Urseltje Schepmoes Van Dyck was of an armorial family in Delft. In 1615 her uncle, Willem Jans Schepmoes, joined the Goldsmith's Guild of that city. His distant cousin, Pieter Huygens Schepmoes, is one of the registered craftsmen mentioned in Havard's work on the Delft potters. It is there stated that he married into the famous VanderBurch family of potters, who were in turn kinsmen of Pieter de Hoogh, the painter (*c. 1630–c. 1677*). Peter Van Dyck's paternal uncles appear to have spent much time in Holland. If we discover in time that Peter's mother sent him to her relatives abroad for his education, it will not be a great surprise.

Fig. 24 — Rare Autograph of Peter Van Dyck

Shows how meticulously Van Dyck clung to his mother tongue in 1713, the date of the deed of which he was a witness. We have taken the liberty of anglicizing his name. A deathbed signature is illegible and hence is not proof of whether or not he had accepted the change

ALBANY SILVER

By ROBERT G. WHEELER

Except as noted, all illustrations from the Albany Institute of History and Art. Left, Mug *by Koenradt Ten Eyck (1678-1753). Mabel Brady Garvan Collection, Yale University Art Gallery. Right,* Bowl *by Jacob Ten Eyck (1705-1793).*

Mr. Wheeler is Director of the Albany Institute of History and Art, one of the oldest museums in the country, founded in 1791. It specializes in the arts and crafts of the Upper Hudson, with emphasis on the silver, furniture, paintings, and textiles of the area.

From its earliest days, and even in some degree to the present, the Albany tradition is basically Dutch. The descendants of the original settlers kept up their contact with Holland long after New Amsterdam had come under English rule. The Dutch language was used in churches and for business until well past the mid-eighteenth century, and long after that the traditional Dutch holidays like St. Nicholas Day and the Pinksterfest were still observed. It was not until close to 1800 that there was any considerable influx of New Englanders to Albany, bringing English ways and customs.

The Dutch, thrifty by nature, proved themselves good businessmen. True to the customs of their homeland, they showed a fondness for substantial possessions. A manuscript owned by the Albany Institute of History and Art contains a record of some of the silver owned by Margaret Schuyler of Albany, the widow of Philip Schuyler: "Albany ye 27 January 1709/10 Put up into this Trunk at ye request of mother by ye/hands of John Schuyler, margret Collins, maria/Schuyler, Elizabeth Schuyler & maria van Rensselaer/ viz/in a box 8 dozyn & five new Silver Spoons/8 new silver forks/6 round handed Spoons/1 Silver Tankard/1 Silver Beeker/1 do mustard Pott/1 Large Silver cup with 2 handles/ 1 Silver Salt Seller/ . . ."

The earliest silversmith working in Albany appears to have been Kiliaen Van Rensselaer, grandson of the first Van

Far left, Lansing Family Tankard *engraved with family coat of arms, by Jan Van Niewkirke (c. 1716).*

Tankard *by Bartholomew Schaats (1670-1758) and Jacob Ten Eyck (1705-1793).*

TEAPOT by Jacob Gerrit Lansing *(1736-1803)*. This piece bears the initials of nine successive generations of owners in the same family line.

COVERED SUGAR by Jacob Gerritse Lansingh *(c. 1700)*, with cast eagle finial. This piece is initialed *NDF* for Neltze Quackenbos who married Jesse de Forest.

Rensselaer Patroon. He served at least part of his apprenticeship under Jeremiah Dummer in Boston. In 1683, Kiliaen's mother wrote, "He is an able young man. I let him set up the silversmith's shop in the country. He does not waste his time."

Among the early settlers in Albany was the Widow Lansing, who arrived in 1641 with her four sons. The Lansing silversmiths descended from this family. They are something of a mystery. Jacob Gerritse Lansingh was active in Albany about 1700, and another Jacob Gerrit (se) Lansing (h) was working about 1765. Some confusion surrounds the use of the Lansing names and marks. One theory (not proved) holds that the same marks were used by both members of the family, having been passed down from one to the other.

The best-known Albany silversmiths are probably the Ten Eycks (see ANTIQUES, December 1942). Among the most

outstanding were Koenradt *(1678-1753)*, Jacob *(1705-1793)*, and Barent *(1714-1795)*.

Koenradt, whose public career extended from 1702 to 1750, was adjustor of weights and measures, juror, assessor, constable, and was a representative to the Colonial Assembly. According to John Marshall Phillips' *American Silver*, sometime before 1746, when "the Deacons of the Reformed Church at Albany bought a piece of land adjoining the Church pasture, they paid the several grantors at the rate of 90 guilders each, in plate. . . . Each grantor received a silver cup made of 6 heavy pieces of eight valued at 81 guilders by the Albany silversmith, Koenradt Ten Eyck, who was paid at the rate of 9 guilders per cup for the fashioning, making a total of 90 guilders." This provides an insight into the demand for plate and the important place of the silver-

THREE-PIECE TEA SET by Jacob Gerrit Lansing *(1736-1803)*. Teapot made for Neltze Roseboom, his first wife *(c. 1767)*, the covered sugar for his second wife, Femmetze Lansing *(c. 1771)*, and the creamer for his mother-in-law, Maria Lansing.

THREE SPOONS by Isaac Hutton *(1767-1855)*. Tablespoon, dessert spoon and teaspoon initialed *MH.*

Koenradt's fifth child, Barent, who also became a silversmith, was less active in civic affairs, though he did serve as firemaster for the Second Ward in 1742 and as assistant alderman for the same ward in 1746 and 1747. Little of Barent's silver remains, but it is quite possible that much of his effort went into silver used in the Indian fur trade. Barent Ten Eyck is mentioned in the papers of Sir William Johnson, who carried on barter with the Indians, in 1756, 1758, and 1769. Johnson records that a "silver armband of ye largest" was equal to three beaver skins, and also lists gorgets, silver medals, breast buckles, silver crosses, and wrist bands as items of barter.

Another prominent Albany silversmith was Isaac Hutton (see ANTIQUES, January 1945). Little is known about his background, but in 1790, when he was twenty-three, Hutton had a jewelry store on Market Street in Albany. By 1797 he had prospered to the extent that he could advertise that "three silversmiths may have constant employment in a very convenient shop and receive prompt pay." Hutton was a highly talented craftsman, and all of his silver is beautifully and honestly made.

In addition to being a silversmith, Hutton carried on many other enterprises. At intervals he advertised the sale of such varied items as sheep wool, glass, gunpowder, and pianofortes. He lived in a time of great expansion, when the West was opening up and progressive schemes of all kinds were afoot. Becoming infected with the prevalent speculative fever, he put his money into the manufacture of cotton goods. This interest eventually brought about his financial ruin and ended his career as a silversmith.

Robert Shepherd and William Boyd, two Albany silversmiths who were quite probably trained by Hutton, advertised from 1810 to 1829. Their early work somewhat resembles Hutton's, but their later products were heavy and clumsy. A few silversmiths worked in Albany after Shepherd and Boyd, but little of worth was produced.

In the century and a half that separated Shepherd and Boyd from Kiliaen Van Rensselaer, Albany had developed from a tiny isolated community to a thriving city that had become the capital of a great state. This change was inevitably reflected in the silver made there. The hand fashioning of silver is an intimate craft. Isaac Hutton was one of the last of the old-time silversmiths working in this tradition. By the time his career ended, hand craftsmanship could no longer carry its own weight in supplying the demand. From the beginning of the nineteenth century, new production methods began to spell the end of the way of life that included the hand craftsman and the beginning of the industrial era.

smith in the life of the eighteenth-century community.

Koenradt's eldest son Jacob, whom Dr. George B. Cutten has called one of the best of the Ten Eyck smiths, was also prominent in the public life of Albany. In 1732 he was appointed high constable, from 1743 to 1747 he was alderman for the First Ward, from 1748 to 1750 mayor and coroner for the city, and in 1767 a judge of the Court of Common Pleas. He received his training as a silversmith under Cornelius Kierstede and Charles LeRoux, and was an expert engraver, as may be judged by the bowl illustrated.

THREE-PIECE TEA SET by Isaac Hutton.

COVERED MILK PITCHER *(c.1826)* and cups *(c.1815)*, by Shepherd and Boyd.

Fig. 1. Demihorse mark on Schuyler teapot, here tentatively attributed to Kiliaen Van Rensselaer III. *New-York Historical Society.*

Fig. 2. Seventeenth-century silver teapot with Schuyler arms and demihorse mark; possibly by Kiliaen Van Rensselaer III. *New-York Historical Society.*

BY JOHN D. KERNAN JR.

The demihorse: mark of a silversmithing Van Rensselaer?

THE SILVERSMITH'S PRACTICE OF using a pictorial device to identify his work died out gradually in England in the course of the seventeenth century: the last one recorded in Jackson's *English Goldsmiths and Their Marks* is three storks, used in London in 1692/3. It is somewhat surprising, therefore, since this was long after silversmithing had begun in the Colonies, that no instance of the use by a colonial silversmith of such a device alone has heretofore been generally recognized; and it seems not at all improbable that there are pieces of colonial silver not thought to be such simply because they are stamped with a device, rather than with initials.

At least one piece of silver, a teapot of primitive type marked (Fig. 1) four times on the bottom with a demihorse, placed crestlike on a torse (a wreath composed of twisted strands), was classified by C. Louise Avery as of early New York workmanship when on loan to a special exhibition at the Metropolitan Museum of Art from December 8, 1931, to January 31, 1932. But to its owner, the New-York Historical Society, the teapot (Fig. 2) remained "Possibly Dutch or German" and was so labeled until recently, even though its mark does not appear in the standard reference books on silver of those countries.

Seventeenth-century teapots of any nationality are so rare that no one can say that the form of this one is distinctively of the Continent, of the mother country, or of the Colonies. Nonetheless, its decoration as well as its background fully justify Miss Avery's attribution: the mantling in which its Schuyler arms are engraved has a definite New York flavor, it bears the chaplet of leaves and roses seen only on New York pieces, and it is decorated at the top with wriggle wire and at the bottom with graduated ridges. (See ANTIQUES, January 1947, p. 35, where this same pot is referred to in an article on a then newly discovered New York teapot.) In addition to the Schuyler arms, the teapot is engraved, in reverse cipher, with the initials *JES*—probably those of Johannes and Elizabeth (Staats) Schuyler, who were married in 1695. On the basis of its style it could have been made in that very year.

The recent emergence of another piece of silver, identically marked, of a form that is unmistakably in the English tradition and quite unknown in the Netherlands or Germany, of a size that all but precludes its being English, and with engraving also pointing to a New York background, affords a firm basis for recording the mark as that of a colonial smith and confirms the Metropolitan's recognition of the pot as American.

This other piece of silver is the finely made porringer shown in Figures 3 and 4. It bears the demihorse touch on the rim at either side of the handle, and on the front in an early-style frame of feathery leaves is skillfully engraved a crest that is, oddly enough, also a demihorse, but facing in the other direction as is heraldically correct. On the handle are the initials VH conjoined, much less skillfully and probably more recently cut. Since the crest is that of both the Bayard and the Ten Broeck families (see Bolton's *American Armory*, Boston, 1927, pp. 11 and 162), and the conjoined initials point to a Dutch surname, its manufacture and original ownership in the colony of New York are all but certain.

It is possible to surmise from the crest and added initials that the porringer was made for Samuel and Margaret (van Cortlandt) Bayard, who were married in 1696, and later became the property of their daughter Margaret who married James van Horne in 1742. (See *The Bayard Family; an address read before the New York Branch of the Order of Colonial Lords of Manors in America*, April 1927, by Mrs. Anson Phelps Atterbury, Baltimore, 1928, p. 16; and Charles Selwyn Williams, *Jan Cornelis Van Horne and his Descendants*, New York, 1912, p. 47). By its style it too could have been made in the 1690's. Because the stamp is the crest in reverse, one might conclude that it is an owner's, rather than a maker's, mark. This would be plausible were the porringer the only piece so marked, but it is unlikely in view of the use of this device on the Schuyler teapot.

The names of virtually none of the silversmiths who used the various devices in England are known, and it is not odd, therefore, that no one, to the best of my knowledge, has ever suggested a name for the user of the demihorse mark. But at least two tempting speculations come to mind. One, that a Bayard or a Ten Broeck used his family's crest as his mark, stumbles because no Bayard or Ten Broeck is known, or suspected, to have been a silversmith.

Another surmise, suggested by the close resemblance of the porringer handle to those used by early Boston makers (see Bigelow, *Historic Silver of the Colonies and Its Makers*, for examples by Dummer, Winslow, and Coney), coupled with the New York and particularly the Albany associations of the two pieces, is that the maker was none other than Kiliaen Van Rensselaer (1663-1719), who after an apprenticeship to an unknown New York craftsman was apprenticed in Boston to "Mr. Jeremy Dommer," and whose mother later "had him put up the silversmith's shop in the country" (*buyten* in this text means outside the town limits of Albany and probably near the family's house at Watervliet). (See *Correspondence of Maria Van Rensselaer, 1669-1689*, translated and edited by A. J. F. van Laer, Albany, 1935,

S. V. Cortlandt to Maria Van Rensselaer, c. August 10, 1682; Maria Van Rensselaer to Richard Van Rensselaer, August 15 (?), 1683; introduction, p. 5). This surmise is not as startling as it might at first seem, when it is recalled that the Van Rensselaers' immediate ancestors in Holland were jewelers. (W. de Vries, "The van Rensselaers in the Netherlands," in *De Nederlandsche Leeuw*, May/June 1949; *Historic Families of America*, edited by Walter W. Spooner, New York, 1707-1708). It is reinforced by Kiliaen's close relationship to both the Van Cortlandts and the Schuylers. It would, furthermore, account for the scarcity of his pieces, because Kiliaen can be supposed to have devoted little time to his craft after 1687 when he inherited the Manor of Rensselaerswyck. However, no reason for his adopting the mark—if his it be—is now apparent; it does not seem, from this heraldic amateur's researches, to have been lifted from any of his ancestors' coats of arms.

Clearly, the emergence of the porringer calls for an intensive search for other demihorse pieces, as well as for further study of silver in colonial forms and with colonial associations but with devices, rather than initials, as marks—if any there be.

Fig. 3. Silver porringer bearing demihorse touch and demihorse engraved crest; possibly by Kiliaen Van Rensselaer III.
Author's collection; photographs by courtesy of Gebelein Silversmiths.

Fig. 4. Detail of porringer showing maker's marks.

THE TEN EYCK SILVERSMITHS

By GEORGE BARTON CUTTEN

KOENRAET TEN EYCK was granted a lot on the west side of what is now Broad Street, New York, in 1651. Presumably he arrived from Holland the preceding year. He brought with him his wife, Maria Boele, his two sons, and a daughter. Eight more children were born to them in New Amsterdam. This wife died about 1681, and in 1682 he married Annetje Daniels, widow of Herman Smeemans. Koenraet was a cordwainer and tanner, and apparently successful. He seems to have taken an active part in the life of his new place of residence and held several appointive positions. He was elder and deacon of the Reformed Dutch Church. He died in 1687.

Koenraet's oldest son, Jacob, was born in Holland. He lived for some years in New Amsterdam with his father, but later moved to Fort Orange (Albany), where he married Geertruy Coeymans, and where he likewise followed the tanner's trade. He was the father of six children, all born in Albany. He died in 1693.

Koenraet Ten Eyck (*1678-1753*) was Jacob's oldest son. Through confusing him with some one of his four first cousins of the same name, he has in the past been regarded as a New York City silversmith; as late as the 1938 exhibition of *Silver by New York [City] Makers* at the Museum of the City of New York, Koenraet Ten Eyck's name was included, three of his pieces were exhibited, and two of the three illustrated in the catalogue. The evidence, however, seems to show that apart from the years of his apprenticeship, which he may have spent in New York, he lived virtually all his life in Albany. In Pearson's *Genealogies of First Settlers of Albany* appears the name, Coenroad Ten Eyck, silversmith (*1678-1753*). He was born in Albany April 9, 1678; October 15, 1704, he married Geertje Van Schaick in Albany; January 23, 1753, he died in Albany.

"Att a Mayor's Court held in ye City Hall of Albany the 29th of January 1702/3," the first name on the list of jurors is *Coonraet ten Eyck*. October 14, 1704, he was appointed assessor and constable in Albany. In the minutes of the

Common Council of the City of Albany, February 28, 1706/7, a memorandum regarding the purchase of lands names *Coonradt ten Eyck* as one of a committee to supervise the matter. April 13, 1706, Robert Livingston and Coenraet Ten Eyck were appointed to see that the bridge over Rutten Kill be repaired. September 28 of the same year they brought in "their account for same, amounting in all to £7:14:4½ which is approved by council and ordered that they have credit in ye City book for what is due them."

In a 1720 list of freeholders of the city and county of Albany is the name *Coonrodt Tennyck*.

July 4, 1744, "Coenraet Ten Eyck, Gerrit Lansing and Christopher Yates being sent for according to the directions of an Act of Assembly, entitled an Act for the more effective fortifying of the City of Albany, to agree for as much of their ground as the fortifications of this city are directed to be built upon, who all appeared at this board, and as the price cannot be agreed upon, it is Resolved that warrants issue to the Sheriff to summon jurors to appraise the same according to the said Act of Assembly." He was a representative to the Colonial Assembly for 1747 to 1750.

The facts that Koenraet was a freeholder in 1720, in contrast to a leaseholder, and that he participated in these activities and held these offices from 1702 to 1750, which were within the rights of a freeman only, show conclusively that he was a freeman of Albany during this period and presumably did his work there.

Of his ten children born between 1705 and 1728 all but the third were baptized in Albany. The third one was baptized September 17, 1710, in New York. In the record of this baptism the parents are designated *Coenraet Ten Yk, Gerretje Van Schaik, van Albany*. So this New York baptismal record, instead of casting doubt on the Albany residence, really confirms it. It may have been that this birth took place during his apprenticeship, but "van Albany" makes this very doubtful.

Where or with whom this Koenraet learned his trade we

do not know, but it is most probable that it was with some-one in New York. The appearance of his silver has a definite New York character. He was admitted a freeman in New York, May 8, 1716: this is the only known incident in his career which would tie him definitely to New York, and probably means no more than that his master in this way certified him as competent. Edward F. de Lancey gives the following information regarding freedom in New York:

To be admitted . . . as a Freeman, the applicant had to be chosen by the city authorities, take an oath of fidelity to the city, pay the prescribed fees, and be duly registered. The only exception was the case of Apprentices who had served seven years. Hence, closely connected with the Freeman under the charter, were their Apprentices, and the system of binding them out then in vogue. For every apprentice upon duly attaining the end of his apprenticeship was entitled to, and did become a Freeman without the payment of any fees, and able to practice his trade or occupation in the city, and vote, and be eligible to office therein.

While seven years was considered the time required for an apprentice to learn a trade, the common council of New York voted January 16, 1695, that the term required for the completion of apprenticeship and the admission to freedom should be not less than four years, and then only on the recommendation of the apprentice's master.

In the New York City register of freemen, one of the following designations appears after certain names: *R, P,* or *complimented.* These designations are interpreted thus: in the few cases where we find *complimented,* an exalted visitor has been presented with the freedom of the city; *P* means that the man in question was approved by the city authorities and had *paid* his fees; *R* signifies that he was *registered* first as an apprentice and later as a freeman. The *R* which appears after Koenraet Ten Eyck's name indicates, if it does not prove, that he was apprenticed in New York.

There were certain restrictions about the length of time a person could be absent from the city without losing his freedom, but there were no means of forcing a person to remain in the city after having received it. Why Koenraet Ten Eyck should wish to be a freeman of New York while living and working in Albany, we do not know. There must have been some special reason why he should become a free-man when thirty-eight years old. His son, Jacob, who undoubtedly served his apprenticeship in New York, was not admitted freeman there.

Five years before Koenraet became a freeman in New York, the authorities at Albany passed the following ordinance, and re-enacted it in 1712 and 1713:

Whereas complaints are made that severall persons in this city do presume to retaile and use manual occupations without being made freemen or citizens of ye sd City: It is therefore publish^d, ordain^d, and declar^d yt no person or persons shall hereafter sell or expose to sale by retaile any ware or merchandise by themselves or any other person or persons whatsoever, or use any trade or mystery or manuall occupation in ye sd city or liberties thereof, unless he or they shall have his or their freedom and be actuall dwellers and inhabitants of ye City afores^d.

We have no early records or register of freemen of Albany, but, since Koenraet was born there and his father had been long a resident there, it may not have been necessary for him to go through any formality to acquire his freedom.

It is said by Stephen G. C. Ensko and others that he was "Appointed Official Adjuster of Scales and Measures and elected to various minor civil offices," presumably in New York. There is no record of Koenraet Ten Eyck's being appointed to such an office in New York, but in 1702, he was appointed Adjuster of Weights and Measures in Albany, as the following document attests:

Albany ye 21st of Feb. 1701/2. A proclamation proclaimed that all persons within this City and County doe cause their weights and measures be adjusted by Coenraet ten Eyck, in ye space of six months, upon pain of forfeiting ye sum of sixty shillings; and who ever as shall send bags to ye mill with Corn without ye owners mark forfeits ye bags for ye behooffe of ye . . . and sheriffe; Ye sd Coenraet is sworne this day Eyk master, who is allowed for ye stamp on weights ld. and on ye schepel 9d.

The explanation seems to be that Koenraet Ten Eyck of Albany had a cousin of the same name in New York. The latter was the son of Dirck Ten Eyck and Aefje Boelen (a sister of the noted New York silversmith Jacob Boelen).

Fig. 1 (*left*) — Tankard by Koenraet Ten Eyck. Check list No. 1. The engraving on the front is shown above. *Owned by Walter M. Jeffords.*

Fig. 2 (*above, right*) — Trencher Salt by Koenraet Ten Eyck. Check list No. 7. *Owned by Mrs. Henry G. Bartol; photograph from Museum of the City of New York.*

Fig. 3 (*right*) — Mug by Koenraet Ten Eyck. Check list No. 4. *From the Mabel Brady Garvan Collection, Yale University Art Gallery.*

FIG. 4 (*above*) — TEAPOT BY JACOB TEN EYCK. Check list No. 1. *Owned by Edsel Ford.*

FIG. 5 (*right*) — TRENCHER SALT BY JACOB TEN EYCK. Check list No. 12. *From the Metropolitan Museum of Art.*

FIG. 6 (*below*) — MUG BY JACOB TEN EYCK. Check list No. 10. *From the Detroit Institute of Art.*

It is this cousin, Koenraet, to whom C. Louise Avery mistakenly refers as the silversmith. He was baptized June 15, 1684, in New York. His will was dated January 11, 1758, and proved May 3, 1762: it begins, "I, Koenraet Ten Eyck, of New York, Cordwainer."

There are further complications: three other cousins of the same name were living in New York. Five of the sons of the original Koenraet Ten Eyck named a son Koenraet, and four of these five were born and baptized in New York. I have already mentioned two of these five—let us now consider the others.

Koenraet Ten Eyck, the fifth child of Tobias Ten Eyck and Elizabeth Hegeman, was baptized March 6, 1687, and died December 28, 1744. In his will, he calls himself a bolter by trade. Another document refers to him as a baker; at any rate he worked with flour, and not with silver.

Koenraet Ten Eyck, the eldest son of Koenraet Ten Eyck and Belitje Herex, was baptized December 13, 1675, and died March 31, 1762. He was a cordwainer, and became a freeman September 6, 1698. He held several civic offices; in 1714 he was collector of the south ward; in 1722 to 1723 he was asses-

sor of dock ward; in 1732 he was deacon of Collegiate-Reformed Dutch School.

Koenraet Ten Eyck, the third son of Hendrick Ten Eyck and Petronella de Wit, was baptized September 13, 1680. We know little about him: he was married in New Jersey, and both his children were born in that state; the second one was baptized August 11, 1728.

Two of these New York cousins were cordwainers and the third was a bolter. The New Jersey cousin can be excluded from present consideration. This leaves the Koenraet of Albany in exclusive possession of the title of silversmith.

Only twelve years separated the oldest of these five cousins of the same name from the youngest. Any of the three who lived in New York might have received the appointments which have been mentioned as going to Koenraet Ten Eyck, the silversmith.

The following skeleton family tree shows the relationship of the five cousins:

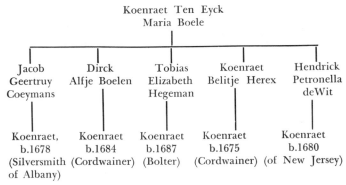

Koenraet Ten Eyck
Maria Boele

Jacob Geertruy Coeymans	Dirck Alfje Boelen	Tobias Elizabeth Hegeman	Koenraet Belitje Herex	Hendrick Petronella deWit
Koenraet, b.1678 (Silversmith of Albany)	Koenraet b.1684 (Cordwainer)	Koenraet b.1687 (Bolter)	Koenraet b.1675 (Cordwainer)	Koenraet b.1680 (of New Jersey)

Fortunately several fine pieces by this craftsman still exist as proof of his skill. His trencher salt (*Fig. 2*) is one of the earliest American salts, and one of the few of its time. His tankards have the typical New York shape and ornamentation, with cockscrew thumbpiece and cut-card ornamentation around the bottom (*Fig. 1*). His lion-rampant handle ornament is not unique. His most original piece is the tapered, straight-sided mug (*Fig. 3*), with molded bands at top and bottom and around the center of the body, but mugs somewhat like this were made by other New York and foreign smiths. Indeed, the shape of the mug and the use of five bands might be attributed to John Coney of Boston; the distinctive feature in Koenraet's creation is the use of a spiral wire in the center of the group of bands—a typical, Dutch detail, never used by a New England smith. Simeon Soumain made a similar mug, but instead of the spiral wire decoration, he used a cut-card border above the set of bands, at the base. Banded mugs of this shape were made as late as Paul Revere's day, but Revere used as many as ten plain bands in a group.

Jacob C. Ten Eyck (*1705-1793*) was the oldest son of Koenraet Ten Eyck, silversmith, and was baptized April 29, 1705. In one document he is referred to as Jacob Coenraedts Ten Eyck. Like his father, he was born in Albany; he married Catharyna Cuyler August 17, 1736; he died September 9, 1793. With the exception of the time served as apprentice, he lived in Albany. He was prominent in civic affairs. In 1732 he was appointed high constable. In the 1742 list of freeholders of Albany Jacob C. Ten Eyck is named in the first ward. In 1743 he is mentioned as alderman for the first ward, an office which he held through 1747. October 14, 1748, "Jacob C. Ten Eyck produced a commission for mayor of the city of Albany . . . for the ensuing year and took the oaths appointed by law, signed the Test and was sworn into office of mayor and coroner for the city, and Justice of the

Peace for the city and county of Albany." He continued in office for the years 1749 and 1750. In one document, dated 1750, he attests, as mayor of Albany, the authenticity of a report. He was also a judge of the Court of Common Pleas in 1767. In 1775 he was a member of the Albany Committee of Correspondence, and of a sub-committee "to receive donations for the Poor at the Town of Boston." An Anti-Federalist, he opposed the adoption of the Constitution in 1788.

As a boy, Jacob Ten Eyck doubtless gained familiarity with silversmithing in his father's shop, but shortly after passing his fourteenth birthday he was apprenticed by his father to Charles LeRoux, goldsmith, of New York. We are fortunate in having a copy of the indenture of apprenticeship. Jacob C. Ten Eyck was a credit to his master, to judge from his silver that survives.

The original of the broad-based, pear-shaped teapots made by the New York smiths in the second quarter of the eighteenth century is traced by some critics to the bulbous pot made by John Coney. But this form seems much more closely related to the octagonal and other pots made in England and Holland a short time before, and is probably a direct adaptation of these. At any rate, we find a fine pot of this style (*Fig. 4*), made by Jacob Ten Eyck, very similar to those made by Peter Van Dyck, Nicholas Roosevelt, John Brevoort, Adrian Bancker, Simeon Soumain, Thauvet Besley, John LeRoux, Charles LeRoux, and others. It is natural that Jacob should follow his master, Charles LeRoux, in using this style, and this pot is more nearly identical with the LeRoux pot than with that of any other smith.

Two other items, a mug (*Fig. 6*) and a trencher salt (*Fig. 5*), display more originality. The slight curvature of this mug seems to show the beginning of the transition from the straight-sided, tapering mug, made by his father, to the bulbous mugs and cans so common in the latter half of the 1700's. Besides some New York examples, similar mugs were made by William Pollard and John Blowers of Boston, but both of the latter approach more closely the later bulbous type. There is a John Coney mug in the Museum of Fine Arts, Boston, less developed than those by Pollard and Blowers, and more like that by Jacob Ten Eyck. Some English mugs are very similar.

Another claim to originality might be made for Jacob Ten

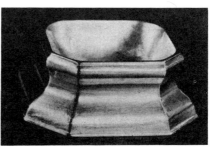

Eyck in connection with his trencher salts. One of these is unusually high and tapering, with a broad rounding band at top and bottom, chased with diagonal lines suggesting gadrooning. Between the bands is a simple design of additional chasing like punchwork. Again we have a somewhat similar example by John Coney, whose trencher salt has gadrooning

on the upper band encircling it, but not on the lower.

Jacob, a disciple of Charles LeRoux, was an expert engraver, and probably deserves to be classed as the best of the Ten Eyck smiths.

Barent Ten Eyck (*1714-1795*) was the fifth child of Koenraet Ten Eyck, the silversmith. He was born in Albany, and was baptized October 3, 1714. He married a woman whose first name was Effie, and who died in 1791. They had no surviving issue. He died February 27, 1795. We do not know with whom he learned silversmithing, but probably it was with his father; as he was nine years younger than his brother Jacob, he may have been apprenticed to him.

Barent seems to have been less conspicuous in civic affairs than Jacob. However, in 1742 he was appointed firemaster in the second ward, and in 1746 and 1747 he was elected assistant alderman in the second ward. In the latter year he was entrusted with an important commission by the City Council. The annals of September 17, 1748, record the following resolution: "Resolved by this board that Barent Ten Eyck and Johannis Vol: Dow go and desire Langaseri and the other French Gent that came with the flag Truces from Canada, to come to Ackerman's to let the Mayor and Corporation know the meaning of their coming to this town." It is later recorded, "French Gent appeared." In 1794 he subscribed £40 toward the establishment of Union College.

In his will Barent directed his estate to be divided into seven parts, one part to go to each of his brothers or sisters, or, where any were deceased, to their heirs. One section of his will reads, "to my nephew John De Wandelaer, £40. I also give him my silver tankard forever."

Scarcely enough silver of his remains to permit of a critical judgment of his craftsmanship. There may, however, be an explanation for the lack of domestic silver made by him: he seems to have taken part in a business of considerable proportions which was carried on with the Indians, and possibly the bulk of his production was trade silver. In Sir William Johnson's papers we find his instructions for barter at Fort Niagara in 1764, listing equivalents in barter to govern Indian trade. A "silver arm band of ye largest" was equivalent to "3 Bever." Also mentioned are silver wristbands, earbobs, brooches, crosses, hair plates for women, gorgets for men, gold lockets, silver medals, and silver breast buckles. As many as forty gorgets were received in one lot. Usually the silver goods are named in the accounts, but not the maker. However, three entries mention Barent Ten Eyck, in 1756, 1758, and 1769.

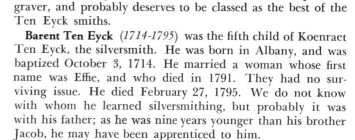

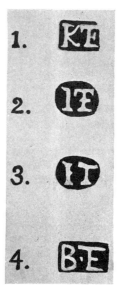

Fig. 7 (*left*) — Gorget by Barent Ten Eyck. Check list No. 2. *From the Museum of the American Indian, Heye Foundation.*

Fig. 8 (*below*) — Trencher Salt by Barent Ten Eyck. Check list No. 3. *Owned by Grace Edith Polgreen.*

Fig. 9 (*right*) — Marks of the Ten Eyck Silversmiths. *1,* Koenraet; *2, 3,* Jacob; *4,* Barent.

The following pieces of silver made by the Ten Eyck silversmiths have been traced. Those starred are here illustrated.

Koenraet Ten Eyck

*1. Tankard (*Fig. 1*). Height, 6½ inches; diameter of base, 5⅝ inches; weight, 30 ounces 18 pennyweight. Initialed *L/IHG*. Made for Johannes Henricus Lidius and his wife Genevieve. Engraved on front with the coat of arms of the Lidius family. Owner, Walter M. Jeffords.

2. Tankard. Height, 7⅞ inches; diameter of base, 5⅛ inches; weight, 25 ounces 14 pennyweight. Initialed *G.V.S.* on handle. Made for Gerrit Van Schaick, born 1650, married Alida Van Slichtenhorst, 1679. Present owner unknown.

3. Mug. Height, 3⅝ inches; diameter of base, 3 7/16 inches; weight, 7 ounces 17 pennyweight. Initialed *S/I*E* on handle. Probably made for Johannes Schuyler and his wife Elizabeth Staats. Cipher on the front. Owner, Metropolitan Museum of Art.

*4. Mug (*Fig. 3*). Height, 3½ inches; diameter of base, 3¼ inches. Rim, midband, and base reeded. Meander wire decoration. Scroll handle with beaded rat tail. Owner, Mabel Brady Garvan collection, Yale University Art Gallery.

5. Mug. Height, 3⅜ inches; diameter of base, 3¼ inches; diameter of top, 2¾ inches. Chased foliated border at top next to which are six bands. At bottom also six bands. Wire handle on which is mark. Owner, Albany Institute of History and Art.

6. Salvers (a pair). Height, 1 inch; diameter, 6½ inches. Plain with Chippendale rim and mask and shell. They stand on three scroll feet. Owner, James B. Neale.

*7. Trencher salt (*Fig. 2*). Height, 2 3/16 inches; diameter of base, 3 5/16 inches; diameter of top, 3⅛ inches; weight, 2 ounces 11 pennyweight. Chased band at top and bottom. Owner, Mrs. Henry G. Bartol; now in the Museum of the City of New York.

8. Tablespoon. Length, 7⅝ inches. Initialed *A*G/G/B*H*. The upper letters are said to have been for Abraham Gouverneur. Trifid end. Elliptical bowl. Rat tail, double-lined along the edges and beaded down the center. Owner, Edmund Bury.

9. Tablespoon. Length, 7 7/16 inches; weight, 1 ounce 18 pennyweight. Initialed *M V V*, possible for Maria Van Vechten. Wavy end. Rat tail. Owner, Metropolitan Museum of Art.

10. Punch ladle. Handle three-quarters wood. Boat-shape bowl. Mark on bottom. Initials in the bowl just under handle. Owner, Arthur Michael.

Jacob C. Ten Eyck

*1. Teapot (*Fig. 4*). Height, 7 inches. Pear shape. High domed cover with molded band hinged to outer part of socket. Wooden knob pierced by ornamental silver bolt. Duck-neck spout, octagonal in section, capped so as to appear like a bird's beak. Owner, Edsel Ford.

2. Tankard. Height, 7 inches. Initialed *C/A*C*. Made for his wife's parents, Abraham and Catherine Cuyler. Plain, typical New York form. No foliated band. Raised flat top, serrated front edge, special thumbpiece, scrolled handle with rat tail, and oval on tip. Mark, No. 3. Owner, Mabel Brady Garvan collection, Yale University Art Gallery.

3. Tankard. Height, 6⅛ inches; diameter of base, 5 7/16 inches; weight, 36 ounces, 7 pennyweight. Initialed *L/P*C* on handle. Belonged to Philip Livingston, second Lord of the Manor (*1686-1749*) and Catherine Van Brugh (*1689-1756*) who were married in 1707. Mark, No. 2. Owner, Arthur Iselin Jr.

4. Wine bowl. Height, 1¾ inches; diameter, 3½ inches. Initialed *M/IVS* and in contemporary script *VS/IM*. Two twisted wire handles. Four-paneled body. Engraved design. Mark, No. 2. Owner, Mabel Brady Garvan collection, Yale University Art Gallery.

5. Bowl. Height, 3¾ inches; diameter, 7¾ inches. Initialed on the bottom *B/D*M*. Made for Dirck Ten Broeck and Margaret Cuyler, who were married November 26, 1714. Plain cylindrical foot with flat rim. Two cast scroll handles with beading and caryatids. Sides chased in six shaped panels, each enclosing repoussé flower. Mark, No. 2. Owner, Elizabeth W. Jackson.

6. Rapier. Length, 36 inches. Silver handle bound with twisted silver wire. Mark, No. 3 on branch. Owner, Mabel Brady Garvan collection, Yale University Art Gallery.

7. Cream jug. Height, 3¾ inches; diameter, 2⅛ inches. Initialed *MS*, and *J E C* in Old English letters. Pear-shaped body, pinched spout, double-scrolled handle, and three scroll legs. Mark, No. 3. Owner, Mabel Brady Garvan collection, Yale University Art Gallery.

8. Cream jug. Similar to No. 7. Sold in the Garvan sale of 1931. but not traced since then.

9. Mug. Height, 4 1/16 inches; diameter, 4 11/16 inches; weight, 9 ounces 12 pennyweight. Initialed on base *J D* in deeply cut script letters, and *P G* in block letters for Jonas Douw and Peter Gansevoort. The arms of the Douw family are engraved on the front. Mark, No. 2. Owner, Metropolitan Museum of Art.

*10. Mug (*Fig. 6*). Height, 4 inches; diameter of base, 3⅜ inches; diameter of top, 2 13/16 inches. Slightly tapering with flaring rim and round foot. Curves in sharply at the bottom. Solid double-scroll handle, with drop on body and extended sharp-pointed tip. Mark, No. 3. Made for Margaret Shipman in 1791. Owner, Detroit Institute of Art.

11. Salt. Height, 2⅜ inches. Initialed *F/H*M*. Owner, Henry F. du Pont.

*12. Trencher salt (*Fig. 5*). Height, 2¼ inches; diameter of base, 4 1/16 inches; weight, 2 ounces 15.6 pennyweight. Initialed *T B* imposed over *D M* in script on drum. Probably made for Dirck Ten Broeck and Margaret Cuyler, as was No. 5. Margaret Cuyler was a sister of Jacob Ten Eyck's wife. Owner, Metropolitan Museum of Art.

13. Basting spoon. Length, 14¾ inches. Initialed *W/I*S*. Forward turn. Rat tail. Mark, No. 2 twice. Owner, Mabel Brady Garvan collection, Yale University Art Gallery.

14. Tablespoon. Length, 7½ inches. Forward turn. Mid rib. Initialed *P G*. Mark, No. 2 twice. Owner, Albany Institute of History and Art.

15. Snuffbox. Length, 2 inches; width, 1⅝ inches; height, ⅞ inches. Engraved cipher *T E* on bottom; also intials *N T E*, probably for Neeltje Ten Eyck, born in Albany, 1726. Top of box is engraved with a decoration of a lion in a forest. Mark, No. 2 on inside of bottom. Owner, Mrs. N. H. Green.

16. Gold ring. Engraved *I V R obit 2 octo: 1730 E 25*. Mark, No. 2. Owner, Albany Institute of History and Art.

Barent Ten Eyck

1. Tankard. Height, 7 inches; diameter of base, 5½ inches; diameter of lip, 4 9/16 inches; weight, 34 ounces. Initialed on applique of hinge *L/P*C*, probably for Philip Livingstone and Christiana Ten Broeck, who were married in 1740. Straight tapering sides, molded lip and applied base band. Flat domed cover with wide rim serrated and engraved at front. Corkscrew thumbpiece. Broad scroll handle. Thick drop below hinge tapering to rat tail. Large, flat, elliptical boss on tip. Owner, Amor Hollingsworth Jr.

*2. Gorget (*Fig. 7*). Hanging in place, height, 4⅝ inches; width, 5⅞ inches. Coat of arms of Great Britain rudely engraved in center where silver is 2⅛ inches wide. A hole is pierced at each end. *Danyel Cryn 1775* engraved on front. Owner, Museum of the American Indian, Heye Foundation.

*3. Trencher salt (*Fig. 8*). Height, 1⅛ inches; length, 2⅞ inches; width, 2⅜ inches; depth of bowl, ⅜ inches. Oblong, octagonal, curved sides. Mark inside bowl. Owner, Grace Edith Polgreen.

4. Funeral spoon. Length, 7 11/16 inches. Initialed *A V S*. Forward turn, leaf drop. Engraved on the back of handle *pat Kyll van Rense gebod 28 Feber 1655 obut dn 3 Mart 1687*. Owner, Metropolitan Museum of Art.

5. Tablespoon. Length, 8 5/16 inches. Initialed *C/M*W*. Forward turn, elliptical shaped bowl with long leaf drop. Owner, George B. Cutten.

6. Teaspoon. Length, 4⅝ inches. Initialed *C T E* (last two imposed); evidently made for a member of the Ten Eyck family. Forward turn, midrib, elliptical-shape bowl with triple drop. Owner, George B. Cutten.

7. Tablespoon. Length, 8⅜ inches. Initialed *E R B*. Believed to have been owned by Elizabeth Roseboom. Forward-turn handle with short molded ridge. Elliptical bowl with long double-molded drop. Owner, Mabel Brady Garvan collection, Yale University Art Gallery.

8. Teapot. John Marshall Phillips reports having seen a teapot by Barent Ten Eyck in Scotland.

The Verplanck cup

BY LOUISE C. BELDEN, *Assistant curator, Henry Francis du Pont Winterthur Museum*

AMONG THE HANDSOME domestic silver objects made by American craftsmen in the eighteenth century is the two-handled covered cup on a pedestal. More than a dozen examples by such silversmiths as John Burt, Jacob Hurd, John Coney, and William Swan have long been admired for their magnificent proportions, imposing contours, and ornate inscriptions. Ordered by men of wealth to mark important occasions, they stand out as high lights not only of America's decorative arts but of its social history.

The Henry Francis du Pont Winterthur Museum has recently added a fine example of this form to the collection of New York silver displayed in its Queen Anne Dining Room (Fig. 1). It was made by the New York Huguenot Bartholomew Le Roux II (1717-1763) for a member of the Verplanck family, in which it has descended through more than two centuries. Family tradition says that it was originally owned by a William Verplanck. Of the three or four Williams (or Gulys, Gulians, and Guilliens) on the family tree, the Gulian Verplanck who was born in New York City in 1698 seems the logical first owner for several reasons. An affluent merchant in extensive trade with Holland and the West Indies and a member of the colonial legislature, he held, between about 1737 and his death in 1751, a position in society enjoyed by other men in the Colonies who ordered similar impressive silver pieces. The period coincides with the years when Bartholomew Le Roux was active in his craft. Furthermore, during those fourteen years, Gulian was married at the advanced age of thirty-nine and his seven children were born—all events giving cause for celebration and the purchase of a fine cup.

Gulian married Mary Crommelin (b. 1712), the daughter of an Amsterdam merchant, and in 1737 brought her from Holland to his house on Wall Street. A history of the Verplanck family says that Gulian owned "houses and buildings" on Wall Street, one of which was "large . . . and of yellow Dutch brick" next to his "lott of ground and stable thereon near the City Hall" (*The History of Abraham Isaacse Verplanck and His Male Descendants in America* by William Edward Verplanck, Fishkill Landing,

Fig. 1. The Verplanck cup. Silver two-handled cup made by Bartholomew Le Roux II (1717-1763), New York, for a member of the Verplanck family, New York probably between 1737 and 1751. The hollow handles, plain face, molded mid-band, and high-domed cover are in contrast to the earlier style of cup with solid cast caryatid handles, *repoussé* acanthus leaves, and flat cover made by Bartholomew Le Roux I (c. 1663-1713) probably for Lord Cornbury, royal governor of New York from 1702 to 1708, which was given by Mr. and Mrs. James S. Bell to the Minneapolis Institute of Arts. Mark: B LR (conjoined) in oval twice on bottom of cup outside. Over-all height, 13¾ inches; over-all width, 12¾ inches; diameter of cup at lip, 6⅝ inches. *Henry Francis du Pont Winterthur Museum; photographs by Gilbert Ask.*

Fig. 1a. Mark of Bartholomew Le Roux II, B LR (conjoined) in oval, struck twice on underside of base of Verplanck cup. A tentative strike of Le Roux's die next to one of the marks has impressed the metal of the cup to form the top two thirds of the R of the B LR mark.

Fig. 2. Silver two-handled cup made by Elias Pelletreau (1726-1810), New York; engraved with the windmill wings and the stars of the Van Cortlandt arms. The finial, which suggests a closed flower or bud, rare in American silversmithing, is like those on a number of French silver objects. The three pairs of handles on Figs. 1, 2, and 3 look as though they could have been cast from the same mold. Mark: E P in rectangle. Over-all height, 12⅞ inches; diameter of cup at lip, 6¾ inches. *Privately owned; on loan to the Museum of the City of New York.*

Fig 3. Silver two-handled cup made by Myer Myers (1723-1795), New York, for a member of the Stuyvesant family of New York. It was given by Elizabeth Stuyvesant (1775-1854), who married Colonel Nicholas Fish in 1803, to their daughter, Elizabeth Fish Morris of New York. It descended through the family to the great-great-granddaughter of Elizabeth Stuyvesant. The finial, a ball with a square flat block fastened horizontally through its center, is, like the finial on the Pelletreau cup, of unusual design. So, too, is the high-domed base. Mark: MYERS in italics in conforming rectangle under foot and on cover. Over-all height, 14 inches. *Collection of Elsie O. and Philip D. Sang; photograph by courtesy of Parke-Bernet Galleries.*

New York, 1892). He also owned a gambrel-roof house, Mount Gulian, which was built at Fishkill, Dutchess County, on part of the Rombout Patent that his grandfather Gulian Verplanck (1637-1684) had bought in 1683. In 1783 the Society of the Cincinnati was formed at Mount Gulian, which burned in the fall of 1931. Besides these two properties, Gulian owned land in what were in his day Albany and Ulster Counties, though they are referred to in the Verplanck history as "the Hardenburgh Patent."

Gulian and Mary Verplanck's first child, Samuel, was born in 1738, a year after their marriage, but lived only ten days. Their second son, also named Samuel, was born the next year. According to the Verplanck biographer, Gulian's will, dated July 5, 1750, gave "to his wife, Mary, all the household furniture, jewels, plate, etc. and four negro slaves, together with an annuity of £200 and the use of the rents and profits of 'my house in Wall street wherein I now live' until his wife marries again or 'until my son (Samuel) shall attain the age of twenty-three.'" Samuel lived to inherit his father's bequest to Mary and to become a wealthy importer and banker, one of the twenty-four founders of the New York Chamber of Commerce in 1768, and a member of the Committee of Safety during the American Revolution. The descendants of Samuel have owned the cup down to the present generation, and the furniture he used in the Wall Street house inherited from his father is preserved in the Metropolitan Museum's Verplanck Room.

The cup, unlike most known American two-handled standing covered cups, bears no inscription and no coat of arms. The arms said by the biographer to have been used by Gulian's branch of the family were "a field ermine, on a chief engrailed sable three mullets argent."

The crest was a demi-wolf proper, and the motto, *Ut vita sic mors.* Why the arms or some dedicatory inscription were not engraved on the cup is a matter for a future biographer to seek. It may be found that it was connected with disappointment over a first son's death.

Cups as capacious as the Verplanck example, which holds two and a third quarts, are often called grace

Fig. 4. Silver two-handled cup made by Charles Le Roux (1689-1745), New York, for a member of the De Peyster family of New York. It was owned by Frederic de Peyster who was christened April 19, 1731, and bears a cipher of the letters *FDP*. Harp handles and bold applied strap decoration were often used by silversmiths of French origin who worked in London and New York. Over-all height, 10¼ inches. *Yale University Art Gallery, Mabel Brady Garvan Collection; photograph by E. Irving Blomstrann.*

cups or loving cups, charming terms that enhance the aura of ceremony and sentiment surrounding the handsome vessels. Large two-handled cups holding wine or beer for the "grace drink" were, as early as English recorded history, passed from diner to diner after the saying of grace, that is, the giving of thanks (*gratias*) at the end of a meal. In the eighteenth century such cups came to be reserved for commemorating state occasions. The known American cups were ordered from silversmiths for a variety of reasons, among them a wedding, a christening, appreciation for services to the state, and a naval victory. The earliest cup by an American silversmith was made by John Coney (1655-1722) for William Stoughton to present to Harvard College at the July 1701 commencement.

So far, only three other New York cups of the style of the Verplanck cup have been located. One of them (Fig. 2) was the work of Elias Pelletreau (1726-1810). It is engraved with the arms and crest of the Van Cortlandt family and is owned by a descendant. The Van Cortlandts owned the vast Philipse Patent on the east bank of the Hudson adjacent to the Verplancks' Rombout Patent. The families were joined by close association in early New Amsterdam and by the marriage in 1718 of Philip, Gulian Verplanck's cousin, and Gertrude, daughter of Johannes Van Cortlandt.

The second cup (Fig. 3) was made by Myer Myers (1723-1795) for the Stuyvesant family. The third (Fig. 4) was the work of Charles Le Roux (1689-1745), Bartholomew's father. It was owned by Frederic de Peyster, son of Abraham and Margaret van Cortlandt de Peyster, and, presumably, was ordered by them for his christening on April 19, 1731. A fourth, also by Charles Le Roux, has not been located. It was made for James and Mary Alexander who were married in 1721, and whose descendants owned it in 1937.

The Le Roux family, like the families of Pelletreau and many New York craftsmen, were descendants of French Huguenots who had left their mother country in the seventeenth century and settled in England. Bartholomew Le Roux I was born about 1663 in London and came to New York where he was made a freeman in 1687. He died in 1713. His sons Charles and John (b. 1695) were both born in New York and became silversmiths. Bartholomew II, whose mark B LR (conjoined) is stamped twice on the Verplanck cup, was the son of Charles.

The work of American and English silversmiths of Huguenot ancestry shows the influence both of richly decorated French domestic objects and of the plainer English forms, their simplicity necessitated by the softness of silver used following the new purity standard of 1697. With their hollow S-curved handle embellished by a cut acanthus leaf, their broad plain areas, and their molded mid-band, cups like this one by Bartholomew Le Roux II are a blending of early eighteenth-century French elaboration and English restraint. That fortunate blending gave the English two-handled cup a new dignity and it became more a ceremonial vessel than ever before. Whatever ceremony the Verplanck cup may have graced, its stunning proportions, its synthesis of the two fine traditions of design, and its association with two early New York families—the Le Roux silversmiths and the Verplanck merchants—make it an object of outstanding interest.

131

New York's two-handled paneled silver bowls

BY JOHN N. PEARCE, *Assistant curator of cultural history, Smithsonian Institution*

ONE OF THE RAREST FORMS in American silver is the type of two-handled paneled bowl illustrated here by several examples. The accompanying table summarizes data concerning the eighteen such bowls to which I have found reference: fifteen in printed sources, two from the notes of John Marshall Phillips, and one, previously unrecorded, brought to my attention by Martha Gandy Fales.

The examples of this form listed in the table exhibit several distinctive features. Each is a roughly hemispherical bowl, divided into six segments, or lobes, by heavy chased lines. Within each panel, in all the bowls except that by Henricus Boelen, is a boldly chased baroque enframement. In about half of the known examples the enframed area has chased and *repoussé* floral ornament (Figs. 1, 2, 8). Except for the example by Cornelius Van Der Burgh, each of the bowls sits on a short circular foot with a flanged lower edge. The scalloped edge of the hitherto unpublished Wynkoop bowl (Fig. 1) is unique, but the engraved latticework design on its footband appears in several other examples, most notably that by Kierstede. All of the bowls have two opposed handles, with a general S curve in the vertical plane. In the majority, these handles take the form of female figures (Fig. 2); but much simpler designs were also used (Figs. 1, 8).

Similar vessels with diameters of less than about 5¼ inches are easily differentiable, as they generally have no foot and invariably have handles of cut sheet or twisted wire, rather than the heavier cast scrolls of the larger bowls.

There has been some discussion among students of silver as to the relationship of these bowls to Dutch work.

The widest spread of opinion has been between C. Louise Avery's belief that they were "typically Dutch in form and decoration" and John Marshall Phillips' conclusion that they were "basically . . . unlike any Dutch prototype with which they have previously been compared." An examination of Dutch and Scandinavian examples (of which two are illustrated, Figs. 3, 4) indicates that the general concept and the specific vocabulary of the New York bowls were taken from north European—and particularly Dutch—examples of approximately the same period as the earliest from New York.

The century-earlier German and Italian examples (Figs. 5, 6), in which many general and specific similari-

1

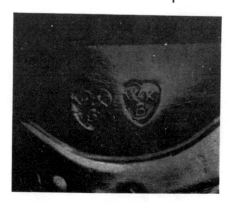

Fig. 1. Previously unpublished example of the very rare lobate type of silver bowl made only in New York, c. 1680-1740. This example, by Benjamin Wynkoop (1675-1728), originally belonged to Nicholas and Hilletje Roosevelt, whose initials appear above the central panel, the surname represented by the conjoined R and V. Note that the surname in the maker's mark, struck twice on the rim of the bowl, is indicated in the same manner as that of the owner in the engraving. The foliate handles and scalloped edge of the foot are unique among the American examples (Table, XIII). *Privately owned and currently on loan to the Smithsonian Institution; photograph by J. Carl Burke Studio.*

2

3

4

5

ties can be seen, suggest that both form and details followed the usual path of artistic inspiration in the Renaissance, from Italy north—in this case via Germany. The closeness of Italian to German silversmithing at this period is suggested by several Renaissance pieces in the Medici silver at the Pitti Palace which have been attributed to both Italian and German masters (see E. Plon, *Benvenuto Cellini*, Paris, 1883, Pls. 38, 40, 47, 49). The ultimate design source for this Renaissance work may have been the lobate metalwork of antiquity. It is interesting in this regard that Raphael's pupil Giovan Antonio Dosio, who was originally trained as a goldsmith, was sketching (as early as the mid-sixteenth century) decorative stuccoes in Hadrian's villa which depicted precisely such antique metalwork.

The use of the New York bowls undoubtedly followed Dutch practice, described by J. W. Frederiks in *Dutch Silver . . . : Wrought Plate of North and South-Holland*: "The majority of the bowls are brandy-bowls, used in Friesland and Groningen on feast-days. They were filled with brandy and raisins. Every guest had a silver spoon, and helped himself to the liquor, after which he passed the bowl to his neighbour. For this reason the bowls had always two handles on opposite sides. This custom lasted until the nineteenth century."

The other aspect of the use of these bowls—the occasion of their coming to their original owners—is not clear. I have been able to trace the wills or inventories of only four of the original owners—Joseph Wardel, Evert Wendell, Dirck Ten Broeck, and Jacob van Dorn; none of these documents specifically mentions the bowls. The Wynkoop bowl has a family history of having been given to its first owners as a twenty-fifth wedding anniversary gift; unfortunately our knowledge of colonial wedding anniversary practices is so limited as to be useless in this connection. The Kip example at the Henry Ford Museum has a family tradition (printed as early as 1906) of having been a racing trophy—an interesting sign of the New York area's penchant for racing, encouraged by the British governor's offering of silver cups beginning in 1665. When we note that the Maryland racing trophy of 1773 shown in Figure 7 copies the lobate, paneled design of these bowls (with the punch-mark decoration matching exactly that on the Soumaine example) it seems reasonable to infer that this form may have been used regularly for racing trophies. This would help to explain the use of these stylistic features at so late a date by the unknown maker of the Maryland bowl. Some further substance is given to this line of thought by the ties of the Maryland and New York areas in both racing and silversmithing.

Final determination of the occasion at which these bowls came to their first owners—whether as trophies or other tokens—must await further evidence. Meanwhile it seems at least clear that the eighteen bowls now brought together in this study, made by Dutch and Huguenot silversmiths in New York, drew their design inspiration from the Dutch version of a north European type, and ultimately from the neoclassical work of the Italian masters of the high Renaissance.

The author wishes to acknowledge the aid he has received from many persons, and particularly the interest and assistance of C. Louise Avery, Kathryn C. Buhler, Martha Gandy Fales, Josephine Setze, Alexander Mackay-Smith, and George H. S. King.

Fig. 2. Silver bowl by Jacob Ten Eyck (1704-1793); presumably no earlier than 1725, when the maker finished his apprenticeship. This late example of the type exhibits only the slightest swelling in the individual segments or lobes. The footband is not decorated and the edge of the foot is perfectly circular, as it is in all but the Wynkoop bowl (Fig. 1). The cast handles, stylized female figures, are typical. *Henry Francis du Pont Winterthur Museum; photograph by Gilbert Ask.*

Fig. 3. Dutch bowl in the lobate style, by the Anonymous Master of the Candlestick, Haarlem, Holland, 1667. Though the bowl has eight lobes and a different handle, its striking similarity to the New York examples bears out C. Louis Avery's opinion that the New York ones were "typically Dutch in form and decoration" (*American Silver of the XVII & XVIII Centuries,* p. 6). Dutch examples with scroll or figural handles are known, as are European examples with only six lobes. Note the scalloped edge of the foot, precisely like that of the Wynkoop example. *Collection of the late A. O. van Kerkwijk; photograph from J. W. Frederiks, Dutch Silver: Wrought Plate of North and South-Holland . . . , No. 362; by courtesy of Martinus Nijhoff, Publishers.*

Fig. 4. Danish bowl in the lobate style, by Hans Thuresen, Aalborg, probably 1672. Again eight-lobed, and differing somewhat in the form of the handles, this bowl illustrates the use of the two-handled lobate bowl-on-foot throughout northern Europe. Other Danish examples used Dutch-style floral ornament, and one such can be seen in Fig. 319 of the book from which this photograph is taken. The use of flat and scroll handles together seems to be a Danish feature, undoubtedly in imitation of ancient Roman silver vessels which used a finger ring beneath a flat thumb-grip. Similar bowls were made in Sweden; see, for instance, G. Upmark, *Guld och Silversmeder I Sverige, 1520-1850,* Figs. 7 and 73. *Privately owned; photograph from G. Boesen and C. A. Boje, Old Danish Silver, Fig. 316; by courtesy of Alfred G. Hassing Publishers Ltd.*

Fig. 5. German bowl in the lobate style, by Hans Karl, Nuremberg, c. 1590. Nearly a century earlier than the examples above, this bowl exhibits most of the features of the type: lobate form, floral decoration (in the earlier manner), a low foot, female figure scroll handles. This bowl suggests that Germany, and particularly the silver center of Nuremberg, may have been the point from which the design spread throughout the north of Europe. The flattened spaces between the lobes suggest very strongly that the form developed from a shell motif. *Schatzkammer der Residenz, Munich; photograph by courtesy of Dr. Herbert Brunner, Konservator, Schloss Nymphenburg.*

Fig. 6. Stylized shell-form agate cup on base, with female figure handles of enameled gold; Italian, second half of sixteenth century. A highly probable design source for the lobate bowls. It is almost certain that the Italian Renaissance use of "grotesques" for handles was copied in the similar handles in northern Europe and, eventually, North America. *In the possession of Georges Wildenstein, by whose courtesy this photograph is reproduced.*

Fig. 7. Bowl with lobate decoration by unknown silversmith, probably from Maryland. This bowl was presented, as the inscription records, to William Fitzhugh (of Chatham, near Fredericksburg, Virginia) for his 1773 winner of the Maryland Jockey Club sweepstakes, Kitty Fisher. The bowl was made with paneled lobes precisely like those on the New York bowls, and the impressed circles in the decoration repeat a detail from the bowl by Simeon Soumaine (Table, XV). *Virginia Museum of Fine Arts.*

Fig. 8. Bowl by Henricus Boelen of New York (1697-1755). The initials are probably for a member of the Van Vechten or Van Vlecht families. This example, with its very simple handles, is unique in that there is not a complete panel outline within each lobe, only curled ends at the base (Table, XVI). *Albany Institute of History and Art.*

134

Known examples of New York two-handled paneled silver bowls

Silversmith	Approx. Diam. Lip	Engraved Initials	Documentation	Publication: Mentioned	Illustrated	Present Ownership
I. CORNELIUS VAN DER BURGH 1653-1699 W.C. 1675 New York	9″	D WA IAVR		12. p. 51 22. 5. p. 86 8. p. 81	Figs. 5, 6 Fig. 69	Anonymous
II. JACOB BOELEN c. 1657-1729 W.C. 1680 New York	5½″	AVV TVV MSR	Formerly in the Remsen family	14. p. 17 1. p. 6 15. p. 38 2.	Fig. fac. p. 18 Fig. 17	Metropolitan Museum of Art
III. JACOB BOELEN	7⅞″	E AS		17. p. 4	Fig. 36	Anonymous
IV. JACOB BOELEN				11. "Bowls"	top	Anonymous
V. JESSE KIP 1660-1722 W.C. 1682 New York	6″	VD 1699 IM	". . . the initials of Jacob and Mary Van Dorn, which was won, by one of their slaves, who trained a colt and ran it successfully, in a race, on the King's Highway, in Middletown [New Jersey]." (Stillwell)	21. p. 355 AQ July '43 p. 21 5. p. 79 AQ Feb. '58 p. 175 8. p. 81 7.	Fig. 7 Fig. 75 Figs. 8, 9 Fig. 179	Henry Ford Museum
VI. JESSE KIP	8½″	S TA	Descended in the Clarkson family, probably from the marriage of Matthew Clarkson and Catharina van Schaik. (MMA)	MMA Bull, June '23 p. 139 AQ Aug. '30 p. 124 2. AQ July '43 p. 21	Fig. 9 Fig. 31 Fig. 6	Metropolitan Museum of Art
VII. BARTHOLOMEW LE ROUX c. 1663-1713 W.C. 1689 New York	9″	G.V.S.B.	Initials "probably for a member of the Bleecker family, possibly Gertje van Schaik Bleecker." (Mrs. Goss)	18. p. 43	Pl. 8a	Mrs. George A. Goss
VIII. BARTHOLOMEW LE ROUX			Phillips 1949 p. 43, states that Le Roux made *two bowls* of the type of the one he illustrated (above), but no trace of the other has been found.			Unknown
IX. BARTHOLOMEW LE ROUX	8¾″	W IS later inscriptions	Initials for Joseph and Sarah Wardel of Shrewsbury, New Jersey, Quakers, married 1696. (Josephine Setze)	3. p. 137 2. 17. p. 18 AQ Dec. '48 p. 415 23. p. 13-14 6. p. 75 8. p. 81	Fig. 38 Fig. 169 Pl. I-A	Mabel Brady Garvan Collection Yale University Art Gallery
X. GERRIT ONCKELBAG 1670-1732 W. 1691 New York	9″	arms and inscription	Twyford arms and inscription, but "may have been a wedding gift to Eva Philipse when she married Jacobus van Cortlandt in 1690." (Owner)	5. p. 82	Fig. 76	Anonymous
XI. GERRIT ONCKELBAG			Josephine Setze tells me that John Phillips' notes contained photographs of another bowl by Onckelbag, but this has not been traced.			Unknown
XII. BENJAMIN WYNKOOP 1675-1728 Kingston and New York W. New York 1698	8¾″	P CM EDP HC	Original initials for Cornelius [Cornelis] and Mary (Bancker) de Peyster, married 1694.	1. p. 6 15. p. 38 3. p. 137 2. 5. p. 89	Pl. VIII-3 Pl. XXI Fig. 94 Fig. 72	New-York Historical Society
XIII. BENJAMIN WYNKOOP	10″	RV NH	Initials for Nicholas and Hilletje (Janse) Kunst Roosevelt, married 1682. (Owner)	3. p. 137 20. p. 303		Mrs. Jack R. Hovey

Silversmith	Approx. Diam. Lip	Engraved Initials	Documentation	Publication: Mentioned	Illustrated	Present Ownership
XIV. CORNELIUS KIERSTEDE 1675-1757 New York, Albany, New Haven W. New York 1696	10″	Q TV	Initials for Theunis Jacobsen Quick and wife, Vroutje Janse Haring, married 1689.	MMA Bull, Oct. '38 pp. 227-228 AQ Oct. '46 p. 248 AQ Dec. '48 p. 415 12. p. 51 9. p. 97 23. 22. 4. pp. 29-30 MMA Bull, Mar. '54 p. 212 16. 10. 6. p. 75 8. 19. p. 326 7. pp. 20, 74	Fig. 3 Fig. 10 Fig. 10 Pl. 2 Fig. 3 Pl. 96 Fig. 43 Fig. 17 Pl. 134 Fig. 178	Metropolitan Museum of Art
XV. SIMEON SOUMAINE c. 1685-c. 1750 W.C. 1706 New York	9¼″	R HC	Initials for Hendrick and Catalina Remsen, married about 1730.	14. p. 49 1. p. 6 15. p. 38 2. 17. p. 28	Fig. fac. p. 18 Fig. 68	Anonymous
XVI. HENRICUS BOELEN 1697-1755 W.C. 1718 New York	6⅛″	TVV	Initials probably for member of Van Vechten or Van Vlecht families.	17. p. 3 Am Coll Sept. '41 cover 5. p. 74		Albany Institute of History and Art
XVII. JACOB TEN EYCK 1704-1793 Trained New York, worked Albany W. 1725	7½″	W EE	Initials for Evert and Engeltie (Lansing) Wendell, married 1710.	AQ Nov. '56 pp. 448-449 13.	Fig. 42	Henry Francis du Pont Winterthur Museum
XVIII. JACOB TEN EYCK	7¾″	TB DM	Initials for Dirck and Margareta (Cuyler) Ten Broeck, married 1714. In an inventory, a "punch bowl"; later, a christening bowl. (Mrs. Davison)	AQ Dec. '42 p. 303 5. p. 85 7. pp. 20, 80	Fig. 86 Fig. 213	George S. Jackson, Mrs. Robert Davison, Mrs. Guy E. Cate; on loan to the Museum of Fine Arts, Boston

Key to publications

1. Avery, C. Louise. *American Silver of the XVII & XVIII Centuries.* New York: Metropolitan Museum of Art, 1920.

2. Avery, C. Louise. *An Exhibition of Early New York Silver.* New York: Metropolitan Museum of Art, 1931.

3. Avery, C. Louise. *Early American Silver.* New York: Century, 1930.

4. Buhler, Kathryn C. *American Silver.* Cleveland: World Publishing, 1950.

5. [Buhler, Kathryn C.] *Colonial Silversmiths, Masters & Apprentices.* Boston: Museum of Fine Arts, 1956.

6. [Buhler, Kathryn C.] *French, English and American Silver.* Minneapolis: Institute of Arts, 1956.

7. [Buhler, Kathryn C.] *Masterpieces of American Silver.* Richmond: Virginia Museum of Fine Arts, 1960.

8. Buhler, Kathryn C. "Silver 1640-1820." *The Concise Encyclopedia of American Antiques,* I, ed. Helen Comstock. New York: Hawthorn, 1958.

9. *From Colony to Nation, An Exhibition of American Painting, Silver and Architecture from 1650 to the War of 1812.* Chicago: Art Institute, 1949.

10. Comstock, Helen. "American Silver." *The Concise Encyclopedia of Antiques,* II, ed. L.G.G. Ramsey. London: The Connoisseur, 1955.

11. [Robert Ensko, Inc.] *17th & 18th Century American Silver.* New York: Ensko [1934].

12. Ensko, Stephen G. C. *American Silversmiths and Their Marks III.* New York: Robert Ensko, Inc., 1948.

13. Fales, Martha Gandy. *American Silver in the Henry Francis du Pont Winterthur Museum.* Winterthur (Del.): Winterthur Museum, 195

14. Halsey, R. T. Haines. *Catalogue of an Exhibition of Silver Used in New York, New Jersey, and the South.* New York: Metropolitan Museum of Art, 1911.

15. Jones, E. Alfred. *Old Silver of Europe & America from Early Times to the Nineteenth Century.* Philadelphia: Lippincott, 1928.

16. *Early American Silver, A Picture Book.* New York: Metropolitan Museum of Art, 1955.

17. Miller, V. Isabelle. *Silver by New York Makers, Late 17th Century to 1900.* New York: Museum of the City of New York, 1937.

18. Phillips, John Marshall. *American Silver.* New York: Chanticleer, 194

19. Rogers, Meyric R. "Americas: Art Since Columbus, I. Art of the United States. The Decorative Arts, a. 1625 to 1850." *Encyclopedia of World Art,* I. New York: McGraw-Hill, 1959.

20. Smith, Helen Burr. "Nicholas Roosevelt-Goldsmith (1715-1769)," *The New-York Historical Society Quarterly* XXXIV, 1950.

21. Stillwell, John E. *Historical and Genealogical Miscellany, Data Relating to the Settlement and Settlers of New York and New Jersey,* New York: 1906.

22. Stow, Millicent. *American Silver.* New York: Barrows, 1950.

23. Wenham, Edward. *The Practical Book of American Silver.* Philadelphia: Lippincott, 1949.

Am Coll—American Collector   AQ—ANTIQUES Magazine   MMA Bull—Metropolitan Museum of Art Bulletin

Further comments on the lobate bowl form

BY JOHN N. PEARCE, *Curator, department of properties, National Trust for Historic Preservation*

FOLLOWING MY ARTICLE on the two-handled lobate bowls produced in New York in the period between 1680 and 1730 and the European antecedents of the form (ANTIQUES, October 1961, p. 341), a number of interesting parallels have been brought to my attention.

Further documentation of the form in New York silver is provided by the two previously unpublished bowls shown in Figures 1 and 2. Figure 1 shows a very fine example by Cornelius Kierstede, with the strongly Dutch chasing typical of this maker. The bowl, originally owned by an unidentified *M G*, is quite similar to the well-known handleless bowl made by Kierstede for presentation to Thomas Darling, now in the Yale Art Gallery. This also illustrates the point made in my earlier article, that when the lip diameter is less than five inches, the cast handles and raised foot of the larger examples are replaced by

details in appropriately smaller scale, such as the twisted-wire handles and the molded foot ring here. Figure 2, a previously unpublished winetaster by the New York silversmith Bartholomew Schaats, shows similarly simplified details in still smaller form.

Further support for the view originally propounded by C. Louise Avery, that this form is essentially Dutch, appears in the handsome still life (Fig. 3) by the Dutch painter Pieter Claesz, in which a lobate bowl is shown as a drinking vessel. As I previously noted, the typical Dutch version has eight lobes rather than six and is likely to use horizontal, or porringer-type, handles, as in this case. (What accounts for the universal use, in the American examples, of S-scroll handles in the vertical plane?) The bowl shown in the still life also repeats the bowl plan in the scalloped foot, as does the Dutch example

Fig. 1. Two-handled silver bowl by Cornelius Kierstede (1675-1757; w. New York 1696); height 2 inches, diameter at lip, 4⅛ inches. *Bayou Bend collection; photograph by courtesy of James Graham & Sons.*

Fig. 2. Silver winetaster by Bartholomew Schaats (1670-1758); height 1¾ inches, diameter at lip, 4⅜ inches. *Collection of Mrs. W. R. Nissen; photograph by Christopher Leggo.*

Fig. 3. Still life dated 1642, by Pieter Claesz (1597/8-1660). *Museum of Fine Arts, Boston.*

Fig. 4. Lobate silver bowl by Paul Storr; London, 1800/1. *St. Anne's Gallery; photograph by Evanston Photographic Service.*

in my article and one American example, the Wynkoop bowl on loan to the Smithsonian Institution.

Paul Storr's bowl shown in Figure 4 presents something of a mystery. Here, in a piece made a century after the peak of the form's popularity, precisely the same shape and panel decoration, with handles of a similar Renaissance type (though in the vertical plane, like the American ones), appear again. The present owner has tried to

trace the earlier history of this bowl, but thus far no facts have come to light which explain the use of the form at so late a date.

There obviously is more to be learned about the history of this lobate bowl form, especially in terms of the differences between the New York Dutch and the Netherlands Dutch examples, in number of lobes or panels, amount of convexity of the lobes, and types of handles.

IV Some Silversmiths in the Quaker City

When Philadelphia was settled in the early 1680s, artisans hoping to emigrate to the New World were presented with an especially attractive destination. In order to compete with New England and New York, William Penn offered liberal land grants and some financial subsidies. He also guaranteed religious freedom. Apparently, these lures worked, for artisans came in droves, and the colony expanded rapidly. Within 75 years, Philadelphia was the largest American city. In population, wealth, and trade connections, this colonial upstart rivaled Bristol which had long held second honors, after London, in the British Empire.

In light of this late settlement, it is hardly surprising that examples of 17th-century Philadelphia silver are exceedingly rare. Only a few pieces, made by two silversmiths, can be assigned 17th-century dates with any certainty. The first silversmith to claim the Philadelphia market was Cesar Ghiselin* (c. 1663-1733), who arrived in 1681 with a group of hopeful artisans on the *Bristol Factor*. Ghiselin, a Huguenot, originally came from Rouen. He seems to have left France for England with his brother, John, but later decided to sail for America. Sometime between 1685 and 1688, Ghiselin crafted the porringer featured in Helen Comstock's article (pp. 140-141). Its early style suggests that it was made for Anthony Morris and his first wife, Mary Jones Morris, and the discovery that Ghiselin was in Philadelphia at the time confirms this. Cesar Ghiselin was still in Philadelphia when the tax assessors made their first round in 1693, but he left sometime before 1705 when he and his wife were registered as church members in Annapolis. At that point, Ghiselin's career became peripatetic: he was back in Philadelphia in 1708, moved again to Annapolis in January, 1717, and returned to Philadelphia about 1726.

Johannis Nys (1671-1734) was another Huguenot craftsman whose family left France to escape persecution. They settled in New York, where Johannis was baptized in 1671. Around 1695 he left for Philadelphia, having served his apprenticeship in New York. One of Nys's earliest commissions, the pair of braziers described by Samuel Woodhouse, Jr. (pp. 142-143), was made between 1693 and 1699 for Anthony Morris and his third wife, Mary Coddington Morris. Both braziers, like the Ghiselin porringer, are inscribed *M/AM*—this time on the bottom of the piece.

Ghiselin used two touchmarks: *CG* in an oval surround, and *CG* in a heart-shaped surround. Johannis Nys apparently had nearly as many touches as the variants on his name. Woodhouse illustrates two marks and describes a third. The interesting rectangular punch with a reversed *N* is more clearly shown in figure 4b (p. 145) of Homer Eaton Keyes's article. Keyes, however, incorrectly describes the four-pellet motif, palced below the initials in Nys's heart-shaped surround, as five pellets. This error indicates the difficulty the reading of touchmarks presents whenever they are poorly struck or badly worn. Another mark, *IN* in an oval surround, has since come to light and has been attributed to Nys.

A deluge of wealthy merchants flooded Philadelphia at the turn of the century. They arrived with the necessary prerequisites: cash, considerable business acumen, and a taste for luxurious goods, especially silver. The number of silversmiths instantly climbed. Among those who headed for Penn's city were Henry Pratt, William Vilant, Daniel Dupuy, Peter David, Philip Syng, Sr., and Francis Richardson, the founder of a dynasty of silversmiths. Ghiselin, meanwhile, continued working until 1732, and Johannis Nys remained in the city until 1723, when he moved to Kent County, Delaware.

Francis Richardson, Jr. (called Frank), and Joseph Richardson inherited their father's business when he died in 1729. Frank, however, was already involved in mercantile activities and these eventually became his first priority. The goldsmithing tools were left to the younger son, Joseph, and it was he who continued the family business for over thirty years. Martha Gandy Fales (pp. 149-152), in her article (and book) on the Richardson family, uses surviving business records and other documentary sources to illuminate nearly every aspect of the craftsman's private and business life.

Philip Syng, Jr., also followed his father's craft. He was something of an activist among the Philadelphia artisans, joining groups with abandon. His best-known piece of silver is the inkstand, commissioned by the Pennsylvania Assembly for the State House (now Independence Hall), which was used in signing both the Declaration of Independence and the Constitution. Several attractive domestic pieces demonstrate Syng's versatility and skill (pp. 33, 42).

By mid-century, when Richardson and Syng were active, there were over a dozen silversmiths supplying Philadelphia households with plate. A great deal of English silver was also imported to satisfy the strong demand, to provide the newest —thus the preferred—English taste, and to serve as models for area craftsmen. The imports continued until the non-importation movement of the 1760s gained political and economic force. Purchasers of English goods, including silver, were socially ostracized.

The preference for American-made objects was voiced too late for Jeremiah Elfreth, Jr. He died eight months before the first non-importation agreement was signed. As Carl Williams (pp. 146-148) points out, Elfreth is not a well-known Philadelphia silversmith. Only eight or nine surviving pieces have been positively identified as his work. Among them is the salver illustrated in figure 5 on p. 148. A few of his better-known Philadelphia contemporaries were William Ghiselin (Cesar Ghiselin's grandson), William Hollingshead, Phillip Hulbert, and John Leacock.

Like furniture made in the Delaware Valley, early silver from the area exhibits broad proportions, massiveness, and a low center of gravity. It is usually plainer than that produced by Boston or New York craftsmen. With the introduction of the rococo style, however, many Philadelphia silversmiths abandoned their tendency toward "Quaker modesty" and produced pieces which complemented the English high style. Long-practiced restraint helped them achieve that controlled tension of vigorous, unstable forms and riotous ornament characteristic of the rococo. Philadelphia was, by mid-century, as sophisticated and worldly as New York. So it was in these two cities that the style found its fullest expression.

*See Beatrice Garvan's biographical essay in *Philadelphia: Three Centuries of American Art*. Philadelphia: The Philadelphia Museum of Art, 1976.

Porringer by Cesar Ghiselin, Philadelphia, made for Anthony and Mary Morris between 1693 and 1699. Length across bowl to tip of handle, 6½ inches.

Porringer by Cesar Ghiselin, active c. 1693-1733, showing his mark in a crude rectangular punch heartshaped at the base. It is without the five-pointed star he sometimes used. Length across bowl to tip of handle, 6½ inches.

A porringer by Cesar Ghiselin

SINCE PHILADELPHIA'S FIRST SILVERSMITHS — Ghiselin, Paschall, and Nys—arrived in the last decade of the seventeenth century, there is little Philadelphia silver that can be dated with certainty before 1700. The discovery of a porringer by Cesar Ghiselin, illustrated here and on the frontispiece, which can be dated between 1693 and 1699 and has never before been recorded, illustrated, or exhibited, is therefore a noteworthy event. The porringer has the additional interest of having been made for Anthony Morris, "the Immigrant," and has been continuously in his family until the present time. It now belongs to Mrs. W. Logan MacCoy, whose home, Greenhill, was illustrated in ANTIQUES for November 1954.

Ghiselin was probably a Huguenot who belonged to a Rouen family of goldsmiths and came to America by way of England. He is recorded as a goldsmith in Philadelphia in 1693, according to the late Harrold E. Gillingham's "Cesar Ghiselin, Philadelphia's First Gold and Silversmith" (Pennsylvania Magazine of History and Biography, Vol. LV, p. 170). Not only was his name on the tax list that year, but he was mentioned as a goldsmith in the will of Peter Dubac dated October 14, 1693. It was formerly thought that Ghiselin was in London as late as 1698, since papers of denization were granted to him in that year; but actually he was resident in Philadelphia at the time. A colonial governor did not have power to grant papers of denization, and these were issued in London after Ghiselin had come to this country.

An account book record shows that Ghiselin made silver for William Penn in 1701. Around 1715 he moved to Annapolis, where he worked until about 1726-1728; he then returned to Philadelphia, where he died in 1733. His largest pieces, and the most important thus far known, are the alms plate and beaker in Christ Church in Philadelphia. A spoon by him formerly owned by R. T. H. Halsey is in the Garvan collection at Yale. His work is severely plain, but in the simplicity of early Philadelphia silver expressing Quaker taste it shows the hand of an able craftsman. The wealthy Quakers sometimes owned large quantities of plate, as the inventory of the estate of Anthony Morris in 1721 shows. He had 242¼ ounces of plate and no fewer than five porringers.

The date of the Ghiselin porringer is established as not later than 1699 by the initials on the handle M/AM, well executed in early block lettering. Morris family records show that while the name Anthony runs through many generations, the only Anthony Morris whose wife's name began with M in the period of Ghiselin's activity was the first Anthony Morris, 1664-1721, who was born in London and came to Philadelphia in 1685 with his first wife, Mary Jones. Her name, however, did not supply the initial on the porringer; she died in 1688, almost certainly before Ghiselin had come to Philadelphia. Anthony's second wife also died early. His third, Mary Coddington, whom he married in Newport in 1693/4, died in Philadelphia in 1699, and it seems definite that it was this Mary for whom the porringer was made—possibly as early as the year of her marriage, which coincided with the appearance of Ghiselin's name on the Philadelphia tax list, and certainly not later than 1699, the year of her death.

The initials HM, which are crowded in below the initials M/AM on the handle of the porringer, obviously by a hand other than that of the original engraver, may stand for Hannah Morris, youngest daughter of Anthony, who was four years old at the time of her father's death. She died unmarried in 1741. Her mother, Elizabeth Watson Morris, fourth wife of Anthony, survived Hannah, dying in 1755. Possibly the porringer reverted to the mother, as the latter's will mentions porringers left to her sons Luke and Israel. This would explain the engraving on the back of the handle, LM to SM, which probably stands for Luke Morris to a nephew Samuel Morris. Samuel was grandfather of Israel Morris (1778-1870), whose family plate and furniture have descended directly to Mrs. MacCoy.

The bowl of the porringer is of the seventeenth century but the form of the handle is typical of the earliest examples of the eighteenth century, so that we probably have in it an example of the genesis of the geometric handle—a characteristically American type not found in Europe.

H. C.

Fig. 1 — Silver Brazier (c. 1680)
Made by John De Nys for Anthony Morris of Philadelphia. The fleur-de-lys piercing suggests French influence, though the construction of the brazier follows Dutch practice.
From Richard Wistar Harvey, a descendant of the original owner

Fig. 2 — Silver Brazier
Made by Philip Syng II of Philadelphia for Andrew Hamilton. Foot and kettle support cast in a single piece, after the English fashion, structurally far superior to that employed by the Dutch silversmiths.
From the Pennsylvania Museum of Art

John De Nys, Philadelphia Silversmith

By Samuel W. Woodhouse, Jr.

THE idea seems to have become prevalent that very little in the way of fine craftsmanship was accomplished in the Delaware Valley until well after 1750. Yet there is no basis for such an assumption. On the contrary, we have a list of nearly sixty well-documented cabinetmakers, and a long list of plate workers, all active in this region during the first half of the eighteenth century. Apparently they catered to a well-to-do and somewhat luxurious clientele, if we may judge from the appraisal and inventory of the goods and chattels left by the Huguenot goldsmith Cæsar Ghiselin, who died in Philadelphia in March 1733. This document mentions such stock as:

85 dwt. 10 grs. gold
912 ounces of silver
6 links of gold buttons
16 silver buttons
a quantity of silversmith's tools, crucibles etc.
an oyl and Touch Stone
a folio Bible in French, together with some small French books.

Ghiselin was the second silversmith recorded in the district. He had been preceded, curiously enough, by another Huguenot, John De Nys. Of this pioneer craftsman very little, until recently, had been known, and that little was mainly incorrect. Thanks, however, to the painstakingly accurate research

Fig. 3 — Silver Brazier from Holland (*late seventeenth century*)
Illustrating the Dutch method of attaching kettle supports to the rim without bracing

of my friend Harrold E. Gillingham (published in the *Pennsylvania Magazine of History and Biography*, April 1931), and the documents here illustrated, it is now possible to correct past errors and to present some reliable data as to De Nys and his work.

One reason for misapprehensions concerning the man is the variety of ways in which his name is spelled. The earliest reference to him, which is found in William Penn's cash book, under date of February 22, 1700, calls him *Johan Nys Goldsmith*. In 1712 Isaac Norris writes of *John DeNoys, the Silversmith*, and two months later of *John Denoys*. In 1716 he alters the name to *John Neys*. The will of Samuel Holton bequeaths to a daughter "My house in Front Street (corner Carpenter's Alley) now in the tenure and occupation of Johan Nys, Silversmith." James Logan's account book, beautifully kept, with a calligraphy clear as copper plate, records transactions with *Jno De Nys*.

But there are more variations to come. The list published in *American Silversmiths and their Marks*, compiled for the Walpole Society by Hollis French in 1917, omits both our man and his mark. But in Maurice Brix's check list of Philadelphia silversmiths, published in 1920, we find the entry *Jan Neuss, Silversmith, 1698, died 1719*; while in the Pennsylvania Museum catalogue of a loan exhibition of silver, issued at the same time, we meet *John De Nise*. Part

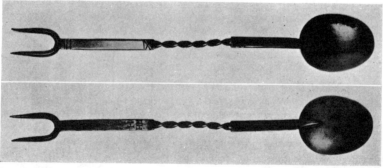

Fig. 4 — Sucket Forks
Made by John De Nys, whose mark appears on the reverse of the handle slightly above the bowl.
From the Pennsylvania Museum of Art

of this muddle is due to Governor Pennypacker's confusion of John Nys, Silversmith, with Jan Neuss, an early Germantown weaver. Having mentally amalgamated these two quite distinct individuals, he knew the result only as Jan Neuss, the Mennonite Silversmith. What the silversmith called himself we learn from his signature as witness to two wills, one dated April 6, 1713, the other, 1723. In both instances he wrote his name *Johannis Nys*. It should be noted in this connection that, if Johannis Nys was witnessing a will in 1723, Mr. Brix's notation of his death in 1719 is incorrect.

As a matter of fact, we cannot determine precisely when De Nys first began to ply his craft in Philadelphia or when he ceased to be. The first mention of his name, as we have already learned, occurs in 1700, the last is his signature on the will of 1723. The evidence of one of his productions, the Anthony Morris brazier, presently to be discussed, would, however, seem to indicate that he was settled in this country as early as 1682. The disappearance of his name from documents subsequent to 1723 argues for his demise in or soon after that year.

Of his origin, we may only guess. The *Bulletin* of the Pennsylvania Museum advances the theory, frequently quoted elsewhere, that De Nys came to America from, or through, Holland, and that he was one of the many Protestant Huguenots who, having sought an asylum in that liberal country, remained there long enough to acquire Dutch variants of their original names. Otherwise, why should Logan, one of the most scholarly Philadelphians of his time, employ the form *De Nys*, as did, also, Isaac Norris, a prominent Quaker?

The brazier made by De Nys for Anthony Morris, first of the name in Philadelphia, has never before been introduced to collectors of early American silver, though it is illustrated in Doctor Moon's *Genealogy of the Morris Family*. Doctor Moon speaks of the item as of English workmanship, and states that it was "brought to this country by Anthony Morris prior to 1780." The error of this statement becomes obvious when an examination of the rare piece itself reveals, below the rim to right and left of the handle, the punched initials I N in a heart shape over a cross of four pellets. Of English

hall mark there is no indication. The French origin of the maker may be signified by the fleur-de-lys that forms the ornamental piercing of the bowl. At the same time, the hornlike rests for the kettle follow the practice of Dutch silversmiths, who attached such supports directly to the brazier's rim without braces of any kind. English and French technique differed from this: in both, the kettle supports become finials topping the elongated legs upon which the brazier itself reposes (*Figs. 1, 2, 3*).

It is from this brazier that we obtain our first clear assurance as to the mark usually employed by De Nys to identify his work — the initials I N in a heart shape over four pellets. On the basis of imperfect examples, this mark had previously been described in the Pennsylvania Museum catalogue of 1920 as the initials I N over a cross in a heart shape. Again in the Museum *Bulletin* for April 1926 it is given as I N in a heart shape with two pellets and a mullet below. If poorly stamped in the first place, or subsequently defaced, the actual four pellets below the initials might easily be interpreted in the ways just quoted. An illustration shows the full De Nys mark, but not with perfect clarity (*Fig. 6*).

The same initials appear, though in a rectangle, on a pair of sucket forks, published in the above-mentioned issue of the Pennsylvania Museum *Bulletin* (*Fig. 4*).

A unique variant of this rectangular mark — shown in Figure 6 — may be found on the porringer illustrated in Figure 5. Here the initials appear in reverse — a circumstance doubtless due to the inexperience or carelessness of the die cutter, who either failed to realize, or forgot, that to show in proper order when stamped or printed, letters must at the outset be cut in reverse. Despite its peculiar aspect, there can be little doubt that the porringer mark in question is that of De Nys. The collateral engraving, the way of handling the graver, the abbreviations *on* for ounce and *p* for pennyweight are all identical in style with the engraving on the bottom of the De Nys tankard at the Historical Society, and on the tankard that our silversmith made for Andrew Hamilton.

The crudely cut letters I R A on the porringer handle are those of John Richardson and Anne Ashton, who were married in 1704.

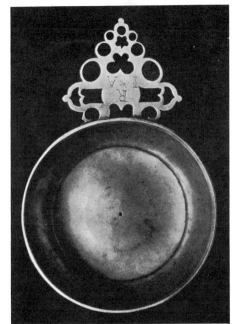

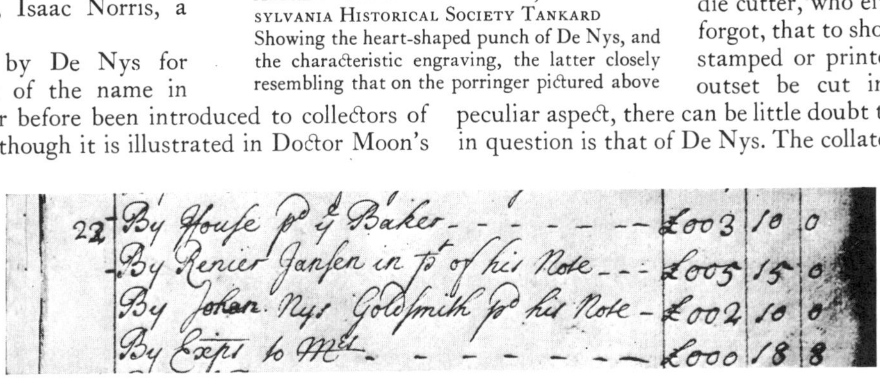

Fig. 5 — Richardson Porringer
Doubtless made by De Nys, though the reversed initials in the mark (shown below) appear in a rectangle instead of a heart

Fig. 6 — Marks from Richardson Porringer, Andrew Hamilton Tankard, and Pennsylvania Historical Society Tankard
Showing the heart-shaped punch of De Nys, and the characteristic engraving, the latter closely resembling that on the porringer pictured above

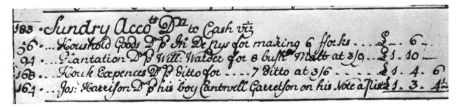

Fig. 7 — From the Cash Book of William Penn, for February 22, 1700
Entry recording "Johan Nys'" payment of a note for two pounds, ten shillings

Fig. 8 — From the Account Book of James Logan for January 13, 1718
Showing entry of a transaction with "Jno De Nys."
From the Historical Society of Pennsylvania

John Nys *vs.* John Newkirke

An Editorial Note

NOTES by E. Alfred Jones, *American Silver Porringers in England* (ANTIQUES for May 1936, *p. 195*), have occasioned some interesting communications. It will perhaps be recalled that the first of the porringers pictured and discussed by Mr. Jones in the notes referred to is obviously of New York type, and carries the mark I N in a rectangle, with the N curiously reversed. Mr. Jones tentatively ascribes this mark, and hence the porringer in question, to "Joseph" Newkirke, "working in New York in the first quarter of the eighteenth century."

This ascription has been questioned by sundry correspondents. It transpires that, while students of American silver formerly inclined to associate with Newkirke the mark described, they now cherish serious doubts regarding that identification. For one thing, Newkirke seems to be little more than a name of record. First listed with the Christian name Joseph, he has latterly been rechristened John. No one has yet delved deep enough in early records to uncover his biography. As for his mark, it is fair to assume that, like the marks of other Manhattan silversmiths of the day, it would have indicated the two parts of the maker's name, *New Kirke*, by corresponding initials. Just as Tobias Stoutenburgh proclaimed his handiwork by stamping it with the letters T S B, Jacob Ten Eyck with I T E, Peter Van Dyck with P V D, so we should expect the contemporary John Newkirke to adopt the symbol I N K. As a matter of fact, in her catalogue of

an exhibition of New York silver held at the Metropolitan Museum through December 1931 and January 1932, Miss Avery cites precisely this combination of letters, in monogram, as the mark on a two-handled covered porringer which she credits to Newkirke. The same combination of letters occurs in the mark on a silver tankard recently acquired by the Mabel Brady Garvan collection at Yale from the firm of Robert Ensko (*Fig. 4a*).

Some students may be inclined to read the cypher as I V K. On the other hand, the cheerful indifference of die cutters, sign painters, and letterers in general — early and late — to the direction of the letter N affords ample ground for accepting the reading I N K, the to-be-expected monogram, or cypher, of John New Kirke.

Under these circumstances we must logically seek another claimant to the I N mark in a rectangle. Quite convincing reasons may be advanced for permitting John Nys to assume that rôle. This elusive silversmith, whose name confusingly appears in sundry records as Neuss, De Nys, De Nise, Nys, and so on, was, we know, content to sign himself simply *Johannis Nys* (ANTIQUES for May 1932, *p. 217*). This form of signature sufficiently accounts for the craftsman's use of the two initials I N rather than the three I D N (for Johannis De Nys) in his silver mark.

In Nys' generally recognized mark the two initials appear above five pellets (so arranged as sometimes to be mistaken for a cross) in a heart-shaped shield. Doctor

Fig. 1 — BEAKER: MIDDLETOWN, DELAWARE, ST. ANNE'S PARISH
Probably by John Nys. Mark, I N in rectangle.
From Jones' "The Old Silver of American Churches"

Fig. 2 — TANKARD: PENNSYLVANIA MUSEUM OF ART
Ascribed to John Nys. Mark, I N over five pellets in heart. Inscribed *A H* (Andrew Hamilton).
Photograph by courtesy of the Pennsylvania Museum of Art

Fig. 3 — TANKARD: PENNSYLVANIA HISTORICAL SOCIETY
Ascribed to John Nys. Mark, I N over five pellets in heart. Inscribed *I R M.* Lid missing.
Photograph by courtesy of the Pennsylvania Museum of Art

Fig. 4a — MARK ON TANKARD BELIEVED TO BE THE WORK OF JOHN NEWKIRKE
Photograph by courtesy of Robert Ensko

Fig. 5 — TANKARD: COLLECTION OF EDSEL B. FORD
Ascribed to John Nys. Mark, I N over five pellets in heart.
Inscribed $\begin{smallmatrix}A\\T*M\end{smallmatrix}$·
Photograph by courtesy of Clapp & Graham

Fig. 4b — MARK ON PORRINGER ASCRIBED TO JOHN NYS, SHOWING THE "N" REVERSED

Woodhouse, however, advances cogent reasons for recognizing the stamped initials I N (the latter sometimes reversed) in a rectangle as likewise signalizing the work of John Nys. This mark occurs on a porringer, and on a pair of sucket forks which Doctor Woodhouse ascribes to Nys (see ANTIQUES as previously quoted).

Somewhere, however, there should be discoverable a missing link connecting examples of silver bearing the Nys heart mark with those disclosing his rectangular device. We venture to suggest that this discovery was long since made by E. Alfred Jones, who in his monumental work *The Old Silver of American Churches* pictures and describes a silver beaker that seems quite to meet the essential specifications of a link. This beaker, cherished by St. Anne's Parish Church in Middletown, Delaware, stands six inches high. Its only ornamental feature is a "band of cut leaves above a molded base" (*Fig. 1*). Its maker's mark as sketched by Mr. Jones is I N in a rectangle with the N apparently reversed.

As in the I N porringer pictured in ANTIQUES for May 1936, the design of this beaker conforms to New York practice. It is at this point that the piece really begins to function as a missing link; *for its band of cut leaves is apparently identical with that on a tankard in the Pennsylvania Museum, whose mark is the well-*

known I N *above five pellets in a heart* (*Fig. 2*). A very similar band occurs on a lidless tankard bearing the I N mark, which is owned by the Pennsylvania Historical Society (*Fig. 3*). Presently we find this same heart mark on a group of three other tankards whose New York implications are decreasingly pronounced (*Figs. 5, 6, and 7*). Hence, though the documentary evidence that we possess concerning John Nys associates that craftsman primarily with Philadelphia, the stylistic features of certain among his works yield striking evidence that he sojourned in New York before moving southward.

Miss Avery (*Early American Silver, p. 175*) considers this likelihood to be a virtual certainty. If, further, we accept the I N in a rectangle as an alternative mark employed by Nys, we have materially lengthened the list of surviving examples of his handiwork — among them the porringer discovered in England by Mr. Jones and published in ANTIQUES for May of 1936.

The accompanying illustrations portray all but one of the known surviving tankards by John Nys. Their arrangement is intended to accord with the chronological sequence indicated by successive alterations in details of form. The item omitted was, at last accounts, owned by Mrs. Maurice Brix of Philadelphia, who has not responded to requests for a photograph.

Fig. 6 — (*left*) TANKARD: PENNSYLVANIA HISTORICAL SOCIETY
Ascribed to John Nys. Mark, I N over five pellets in heart, as shown.
Inscribed $\begin{smallmatrix}E\\G*M\end{smallmatrix}$ (George and Mary Heath Emlen).
Photographs by courtesy of Harrold E. Gillingham

Fig. 7 (*right*) — TANKARD: COLLECTION OF SAMUEL W. MORRIS
Ascribed to John Nys. Mark, I N over five pellets in heart. Inscribed $\begin{smallmatrix}E\\W*D\end{smallmatrix}$ and M*D. A spout, not evident in the illustration, is a late addition.
Photograph by courtesy of the Pennsylvania Museum of Art

AN UNRECORDED GOLDSMITH

Jeremiah Elfreth Junior of Philadelphia

By CARL M. WILLIAMS

No PUBLISHED LIST OF AMERI-
CAN SILVERSMITHS includes
the name of Jeremiah Elfreth
Junior. Today the man and his work are
almost unknown. Yet two centuries ago he
was active among the men who made the
Philadelphia of that day a center of fine
craftsmanship, and the few surviving examples of his work that have been identified
are of a quality to win him a better fate
than the oblivion that has been his so far.

In Philadelphia there is a street called Elfreth's Alley. A
cobblestoned thoroughfare nearly adjacent to the Delaware
River waterfront and extending for a single block westward
from Front to Second Streets, north of Arch, it is known as
perhaps the only surviving early street in the United States
with the majority of its original eighteenth-century buildings
intact and in many cases dating prior to 1750. Elfreth's Alley
took its name from Jeremiah Elfreth Senior, father of the
goldsmith, who made it his lifetime dwelling place. Early
records tell much of the varied activities of Jeremiah Senior,
but these are all but overshadowed by the accounts of his five
marriages and the interesting relationships thus developed
with families prominent in the annals of our
early arts and crafts.

The elder Elfreth, a blacksmith by calling
but not by habitual practice, purchased a
plot at the northeast corner of Second Street
and the Alley in 1716. Walls of the house
he occupied on this corner form part of the
fabric of the present structure. He also
owned lots to the rear and extending for
some distance along the north side of Elfreth's Alley. On one of these, No. 137,
stands an exquisite example of a small mid-
eighteenth-century Philadelphia town dwelling in an untouched and excellent state of
repair (*Fig. 1*). This house, whose interior
shows some plain yet impressive parlor panel-
ing, was the home of the goldsmith's family
for many years.

Jeremiah Elfreth Junior, son of Jeremiah
and his first wife, Sarah Oldman, was born
at Philadelphia in 1723. As early as 1745 he
was active as a silversmith. His apprenticeship indenture has not been found, but
there is strong evidence to indicate that he
was taught his trade by Joseph Richardson
Senior. On August 27, 1752, in Friends'
Meeting at Philadelphia, Elfreth married
Hannah Trotter, an aunt of Daniel Trotter,
cabinetmaker, of Elfreth's Alley. It was this
Trotter who made the remarkable group of
Marlborough furniture for Stephen Girard.
Jeremiah and Hannah had two children,
Jeremiah III (born September 2, 1754), and

A "NEW" Philadelphia silversmith, particularly one who died as early as 1765
and whose work ranks him with the
renowned craftsmen of the American
Chippendale period, is a find indeed.
Through the happy discovery of some
early family papers and at about the
same time of a piece from this smith's
hand, Mr. Williams was led on a quest
whose fruits he reveals in this article.
—THE EDITOR

Josiah (born May 2, 1759). On April 9,
1760, the silversmith and his wife purchased
from Charles Stow Junior a brick dwelling
and shop on the east side of North Second
Street, near Arch Street. There Elfreth
continued as a silversmith until his death
on February 10, 1765. He died intestate,
but among the family papers is a detailed
room-for-room description of the contents
of the Second Street house and shop. On
April 19, 1765, John Browne, a fellow
silversmith of Philadelphia, appraised Jeremiah Elfreth's "Sale
Plate" at £33. "All the Tools for silver smithery including
Coals" were valued at £36. This sum suggests that Elfreth
had a comprehensive assortment of shop tools, capable of
producing a wide variety of silver. The balance of the inventory lists a large and interesting group of household
furnishings.

The Elfreth House (*Fig. 1*) at No. 137 Elfreth's Alley was
built for the goldsmith's widow and occupied by her until her
death in 1791. Both their sons became cabinetmakers, but
Josiah, who established his shop in Philadelphia and produced much fine furniture in the then popular Marlborough

style, became the better known. He worked
continuously from about 1779 until his
death in 1793 in the neighborhood of the
Elfreth house, where he lived. The house
stayed in the Elfreth family until 1818.
Jeremiah III was long the leading cabinetmaker in Haddonfield, Gloucester County,
New Jersey. His life there during the Revolution was a sore trial, for, being a plain
Friend and consequently a man of peace, he
remained neutral during the struggle and
had his home frequently ransacked by men
of both sides. He died March 12, 1825.

Silver by Jeremiah Elfreth is exceedingly
scarce. A silver tablespoon, porringer,
small salver, and pint cann, and a gold
knee-breeches buckle comprise the known
output of this Quaker craftsman who worked in one neighborhood for twenty years.

The spoon (*Fig. 2*) by Elfreth is identical
in design and workmanship with several
bearing the mark of Joseph Richardson
Senior. In fact, they could have come from
the same mold.

While the porringer is of the conven-

Photographs by Philip B. Wallace

FIG. 1 — ELFRETH HOUSE at 137 Elfreth's Alley. A
rare example of a small Philadelphia town dwelling
displaying colorful blue-black glazed headers in the
bond of its brickwork.

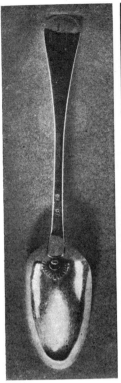
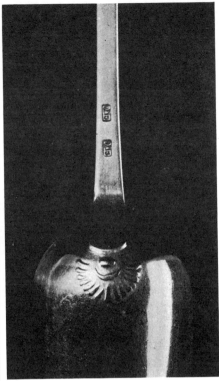

FIG. 2 — TABLESPOON (c. 1760) bearing two clear marks of Jeremiah Elfreth Junior. *Privately owned.*

tional Philadelphia type, it differs from its many fellow pieces in the finely designed ciphering on the handle (*Fig. 3*). The date is a contemporaneous part of the handle design and records the year in which Elfreth fashioned this sturdily made piece for Jeremiah and Mary (Head) Warder. Jeremiah Warder (*1711-1783*) was considered one of the wealthiest of the great Philadelphia merchants and shippers of the mid-eighteenth century. The porringer, dated *1759,* was very likely made in honor of the birth of one of Warder's several daughters, four of whom married into the distinguished Philadelphia families of Morris, Vaux, Emlen, and Maybury.

The gold knee buckle (*Fig. 4*) is inscribed in block letters I. HEAD and was made by Elfreth for John Head of Philadelphia, a brother to Mary (Head) Warder for whom the porringer was made.

The Elfreth salver (*Fig. 5*), now in the Philadelphia Museum of Art, is unfortunately labeled as being the work of an obscure Boston maker. This piece, displaying a beautifully shaped edge and standing on three hoof-feet, was made about 1760 for Abel and Rebecca (Chalkley) James of Chalkley Hall, Frankford, Philadelphia. The inscription *RJ 1782* was added when the salver became the property of their daughter Rebecca (James) Thompson. It forms part of a large bequest of silver and furniture to the Philadelphia

FIG. 3 — PORRINGER made by Jeremiah Elfreth Junior in 1759 for Jeremiah and Mary (Head) Warder of Philadelphia. *Privately owned.*

FIG. 4 — GOLD KNEE-BREECHES BUCKLE made by Jeremiah Elfreth Junior for John Head (obverse and reverse). *Collection of Robert S. Stuart.*

Museum by the late Miss Lydia Thompson Morris. Chalkley Hall was first built by Thomas Chalkley prior to 1723 and its great Georgian wing of cream-colored Manchester stone was added by his son-in-law, Abel James, about 1775. This structure, once considered a country seat of great beauty, is now a hopeless ruin in the midst of a vast industrial section.

When on October 3, 1791, an inventory of the personal estate of Hannah Elfreth was taken at her dwelling in Elfreth's Alley, a list of Jeremiah Elfreth Junior's personal plate was disclosed. It is here given from the original record:

1 Tankard	The whole of Plate Amount.g to
2 Canns	Oz 96-13 dwt-at 8/0 p oz. £38.-13-2.
2 Porringers	
2 Cream Pots	
1 Pepper Box	
1 Punch Strainer	
& Sundry other Pieces of Plate Valued at 8/0 p ounce.	

All of these items with the exception of the tankard and one cream pot are believed to have been fashioned by Jeremiah Elfreth Junior for the use of his family. One of the two canns has been located in the possession of a descendant. One of the cream pots was the property of Hannah Trotter before she became the wife of Jeremiah Elfreth Junior.

Decidedly interesting connections between the Richardson family of silversmiths and the Elfreths are disclosed in important documents lately contained in the Richardson and Elfreth family papers, which I recently had the pleasure of purchasing from descendants of both families. Through two ancient marriage certificates it was learned that Jeremiah Elfreth Junior and Joseph Richardson Senior had the same stepmother. Letitia Swift Richardson Elfreth was first the second wife of Francis Richardson Senior, goldsmith, and father of Joseph Richardson Senior; and secondly the second wife of Jeremiah Elfreth Senior. Thus it was natural that Jeremiah Elfreth Senior should seek the services of Joseph Richardson when in need of a tankard some years before his son was active as a silversmith. On December 7, 1734, Jeremiah Elfreth Senior was charged in the day book of Joseph Richardson with the following entry: "To a Silver Tankard £16.10.1." This piece, which survives today, is marked with the family initials, E/I*E, showing that it was made for Jeremiah Elfreth Senior and his third wife, Elizabeth Massey,

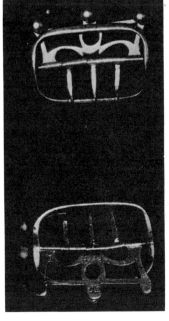

FIG. 5 — SMALL SALVER made about 1760 by Jeremiah Elfreth Junior for Abel and Rebecca (Chalkley) James. *Courtesy Philadelphia Museum of Art.*

whom he married in Friend's Meeting on October 12, 1734.

The family papers include the original marriage certificates of Francis Richardson Senior, goldsmith, to both his first and second wives. His first wife was Elizabeth Growdon, daughter of Judge Joseph Growdon of Trevose, Bucks County, Pennsylvania. The certificate of their marriage is dated April 18, 1705 (Old Style), and in addition to the seldom-seen autograph of Francis Richardson, it bears the very rare signature of Johann Nys, the Philadelphia and Delaware goldsmith, and that of Peter Stretch, clockmaker, as two of the seventy-five witnesses present at this marriage held in Philadelphia.

Among such craftsmen of the eighteenth century, to whom Jeremiah Elfreth Junior was affiliated by ties of relationship, mutual interest, and accomplishment, he deserves to take his place in the annals of craftsmanship.

Note. I wish to acknowledge my indebtedness for valuable assistance to the late Miss Anna E. Elfreth of Chestnut Hill, Pennsylvania, and to Mrs. Florence Redman Engle of Haddonfield, New Jersey. Miss Elfreth, who died August 10, 1946, was one of the few descendants of Jeremiah Elfreth bearing the family name.

Joseph Richardson and family, Philadelphia silversmiths

BY MARTHA GANDY FALES

IN THE SEVENTEENTH century only a few American families could afford to commission a set of silver spoons or, occasionally, a cup and a tankard, and the goldsmith's business was largely confined to making communion vessels for churches or presentation silver for organizations and wealthy individuals. By the eighteenth century, however, the members of the burgeoning middle class could well afford to ornament both their houses and their persons with objects of silver and gold. Joseph Richardson, like many of his fellow artisans, found the demand for his handiwork so great that he had to supplement the production of his own shop with silver bearing London hallmarks. Importations of silver from England to America rose from a value of £28 of plate in 1697 to a value of £4,701 in 1760.[1]

The total value of yearly shipments of silver from England to America is known from records at the Public Record Office in London, and the kinds of objects imported are known from advertisements in American newspapers. Joseph Richardson's letter book, which records his orders for plate from 1758 to 1774, reveals that he ordered silver from London once or twice a year, that it usually took about six months for the goods to arrive in Philadelphia, and that frequently the silver sent was not entirely satisfactory. His purchases were paid for through bills of exchange—a form of money order—or with actual bullion sent by him to the firms with which he dealt. These firms included those of Thomas Wagstaffe, George Ritherdon, Daniel Mildred, and How and Masterman.[2]

This information, together with the detailed accounts in Joseph Richardson's daybooks and the large number of surviving objects that bear his marks, provide an unparalleled picture of the wares and activities of a flourishing goldsmith in mid-eighteenth-century Philadelphia. Richardson's records reveal which objects were most commonly

Fig. 1. Pair of sauceboats made by Joseph Richardson (1711-1784), Philadelphia, c. 1755. Marked on the bottom IR in a rectangle with an asymmetrical scroll above. They bear the Pemberton crest. These are similar to the Logan sauceboats at the Metropolitan Museum of Art except for an extra furl at the base of the handle. Length 8¼ inches. *Historical Society of Pennsylvania; gift of Henry R. Pemberton.*

Fig. 2. One of a pair of tea canisters by Richardson, c. 1740. Marked twice on the bottom IR in an oval. Engraved in later block letters on narrow end *Oswald/and/Lydia Peel* and on top in script *Green Tea.* The two "square" canisters were bequeathed by Lydia Peel in 1785 to her daughter Grace. The matching canister is also still owned by Lydia's descendants. Scratched on the bottom is the weight *12 oz. 5 dwt.* Height 5¾ inches. *Private collection.*

Fig. 3. Pair of half-pint cans by Richardson, c. 1737. Marked twice at the left of each handle, IR in an oval. Engraved on the bottom of each is *R/HM* and on the front opposite the handle in later script, *ER*. Also engraved on the bottom is the original weight: *8 oz. 2 dwt.* on one and *8 oz. 5 dwt.* on the other. Hugh Roberts married Mary Calvert in 1735 and was credited in Richardson's accounts in 1737 for 12 oz. 14 dwt. 12 gr. of silver towards making a pair of half-pint cáns. Height 4⅜ inches. Present weights 7 oz. 14 dwt. 11 gr. and 7 oz. 16 dwt. 21 gr., showing a loss of about 8 dwt. for each can over the years. *Historical Society of Pennsylvania; photograph by Gilbert Ask.*

made in the goldsmith's shop (spoons, cans, and porringers), and which were more frequently imported from abroad. Joseph apparently did not carry a few items, such as candlesticks; and he only rarely sold such things as fountain pens, cranes, and harness bosses. It is evident that such objects as cans, tankards, porringers, tea sets, and trays were in great demand, while teakettles, spoon boats, and pannikins were sought only occasionally. No American examples of spoon boats (the small elongated footless trays used to hold teaspoons) are known to survive, but his daybooks reveal that Joseph Richardson did make them for at least three customers between 1737 and 1738. Another rare form in American silver which until recently Richardson was not known to have made is the tea canister (Fig. 2).

Joseph's records also indicate that his customers preferred pint cans over half-pint cans as drinking vessels. A study of the relative weights of various cans indicates that the average pint can weighed about twelve ounces, while the half-pint can usually weighed about seven ounces (Fig. 3). Such comparative weights can help in determining the approximate size of an object when only its weight is known.

The weights given in Richardson's accounts and orders also help to identify objects that survive today (Fig. 4). Since examples of a given form are rarely identical in weight, a piece with the original weight scratched on the bottom can sometimes be linked to the record of an object of the same weight. Even if only the present weight of an object is known, its history may be traced by allowing for the normal pennyweight loss of silver over the years.

Weights are also useful in determining which pieces recorded in Joseph's accounts were made by his apprentices, and therefore what part they played in the actual making of the silver sold in his shop. Because weight was of primary importance in determining the price of an object—not only because of the cost of the metal used, but also because the goldsmith figured the cost of his labor at so many pennies per ounce of metal—it takes on greater significance to the student of American silver.

It is general knowledge that American silver followed European styles, reflecting the Renaissance tradition in the seventeenth century, the baroque tradition at the turn of the eighteenth century, the rococo characteristics of the mid-eighteenth century, and the neoclassical taste of the late eighteenth century. In fact, silver was probably the

Fig. 4. Porringer by Richardson, 1739. Marked twice at the left of the handle IR in an oval. Engraved on top of the handle *P/IE* for Joseph and Elizabeth Paschall, whose names appear in later backhand script on the porringer. Two weights appear on the bottom: *7 oz. 18 dwt.* deeply scribed and *7 oz. 15 dwt.* lightly scratched. In Richardson's accounts for 1739 Joseph Paschall was charged £2/8/0 for the work involved in making four porringers weighing 31 oz. 13 dwt. Length 7½ inches. *Philadelphia Museum of Art; gift of Lydia Thompson.*

first art form in the Colonies to be affected by stylistic changes, for it was a more widely patronized art than painting or sculpture and the American artisan could be easily and quickly supplied from London with models of changing taste.[3] Joseph Richardson ordered and received within six months fashionable London silver; he could then copy these designs for his customers, who frequently specified that their plate be made in the newest taste.

The appearance of new styles in American silver has not been precisely dated because colonial silver, unlike English silver of the time, does not bear marks indicating the year it was made. However, the records of Joseph Richardson and the objects made by him which can be dated through these records, or through the dates engraved on them, provide a detailed picture of the development of various stylistic elements in mid-eighteenth century American silver.

Many of Richardson's masterpieces have been identified and often published (Fig. 5). However, new examples of his work are still coming to light. A fifteen-year search for the two salvers recorded in his accounts for 1737 that were to bear the inscription *The Gift of Samuel Sherlock Esqr. to Devontribe* finally led to their discovery as unidentified pieces belonging to the Old Devonshire Church in Bermuda, where Samuel Sherlock was a chief justice and where the early parishes were called tribes (Fig. 6).

An equally fortuitous combination of documents and silver objects exists for Joseph Richardson's father Francis (1681-1729), his brother Frank (1705-1782), and his two sons Joseph (1752-1831) and Nathaniel (1754-1827), all of whom were silversmiths at one time. The history of the art of the goldsmith in America can be recreated and preserved through this wealth of silver and documentary evidence. Joseph Richardson Jr. himself summarized the importance these relics might have for us in the future when

Fig. 5.   Teakettle on stand by Richardson, c. 1755. Marked on the bottom of both kettle and stand, IR in a rectangle with a scroll above. Engraved on one side are the Plumsted arms and crest. Not mentioned in the 1745 will of Clement Plumsted, the teakettle was left by his wife Mary to her granddaughter Elizabeth Plumsted. The handle was probably originally wrapped with wicker. Height over all, 15⁵⁄₁₆ inches. Weight engraved on base of kettle, *62-14* and on stand, *30-16*, a total of more than 93 ounces of silver. *Yale University Art Gallery, Mabel Brady Garvan Collection.*

Fig. 6. Pair of salvers by Richardson, 1737. Marked twice on the bottom, IR in an oval, and engraved *The Gift of Samuel Sherlock Esqr. to Devontribe.* Samuel Sherlock, chief justice in Bermuda, died in 1736. In his will he gave "unto the Church in Devon Tribe [i.e., parish] aforesaid ten pounds money to be disposed and laid out for that use as my Executor and Executrix thinks fitt." In his account book for 1737 Joseph Richardson recorded receiving from Captain William Bell silver and two gold coins (a moidore and a pistole) valued at almost £10 in payment for these two salvers, or "weighters." Diameter of each, 5½ inches. *Christ Church, Devonshire, Bermuda.*

he described the Indian medal (Fig. 7) made by his father: "I have no doubt in a future day, it will be considered as interesting . . . as it may serve to show the progress of the arts in our country."[4]

This article has been adapted from *Joseph Richardson and Family, Philadelphia Silversmiths,* by Martha Gandy Fales, which is to be published this month for the Historical Society of Pennsylvania by the Wesleyan University Press.

Fig. 7. Medals cut by Edward Duffield and struck by Richardson. Left, obverse and reverse of Indian peace medal, 1757, given by the Friendly Association of Regaining and Preserving Peace with the Indians by Pacific Measures. Right, obverse and reverse of medal presented by the city of Philadelphia to Colonel John Armstrong of Carlisle, Pennsylvania, who was wounded while leading a party that destroyed the Indians' village at Kittanning in a surprise attack in 1756. On one side is shown the village being burned and on the other side the corporation arms of Philadelphia. Diameter 1¾ inches. *Historical Society of Pennsylvania.*

[1] R.W. Symonds, *The English Export Trade in Furniture to Colonial America,* Part II, ANTIQUES, October 1935, p. 156.

[2] Thomas Wagstaffe was a London clockmaker. How and Masterman and George Ritherdon were goldsmiths, while Daniel Mildred was a supplier of many different sorts of goods. See also Martha Gandy Fales, "Thomas Wagstaffe, London Quaker Clockmaker," *Connoisseur,* November 1962, pp. 193-201.

[3] Martha Gandy Fales, *English design sources of American silver,* ANTIQUES, January 1963, pp. 82-85.

[4] "Register of the Medal Dies of the United States," Historical Society of Pennsylvania.

Some forged Richardson silver

BY MARTHA GANDY FALES

Editor's note. Fakes of various kinds in English silver were discussed and illustrated by Graham Hughes of the Worshipful Company of Goldsmiths in ANTIQUES for April. The equally tricky subject of American forgeries is investigated here by Martha Gandy Fales, who presents an instructive case history comparing the work of a Philadelphia silversmith with the modern fakes purporting to be his work.

FORGING SILVER, not just in the old handicraft sense, but in the sense of premeditated malfeasance, can be a lucrative business. In the past there have been some who, like the few early silversmiths who turned counterfeiters, have been unable to resist temptation.

Faked silver is often very skillfully done and requires very careful study, but inevitably flaws appear. Experience is the best protection against forgeries; since my personal experience is still limited I welcomed an opportunity to study some of the relatively large number of forgeries purporting to be the work of Joseph Richardson Sr. (1711-1784) of Philadelphia. It appears that a few decades ago several people in that city endeavored to augment the silver belonging to the colonial Morris family and others. Some of the forgeries are preserved by the Historical Society of Pennsylvania, whose director, Richard N. Williams II, hopes it will provide a lesson in detecting fakes.

An article on some of the Morris family silver appeared in the *American Collector* in October 1940; and the cover of that issue illustrated an imposing grace cup said to be by Joseph Richardson and to have been presented to Samuel Morris by the Schuylkill Fishing Company of the State in Schuylkill, although a history of that organization fails to mention any such presentation. Perhaps for the benefit of all, this grace cup has mysteriously retired from the scene and today no one knows its whereabouts.

There are definite ways of determining a forgery, since the artificer almost always lacks some bit of necessary

Fig. 1. Caster.
Historical Society of Pennsylvania.

Fig. 2. Sauceboat.
Historical Society of Pennsylvania.

information about what he is doing. One of the best keys is provided by a thorough knowledge of how the colonial craftsman worked. An example of how this knowledge proves helpful can be seen in the case of the center punch. Generally, early American silversmiths marked the center of the disk of silver with a point or dot before they started to hammer the body of the lid of an object. Frequently this point was conspicuously punched into the silver, and from it the silversmith could check with his calipers as he finished his courses of hammering to see that the silver was being worked evenly and not getting out of line. The forger of the caster shown here (Fig. 1) evidently had seen the punch mark, knew it existed, but either did not understand its purpose or else did not refer to it as he worked, since the center punch in the base of this caster is *off* center.

A thorough knowledge of the work of a particular silversmith is useful too. Even totally different forms made by a craftsman should have some similarities to well-documented and authenticated examples by the same man. If the sauceboat illustrated (Fig. 2) is compared with the authentic Logan sauceboats in the Metropolitan Museum of Art (Fig. 3) and the fine pair of sauceboats owned by Mr. and Mrs. Mark Bortman (ANTIQUES, December 1956, p. 554), a number of differences are at once apparent.

It will be noted that the design of the feet and legs is quite different on the Morris sauceboat; in fact, it is more like the work of such New England silversmiths as Paul Revere, or of John David of Philadelphia. Nor do these legs, which are very awkwardly placed, appear to support the bowl as do the legs on the authentic boats.

By comparison with the authentic sauceboats, whose rims show a boldly cut outline, the forged flange appears flaccid. Nor is the handle of the latter boat like any other handle known to be the work of Joseph Richardson—and in the case of a cast part such as this, it is likely that after going to the trouble of procuring the pattern the silversmith would use it a number of times. The manner of the attachment of the handle at the top of the bowl is not at all in keeping with the asymmetrical shells of the legs and feet, nor is it a customary method of attachment on American sauceboats of the period.

Fig. 4. Tankard.
Historical Society of Pennsylvania.

Fig. 5. Authentic tankard by Joseph Richardson Sr.
Collection of Boies Penrose;
photograph by courtesy of the
Philadelphia Museum of Art.

Fig. 3. Authentic sauceboat by Joseph Richardson Sr.
Metropolitan Museum of Art.

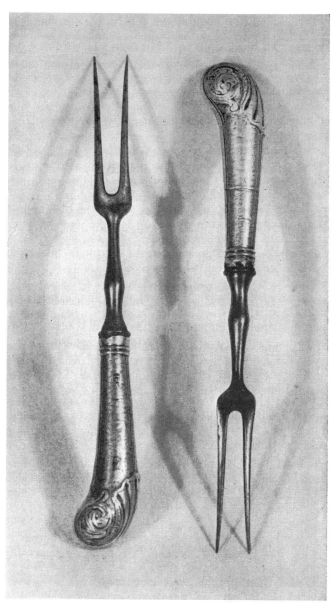

Fig. 7. Spurious mark on sauceboat shown in Fig. 2.

Microphotographs by Gordon Saltar, by courtesy of the Winterthur Museum.

Fig. 8. Authentic mark of Joseph Richardson Sr., on spoon in author's collection.

This brings up the point of how this forgery was made. When considering cast parts, it is not easy to distinguish between the old and the new. Here the handle, legs, and feet may have been taken from an authentic eighteenth-century example and applied to a newly formed body. More likely, patterns were made from authentic examples and then newly cast. The body is probably modern, because it feels uniformly thin as though it were raised from a rolled sheet of silver. Flatting mills were used in Richardson's day but the thinly rolled sheets of silver are later than his working period.

The tankard illustrated (Fig. 4) shows several other departures from Joseph Richardson's normal method of working, and may be contrasted with an authentic tankard (Fig. 5). In addition to the absence of center punches on both lid and base, the handle ending of the spurious tankard is slightly off center. Also, the heart-shape handle ending used by other colonial silversmiths is not as much to be expected in the work of Joseph Richardson as the shaped-shield ending found on well-authenticated examples of his work. The thumbpiece, on the other hand, is in the design of most of the Richardson thumbpieces, but when the lid is pulled back toward the handle, the purchase and the handle do not show the wear any normal tankard would show from the customary and cumulative collision of these two parts.

The base band, rounded in profile rather than gradually molded, is one of the most suspicious features of the tankard. Most revealing of all is the fact that this band is placed at the very bottom of the body instead of overlapping it for half its width. Since the body of a mid-eighteenth-century tankard was generally made of one piece of silver and this tankard has a base set into the body, it would appear that the original has been

155

cut out along the edge where the body joins the base band, to dispose of authentic marks, and has been replaced by a new base given a fake mark.

Another false note is the use of scribing to outline the mid-band and the steps of the lid (contrast Figs. 4 and 5). While Richardson used scribing to accentuate the molding of the base, and the rim of the body and lid, it was not common for him to incise the steps of the lid or the mid-band.

When one has other examples of the same form by the same maker with which to compare a piece of silver, the ground is fairly sure. It is with the unique example that the collector may suffer most or find his greatest rewards: it is either the most wonderful rarity or the most horrible fraud. The forks illustrated in Figure 6 represent such a case. Forks by American makers are rare and no examples are known to be the work of Joseph Richardson. These bear in their design no startling similarity to his recognized work and in addition show clearly on the upper end of the handle the remnants of a STER/LING mark—a mark not commonly used on American silver until the nineteenth century. It is quite likely that these forks are authentic eighteenth-century examples, but the IR mark which appears on them is unlike any other definitely attributable Joseph Richardson mark and may in fact be that of a contemporary English silversmith.

Marks are one of the surest guides to the authenticity of the unique piece. During the course of his career a silversmith might use as many as six different dies to strike his mark. Identifying authentic marks is the most challenging area of research in the field of American silver today. Meanwhile the unique mark throws a question upon the unique piece of silver.

The marks on the caster, the tankard, and the sauceboat are all struck from the same spurious die. Illustrated as it appears on the sauceboat (Fig. 7), it may be contrasted with an authentic Richardson mark (Fig. 8) and identified by its flat, crudely cut letters and the file cuts which appear along the base line, particularly below the R. This spurious mark has been seen only on questionable pieces, including two rare forms in American silver, a vinaigrette and a mote spoon; these are among the eight pieces of Morris silver at the Historical Society of Pennsylvania which bear it. It is a mark to be remembered and avoided.

As the mark is a signature of the silversmith, so is any engraving done by him. Many of the examples of Morris silver are conveniently engraved with initials of members of the Morris family, most of them apparently cut by the same modern hand since the same style of lettering appears indiscriminately on objects purporting to be the work of Philip Syng, Richard Humphreys, Richardson, and others. Typical of the lettering of the man we may call the Morris engraver are the initials on the caster (Fig. 1). Stiff, rigid letters with imposing shading and ruled serifs such as these may be compared with authentic engraving of Joseph Richardson (Fig. 9), which is more flexible, less precise, but at the same time more surely done, not so tall or proportionately thick—in every way the work of a lighter touch. The initials on the caster match those on the sauceboat and the tankard; the latter even has the flagrant mistake of shading in the dot between the initials.

From these examples of forged Richardson silver, then, it is possible to work out some means of identifying genuine examples of American silver. We should look for (1) true and proven maker's marks, (2) technical similarities in the handiwork of a particular silversmith and consistency with the methods of his day, (3) design similarities both in cast elements and in formed areas which were determined largely by the molds and anvils or stakes owned by the maker, and (4) similarities in the style of engraving. All these points can be greatly reinforced by documentation through bills, account books, and continuous family history over a period of many years. Any one of these points may be argued, but when all are considered, the verdict for or against the piece should be apparent. Let us hope that our continually increasing knowledge in these areas will discourage all modern silversmiths from becoming forgers of old silver.

Fig. 9. Authentic engraving of owners' initials done by Joseph Richardson Sr., on a porringer handle. *Historical Society of Pennsylvania.*

Fig. 10. Detail of engraving on spurious caster shown in Fig. 1. *Historical Society of Pennsylvania.*

Bibliography

Avery, C. Louise. *Early American Silver.* New York: Russell and Russell, 1969.

Bigelow, Francis Hill. *Historic Silver of the Colonies and Its Makers.* New York: Tudor Publishing Co., 1948.

Bigelow's book places American work within its context by showing dated English pieces alongside the undated American examples. Similar forms are grouped together, simplifying comparison.

Buhler, Kathryn C. *American Silver, 1625-1825, in the Museum of Fine Arts, Boston.* 2 vols. Boston: The Museum of Fine Arts, 1972.

This interesting and well-designed catalogue illustrates the work of many early silversmiths and their marks. Marks on the featured pieces are clearly photographed and other known marks described. Short biographical sketches accompany each entry.

Davis, John D. *English Silver at Williamsburg.* Williamsburg, Va.: The Colonial Williamsburg Foundation, 1976.

English plate and silverplate is grouped by form under general categories of use. The volume clearly delineates English antecedents of American work.

Ensko, Stephen G. C. *American Silversmiths and Their Marks.* New York: privately printed, 1948.

Fales, Martha Gandy. *Early American Silver.* Revised ed. New York: E. P. Dutton & Co., Inc., 1973.

Interesting book on the whole gamut of silversmithing—the craftsmen, craft practices, techniques, and final products. Includes an excellent bibliography.

————. *Joseph Richardson and Family: Philadelphia Silversmiths.* Middletown, Conn.: Wesleyan University Press, 1974.

A carefully researched account of this dynasty of Philadelphia craftsmen, the book is useful as a guide to business practices of 18th-century silversmiths.

Flynt, Henry N., and Fales, Martha Gandy. *The Heritage Foundation Collection of Silver: with Biographical Sketches of New England Silversmiths, 1625-1825.* Old Deerfield, Mass.: The Heritage Foundation, 1968.

Hood, Graham. *American Silver: A History of Style, 1650-1900.* New York: Praeger Publishers, 1971.

Hood's fascinating account of the development of a continuing market for silver in America details a number of pieces which appear in *Early American Silver and Its Makers.* The objects illustrated in Graham's book, however, tend to be early examples of particular fashions. That is, they are in the American high style. For every avant-garde piece, hundreds were made on more conservative lines.

Kovel, Ralph M. and Terry H. *American Silver, Pewter and Silverplate.* New York: Crown Publishers, 1961.

Philadelphia Museum of Art. *Philadelphia: Three Centuries of American Art.* Philadelphia: The Philadelphia Museum of Art, 1976.

This exhibition catalogue is the definitive source for information about Philadelphia craftsmen.

————. "Philadelphia Silver, 1682-1800." *The Philadelphia Museum Bulletin,* vol. LI, no. 249, Spring 1956.

Index